PowerScore®

LSAT

READING COMPREHENSION
PASSAGE TYPE TRAINING

VOLUME 1: LSAT PREPTESTS 1 THROUGH 20

The complete text of every LSAT Reading Comprehension question from PrepTest 1 through 20 sorted according to PowerScore's famous LSAT Reading Comprehension Bible system.

POWERSCORE®
TEST PREPARATION

Published by
PowerScore Publishing, a division of PowerScore Incorporated
57 Hasell Street
Charleston, SC 29401

Authors: David M. Killoran
　　　　　Steven G. Stein

Manufactured in Canada
08 18 20 16

ISBN: 978-0-9826618-4-0

MIX
Paper from
responsible sources
FSC® C004071

You might also be interested in...

The LSAT Bible Workbook Trilogy

With official LSAC-released LSAT questions and multiple practice drills, *The Logic Games Bible Workbook, The Logical Reasoning Bible Workbook*, and *The Reading Comprehension Bible Workbook* are the ideal companions to the renowned PowerScore Bibles.

The LSAT Setups Encyclopedia Trilogy

With expansive discussions of 60 full game sections (for a total of 240 logic games explained) from LSAT PrepTests 1 – 60, *The PowerScore LSAT Setups Encyclopedia Trilogy* provides the most complete and effective solutions available.

Available at PowerScore.com

CONTENTS

CHAPTER ONE: INTRODUCTION

CHAPTER TWO: DIVERSITY I: AFFIRMING UNDERREPRESENTED GROUPS PASSAGES

CHAPTER THREE: DIVERSITY II: UNDERMINING OVERREPRESENTED GROUPS PASSAGES

CHAPTER FOUR: DIVERSITY III: MIXED GROUP PASSAGES

CHAPTER FIVE: LAW RELATED PASSAGES

CHAPTER SIX: LAW-REGULATION PASSAGES

CHAPTER SEVEN: SOCIAL SCIENCE PASSAGES

CHAPTER EIGHT: HARD SCIENCE PASSAGES

CHAPTER NINE: HUMANITIES PASSAGES

ANSWER KEY AND LINE REFERENCE NOTES

APPENDIX

About PowerScore

PowerScore is one of the nation's fastest growing test preparation companies. Founded in 1997, PowerScore offers LSAT, GMAT, GRE, SAT, and ACT preparation classes in over 150 locations in the U.S. and abroad. Preparation options include Full-Length courses, Weekend courses, Live Online courses, and private tutoring. For more information, please visit our website at www.powerscore.com or call us at (800) 545-1750.

For supplemental information about this book, please visit the *LSAT Reading Comprehension: Passage Type Training* website at www.powerscore.com/lsatbibles.

Chapter One: Introduction

Welcome to *LSAT Reading Comprehension: Passage Type Training* by PowerScore. In this book you will find every Reading Comprehension passage from LSAT PrepTests 1 through 20, arranged in groups according to the classification system used in the renowned *PowerScore LSAT Reading Comprehension Bible*.

Grouping each passage by type provides a number of practical benefits:

- The 80 passages in this book are an excellent practice resource, and an ideal supplement to the *LSAT Reading Comprehension Bible*.

- By examining passages with certain basic similarities, you can analyze the features of each passage type in order to better understand how passages are constructed, how they can be most quickly recognized, and how they can be most easily solved. This is especially the case if you have already read the *PowerScore LSAT Reading Comprehension Bible*.

- Alternatively, for more general practice with passages of all types, you can use the appendix in the back of the book and do complete passage sections from individual tests. The appendix on page 211 gives directions for taking that approach.

- Even if you have not already read the *LSAT Reading Comprehension Bible*, this book provides an excellent practice resource, allowing you to develop your familiarity with various passage types and with the Reading Comprehension section in general.

If you are looking to further improve your LSAT score, we also recommend that you pick up copies of the PowerScore LSAT Logic Games Bible and PowerScore LSAT Logical Reasoning Bible.

At the end of this book a complete answer key is provided. While complete explanations of each passage and question are not provided, each answer key is accompanied by Line Reference Notes that indicate the location in the passage where the source for the correct answer can be found.

In our LSAT courses, our admissions counseling programs, and our publications, we always strive to present the most accurate and up-to-date information available. Consequently, we have devoted a section of our website to *LSAT Reading Comprehension: Passage Type Training* students. This free online resource area offers supplements to the book material, answers questions posed by students, offers study plans, and provides updates as needed. There is also an official book evaluation form that we strongly encourage you to use. The exclusive *LSAT Reading Comprehension: Passage Type Training* online area can be accessed at:

 powerscore.com/lsatbibles

If you wish to ask questions about items in this book, please visit our free LSAT discussion forum at:

 forum.powerscore.com/lsat

The forum offers hundreds of answers to student questions, including many lengthy answers and conceptual discussions from the authors of this book.

If you have an issue that you prefer not to discuss on the public forum, please do not hesitate to email us at:

 lsatbibles@powerscore.com

We are happy to assist you in your LSAT preparation in any way, and we look forward to hearing from you!

The Law School Admission Test is administered four times a year: in February, June, September/October, and December. This standardized test is required for admission to any American Bar Association-approved law school. According to LSAC, the producers of the test, the LSAT is designed "to measure skills that are considered essential for success in law school: the reading and comprehension of complex texts with accuracy and insight; the organization and management of information and the ability to draw reasonable inferences from it; the ability to think critically; and the analysis and evaluation of the reasoning and arguments of others." The LSAT consists of the following five sections:

- 2 Sections of Logical Reasoning (short arguments, 24-26 questions each)

- 1 Section of Reading Comprehension (3 long reading passages, 2 short comparative reading passages, 26-28 total questions)

- 1 Section of Analytical Reasoning (4 logic games, 22-24 total questions)

- 1 Experimental Section of one of the above three section types.

You are given 35 minutes to complete each section. The experimental section is unscored and is not returned to the test taker. A break of 10 to 15 minutes is given between the 3rd and 4th sections.

The five-section test is followed by a 35-minute writing sample.

The Logical Reasoning Section

Each Logical Reasoning Section is composed of approximately 24 to 26 short arguments. Every short argument is followed by a question such as: "Which one of the following weakens the argument?", "Which one of the following parallels the argument?", or "Which one of the following must be true according to the argument?". The key to this section is time management and an understanding of the reasoning types and question types that frequently appear.

Since there are two scored sections of Logical Reasoning on every LSAT, this section accounts for approximately 50% of your score.

At the conclusion of the LSAT, and for five business days afterwards, you have the option of cancelling your score. Unfortunately, there is no way to determine exactly what your score would be before cancelling.

The Analytical Reasoning Section

This section, also known as Logic Games, is often the most difficult for students taking the LSAT for the first time. The section consists of four games or puzzles, each followed by a series of five to eight questions. The questions are designed to test your ability to evaluate a set of relationships and to make inferences about those relationships. To perform well on this section you must understand the types of games that frequently appear and develop the ability to properly diagram the rules and make inferences.

The Reading Comprehension Section

This section is composed of three long reading passages, each approximately 450 words in length, and two shorter comparative reading passages. The passage topics are drawn from a variety of subjects, and each passage is followed by a series of five to eight questions that ask you to determine viewpoints in the passage, analyze organizational traits, evaluate specific sections of the passage, or compare facets of two different passages.

The Experimental Section

Each LSAT contains one undesignated experimental section, and it does not count towards your score. The experimental can be any of the three section types previously discussed, and the purpose of the section is to test and evaluate questions that will be used on *future* LSATs. By pretesting questions before their use in a scored section, the experimental helps the makers of the test determine the test scale.

The Writing Sample

For many years the Writing Sample was administered before the LSAT.

A 35-minute Writing Sample is given at the conclusion of the LSAT. The Writing Sample is not scored, but a copy is sent to each of the law schools to which you apply. In the Writing Sample you are asked to write a short essay that defends one of two possible courses of action.

You must attempt the Writing Sample! If you do not, LSAC reserves the right not to score your test.

Do not agonize over the Writing Sample; in law school admissions, the Writing Sample is not a major determining element for three reasons: the admissions committee is aware that the essay is given after a grueling three hour test and is about a subject you have no personal interest in; they already have a better sample of your writing ability in the personal statement; and the committee has a limited amount of time to evaluate each application.

The LSAT Scoring Scale

Each administered LSAT contains approximately 101 questions, and each LSAT score is based on the total number of questions a test taker correctly answers, a total known as the raw score. After the raw score is determined, a unique Score Conversion Chart is used for each LSAT to convert the raw score into a scaled LSAT score. Since June 1991, the LSAT has used a 120 to 180 scoring scale, with 120 being the lowest possible score and 180 being the highest possible score. Notably, this 120 to 180 scale is just a renumbered version of the 200 to 800 scale most test takers are familiar with from the SAT and GMAT. Just drop the "1" and add a "0" to the 120 and 180.

Although the number of questions per test has remained relatively constant over the last eight years, the overall logical difficulty of each test has varied. This is not surprising since the test is made by humans and there is no precise way to completely predetermine logical difficulty. To account for these variances in test "toughness," the test makers adjust the Scoring Conversion Chart for each LSAT in order to make similar LSAT scores from different tests mean the same thing. For example, the LSAT given in June may be logically more difficult than the LSAT given in December, but by making the June LSAT scale "looser" than the December scale, a 160 on each test would represent the same level of performance. This scale adjustment, known as equating, is extremely important to law school admissions offices around the country. Imagine the difficulties that would be posed by unequated tests: admissions officers would have to not only examine individual LSAT scores, but also take into account which LSAT each score came from. This would present an information nightmare.

The LSAT Percentile Table

It is important not to lose sight of what LSAT scaled scores actually represent. The 120 to 180 test scale contains 61 different possible scores. Each score places a student in a certain relative position compared to other test takers. These relative positions are represented through a percentile that correlates to each score. The percentile indicates where the test taker ranks in the overall pool of test takers. For example, a score of 165 represents the 93rd percentile, meaning a student with a score of 165 scored better than 93 percent of the people who have taken the test in the last three years. The percentile is critical since it is a true indicator of your positioning relative to other test takers, and thus law school applicants.

Charting out the entire percentage table yields a rough "bell curve." The number of test takers in the 120s and 170s is very low (only 1.6% of all test takers receive a score in the 170s), and most test takers are bunched in the middle, comprising the "top" of the bell. In fact, approximately 40% of all test takers score between 145 and 155 inclusive, and about 70% of all test takers score between 140 and 160 inclusive.

Since the LSAT has 61 possible scores, why didn't the test makers change the scale to 0 to 60? Probably for merciful reasons. How would you tell your friends that you scored a 3 on the LSAT? 123 sounds so much better.

There is no
penalty for
answering
incorrectly on the
LSAT. Therefore,
you should guess
on any questions
you cannot
complete.

The median score on the LSAT scale is approximately 151. The median, or middle, score is the score at which approximately 50% of test takers have a lower score and 50% of test takers have a higher score. Typically, to achieve a score of 151, you must answer between 56 and 61 questions correctly from a total of 101 questions. In other words, to achieve a score that is perfectly average, you can miss between 40 and 45 questions. Thus, it is important to remember that you don't have to answer every question correctly in order to receive an excellent LSAT score. There is room for error, and accordingly you should never let any single question occupy an inordinate amount of your time.

The Use of the LSAT

The use of the LSAT in law school admissions is not without controversy. It is largely taken for granted that your LSAT score is one of the most important determinants of the type of school you can attend. At many law schools a multiplier made up of your LSAT score and your undergraduate grade point average is used to help determine the relative standing of applicants, and at some schools a sufficiently high multiplier guarantees your admission.

For all the importance of the LSAT, it is not without flaws. As a standardized test currently given in the paper-and-pencil format, there are a number of skills that the LSAT cannot measure, such as listening skills, note-taking ability, perseverance, etc. LSAC is aware of these limitations and as a matter of course they warn all law schools about overemphasizing LSAT results. Still, since the test ultimately returns a number for each student, it is hard to escape the tendency to rank applicants accordingly. Fortunately, once you get to law school the LSAT is forgotten. Consider the test a temporary hurdle you must leap in order to reach the ultimate goal.

For more information on the LSAT, or to register for the test, contact LSAC at (215) 968-1001 or at their website at www.lsac.org.

The Reading Comprehension Section

The focus of this book is on the Reading Comprehension section of the LSAT, and each Reading Comprehension section contains four passage sets with a total of 26 to 28 questions. Since you have thirty-five minutes to complete the section, you have an average of approximately eight minutes and forty-five seconds to complete each passage set. Of course, the amount of time you spend on each passage set will vary with the reading difficulty of the passage, the difficulty of the questions, and the total number of questions per passage set.

On average, you have 8 minutes and 45 seconds to complete each passage set.

Why Reading Comprehension?

Each section of the LSAT is designed to test abilities required in the study and/or practice of law. The Logical Reasoning sections measure your skills in argumentation and logic. The Logic Games section tests your ability to understand the interaction of different variables and the laws which govern their actions. Reading Comprehension, a section included in many standardized tests, provides a test of skills particularly important to both law students and attorneys. Law students are required to read significant portions of dense text throughout their legal studies, and lawyers must often be ready to do the same in their normal course of business; given that the misreading of a contract or legal judgment could lead to disastrous results for a lawyer's clients (not to mention the lawyer), it should not be surprising that Reading Comprehension is an integral part of the Law School Admission Test.

The Section Directions

Each Reading Comprehension section is prefaced by the following directions:

> "Each set of questions in this section is based on a single passage or a pair of passages. The questions are to be answered on the basis of what is stated or implied in the passage or pair of passages. For some questions, more than one of the choices could conceivably answer the question. However, you are to choose the best answer; that is, the response that most accurately and completely answers the question, and blacken the corresponding space on your answer sheet."

Because these directions precede every Reading Comprehension section, you should familiarize yourself with them now. Once the LSAT begins, *never* waste time reading the directions for any section.

Let us examine these directions more closely. Consider the following sentence: "The questions are to be answered on the basis of what is stated or implied in the passage or pair of passages." Thus, the test makers indicate that you are to use the statements of the author of the passage to prove and disprove answer choices. You do not need to bring in additional information aside from the typical ideas that the average American or Canadian would be expected to believe on the basis of generally known and accepted facts. For example, you would be expected to understand the *basics* of how the weather works, or how supply and demand works, but not the specifics of either. Please note that this does not mean that the LSAT cannot set up scenarios where they discuss ideas that are extreme or outside the bounds of common knowledge, such as a passage about a difficult scientific or legal concept. The test makers can and do discuss complex or extreme ideas; in these cases, they give you context for the situation by providing additional information.

The other part of the directions that is interesting is the sentence that states, "For some questions, more than one of the choices could conceivably answer the question. However, you are to choose the <u>best</u> answer; that is, the response that most accurately and completely answers the question." By stating up front that more than one answer choice could suffice to answer the question, the makers of the test compel you to read every single answer choice before making a selection. If you read only one or two answer choices and then decide you have the correct one, you could end up choosing an answer that has some merit but is not as good as a later answer. One of the test makers' favorite tricks is to place a highly attractive wrong answer choice immediately before the correct answer choice in the hopes that you will pick the wrong answer choice and then move to the next question without reading any of the other answers.

The Two Passage Types

The section directions also state that "Each set of questions in this section is based on a single passage or a pair of passages." Prior to June 2007, all LSAT Reading Comprehension sections consisted of four total passages, each accompanied by a series of five to eight questions. Each passage and its accompanying questions are known as a "passage set."

Starting with the June 2007 LSAT, the test makers introduced a new element to the test known as a Comparative Reading passage set, wherein two passages generally addressing the same topic are presented, and a set of questions follows. Because Comparative Reading passage sets did not appear within LSAT PrepTests 1 through 20, there are none in this book. However, a complete discussion of Comparative Reading passage sets is found in Chapter Seven of the *LSAT Reading Comprehension Bible*.

Passage Topics

Reading Comprehension passages are drawn from a wide variety of disciplines, including science, law, and humanities. Thus, you will typically encounter four passage sets with widely varying topical matter. However, even though passage subject matter differs, most sections are constructed from the same consistent set of topics, as follows:

4 Passage Sets
1 Law-related passage
1 Science-based passage
1 Humanities passage featuring diversity
1 Random passage, often Humanities

So, even though the exact subject matter of each passage changes from test to test, the typical LSAT contains one science passage, one law passage, and one humanities passage featuring diversity. The remaining passage is usually drawn from a humanities field such as history or economics, but occasionally the passage comes from science or law.

For a typical example, consider the topics from the December 2007 LSAT:

Topic	Subject Matter
Humanities/Diversity	Asian-American Poetry of Wing Tek Lum
Law	British Common Law
Humanities	University Research Commercialization
Science	Natural Predation and Cyclamen Mites

Please note that the topic of the passage is not necessarily indicative of the level of difficulty. That is, some Science passages are easy, some are difficult. The same goes for Law passages, Humanities passages, etc. In the next chapter we will discuss how to attack any type of passage, and we will discuss how the underlying structure of passages can be analyzed regardless of the passage topic. Topic is examined here so that you understand the nature of what you will be reading. In some cases, knowing the topic can help you make informed decisions about the viewpoints that will be presented therein, and in many cases, students perform better on passages that contain a subject matter that is familiar to them. And, although our primary analysis will focus on viewpoints and structure, later in this chapter we will examine passages from the most commonly occurring topics as a way to calibrate your test radar to the types of mechanisms and viewpoints put forth by the makers of the test.

To locate passages written in the desired style, test makers draw from various sources, which they adapt for use in the Reading Comprehension section. Academic, scientific, and scholarly journals tend to be written in a fairly sophisticated manner, and thus routinely provide materials for the LSAT; recent passage sources have included The University of California, Scientific American Library, and Johns Hopkins University. Articles are also drawn from publications devoted to the arts, including recent offerings from the American Academy of Arts and Sciences, and Poetry in Review Foundation. While the passages are drawn from a wide variety of sources, including newspapers, magazines, books, and journals, they tend to be written in a recognizable, academic style that generally evades simple analysis.

Approaching the Passages

Every Reading Comprehension passage set contains two separate parts: the passage(s) and the questions. When examining the two parts for the first time, students sometimes wonder about the best strategy for attacking the passages: Should I read the questions first? Should I skim the passage? Should I read just the first and last sentence of each paragraph of the passage? The answer is *Read the passage in its entirety and then attack the questions*. That is, first read the entire passage with an eye towards capturing the main ideas, viewpoints, tone, and structure of the passage, and then proceed to the questions, answering them in order unless you encounter a question too difficult to answer. Although this may seem like a reasonable, even obvious, approach, we mention it here because some LSAT texts advocate reading the questions first or skimming the passage. Let us take a moment to discuss some of the various reading approaches that you *might* consider using, but should avoid:

1. **DO NOT** skim the passage, then do each question, returning to the passage as needed.

   In theory, it might seem that skimming could add some degree of efficiency, but in practice this is not the case. In fact, this approach actually reflects a fundamental misunderstanding of the nature of the Reading Comprehension section.

   Skimming might be sufficient to absorb lighter materials, such as newspapers or magazines, but that is because those types of materials are written with simplicity in mind. A newspaper editor wants readers to know half the story by the time they have read the headline, and magazines put the most attention-grabbing pictures on their covers; these publications are trying to draw you in, to entice you to make a purchase. The makers of the LSAT, on the other hand, are well aware that they are dealing with a captive audience; they do not feel any pressure to entertain (as you may have noticed), and passages are chosen based on completely different criteria.

   For many, skimming is a natural reaction to a time-constrained test, but unfortunately the test-makers are well aware of this tendency—the passages they use are chosen in part because they evade quick and simple analysis. In practice, the time "saved" on the front end skimming a passage is more than lost on the back end. In the question section, the skimmer invariably finds the need to go back and re-read, and is often not sufficiently familiar with the passage structure to locate relevant reference points quickly.

2. **DO NOT** read just the first and last sentence of each paragraph of the passage, and then do each question, returning to the passage as needed.

This type of "super-skimming" may also sound good in theory; the idea of breezing through the passages, trying to pick up the big picture ideas, may sound appealing, but again, these passages unfortunately do not work that way. This shorthand and ineffective approach is based in part on the common misconception that the main idea of every paragraph appears in the first or last sentence. While this may often hold true, we will see that this is not always the case. After all, the makers of the LSAT are extremely sharp, and they are familiar with these common approaches as well. That may be why many passages will not follow this general rule—the test makers do not like for passages to follow such a simple prescribed formula.

This approach is basically an even more simplistic and ineffective variation of skimming that provides neither substantive knowledge of the information in the passage nor familiarity with the structure sufficient to locate important reference points.

3. **DO NOT** scan the questions first, then go to the passage and read it, answering questions as you come upon relevant information.

Like the two methods discussed previously, this approach may have some initial appeal. Proponents claim that a preview of the questions gives readers more direction when approaching the passage—if they know what will be asked, perhaps students can get a sense of what to look for when reading the passage. Then, proponents argue, students can save time and effort by skimming through the material that is not pertinent to any of the questions.

There are several problems with this approach: Because there are between five and eight questions per passage, students are forced to try to juggle a large amount of disparate information before even starting the passage. Not only does this make retaining the details of the questions challenging, but it also detracts from one's attention when reading the passage. Second, reading the questions first often wastes valuable time, since the typical student who applies this flawed approach will read and consider the questions, read the passage, and then go back and read each question again. This re-reading takes time without yielding any real benefit.

The bottom line is that your reading approach must be maximally effective for all passages. The flawed strategies above, although perhaps effective in some limited contexts, do not consistently produce solid results. Having discussed some common practices to avoid, let us now consider the proper way to attack an LSAT passage:

1. Always read the passage first. Read for an understanding of structure and detail, for viewpoints and themes, and for the author's tone. Make notations as needed.

2. After reading the passage, consider the questions in the order given. Return to the passage when necessary to confirm your answers.

3. If you encounter a question too difficult to answer, skip it and return to the question after completing the other questions in the passage set.

These are the basic steps to a proper approach to the Reading Comprehension section.

Your Focus While Reading

Have you ever reached the second, or even third, paragraph of an article or reading passage and suddenly realized that you had no idea what you had just been reading? Many students have had this uncomfortable experience at some point. How are we able to read with our eyes while our minds are elsewhere? Ironically, it is our familiarity with the act of reading that has allowed many to develop the "skill" to do so without 100% focus. This approach might be fine for the morning newspaper or a favorite magazine, but these publications tend to be more simply written and they are unaccompanied by difficult questions. LSAT passages, on the other hand, are chosen for their tendency to elude this type of unfocused approach. Faced with this type of reading, many people "zone out" and lose concentration. Thus, your state of mind when approaching these passages is extremely important.

Giving yourself the simple instruction, "read the passage," allows your mind too much free reign to wander as your eyes gloss over the words. Instead, you should take a more active approach, breaking down the passage as you go, creating something of a running translation, and effectively outlining and notating, as we will discuss further. Yes, it can be difficult to focus for long stretches of time, but you must train yourself through practice to keep your concentration at as high a level as possible.

In our experience, virtually all high-scoring LSAT takers read the passage before looking at the questions.

LSAT reading is unlike the reading most people engage in on a day-to-day basis. For example, newspapers and magazines, and even most novels, are written with an eye towards presenting the material in the clearest and most interesting fashion possible. LSAT Reading Comprehension passages, on the other hand, are not written in this manner. They are often written in an academic style that is, at times, dense and complex.

When starting a section, keep the following mindset tips in mind:

- Channel any nervous energy into intensity.

- Enjoy reading the passages—make them into a game or learning exercise.

- If you lose focus, take a deep breath, refocus, and then return to the task at hand.

- Read aggressively, not passively. Actively engage the material and think about the consequences of what you are reading.

Note: Strong readers have many advantages on this test, but becoming an effective reader obviously has significant value in many contexts. As you practice applying the approaches discussed in this book, keep in mind that they are applicable to reading in general, and not meant solely to help you achieve a high LSAT score (although this is obviously one of the benefits of having an effective approach to reading).

Your Attitude While Reading

Many students approach the Reading Comprehension section with anxiety, concerned about the prospect of reading dense passages with difficult structures and unfamiliar terminology. As is the case with every section of the LSAT, maintaining the proper mindset is vital; in this section, expectations of boredom or anxiety can become self-fulfilling prophecies. If you wish to perform well, you must approach the passages with a positive, energetic, and enthusiastic attitude.

It is vital that you avoid a negative attitude as you practice and improve your approach to reading. Some passages might cover topics that you do not find inherently interesting, but you should not resent the authors for it! These passages are presented not to delight and amuse, but rather to test your reading comprehension skills. Some students approach the passages as puzzles to solve, while others read the passages and try to learn new things from them. Either way, the truth of the matter is that if you do not try to enjoy reading the passages or get some value from them, you will be hard-pressed to perform well.

Some students get annoyed by the academic style of writing of the exam, but this is just part of the test. The passages in this section are not meant to be easy, and the test makers know that the way the passages are written and constructed can be off-putting to many students. You must simply ignore this situation, and take on the passages as a challenge.

Many passages in the Reading Comprehension section discuss conflicts between different viewpoints, and this makes the reading inherently more interesting. Getting involved in the argument will make the passage more enjoyable for you and will also allow you to focus more clearly on the material.

A positive attitude is perhaps the most underrated factor in LSAT success. Virtually all high-scoring students expect to do well on the LSAT, and this mind set helps them avoid distractions during the exam, and it helps them overcome any adversity they might face.

Reading Comprehension Classifications Explained

Each passage type is explained here in basic terms. For a comprehensive discussion of each classification, and how to best solve each type, we recommend that you pick up a copy of the PowerScore LSAT Reading Comprehension Bible.

In the following chapters, the Reading Comprehension passages from PrepTests 1 through 20 are presented in groups by classification type. The classification system we use is explained in detail in the *PowerScore LSAT Reading Comprehension Bible*. The following is a brief description of each classification type.

Diversity Passages

The LSAT Reading Comprehension section tends to include at least one passage about a group (or member of a group) that has been traditionally viewed as underrepresented. As these passages tend to deal with the merits of cultural diversity and the value associated with the representation of diverse perspectives, we term them Diversity passages. There are three primary types of Diversity passages, and they have been separated in this book into Chapters Two, Three, and Four.

Chapter Two—Affirming Underrepresented Groups

Given the history of bias in standardized testing, it is no surprise that LSAC is very careful to avoid any perceived bias in their representation of traditionally underrepresented groups. What is surprising is the consistency in the tone used by the test writers. In the dozens of passages addressing traditionally underrepresented groups that have appeared on the LSAT in the past 15+ years, every single passage has addressed these groups in a positive manner. That is, in each instance, the attitude of the author toward the person or group under discussion has been positive or encouraging. This type of consistency goes beyond mere chance, and reveals one of the core attitudes of the test makers. Knowing how the test makers will approach a traditionally underrepresented group then allows you to predict the general direction of certain answer choices.

Chapter Three—Undermining Overrepresented Groups

Let us take a moment to examine the other side of the coin. If the test makers consistently take a positive attitude towards traditionally underrepresented groups, then what attitude would you expect the test makers to take towards traditionally overrepresented groups? As you might expect, the attitude is often critical—if not wholly, then at least partially. This does make some sense, of course. If a test has been historically biased in favor of a certain group, one method to reverse that bias is to present a greater number of passages critical of that group. On the LSAT, this criticism most frequently appears in passages devoted to assessing the work of scholars, who, under the description of the overrepresented group we used earlier, are typically Caucasian males versed in Western thinking.

While this assertion may seem surprising, an analysis of every released LSAT from the modern era (1991 to the present) shows that usually when the test makers are critical of an individual or viewpoint, that person or perspective belongs to an historically well-represented group, that of Caucasian male authors.

Chapter Four—Mixed Group Passages

There are many passages based primarily on single groups, either traditionally underrepresented or traditionally overrepresented groups. What happens, though, when a passage contains both groups? How do the test makers handle a situation, for example, when one of the members from the overrepresented group addresses one of the traditionally underrepresented groups, or vice versa? Let us take a moment to briefly discuss each scenario:

1. Member of an underrepresented group addresses a member of an overrepresented group.

   These scenarios occur relatively rarely, and thus they are not the focus of this section. When they do occur, it is normally because the member of the overrepresented group was critical of the member of the underrepresented group. Thus, the member of the underrepresented group is typically presented as being somewhat dismissive of the member of the overrepresented group (which is quite reasonable—who wouldn't be dismissive toward someone who criticized them?).

2. Member of an overrepresented group addresses a member of an underrepresented group.

   Although we find passages where members of an overrepresented group criticize a member of an underrepresented group, the response in those passages is predictable: that group or individual is then attacked. More interesting—and the focus of this section— are passages where members of an overrepresented group praise or commend members of an underrepresented group. For example, how would you expect the test takers to treat a Western Caucasian male scholar who wrote a study about the positive developments within a native culture? Such a scenario presents a bit of a dilemma for the test makers. Because the scholar is writing in a positive manner about a traditionally underrepresented group, the test makers endorse that position. But, perhaps because of the source of the commentary, the test makers usually also insert at least some mild criticism of the scholar. Thus, passages of this type, which we term "Assessing the Scholars," contain a fascinating display of the competing values of the test makers.

The LSAT Reading Comprehension section usually features one passage based on a law related issue, and these passages are presented in Chapter Five.

Many students assume that because the LSAT is the test to gain admission to law school, the makers of the test must defend the legal system at every turn in the passages they present. This assumption is incorrect. Instead, the test makers treat the Law as a positive, benevolent, dynamic, and at times flawed system.

Seeing the legal system as having flaws is not unreasonable. A system as complex as law is bound to have areas where confusion, uncertainty, or change arises. This uncertainty within law can come from the rules, the witnesses, the attorneys, or even the judges. The test makers are happy to engage in frank discussions of the issues related to improving any aspect of the judicial system, and passages have addressed the following issues:

> Inferential errors made by juries

> How the Web affects copyright holders

> The blandness of legal writing

> Possible bias introduced by computer displays in court

> Indeterminacy in legal outcomes

The above is just a small sampling of issues that the LSAT has addressed regarding the legal system.

On the other hand, the test makers show no hesitation in discussing the law as a positive force, and as a remedy to right social injustice. For example, passages have addressed some of the following topics where the law is used as a remedy or an aid:

> The benefits of bankruptcy law revisions

> Native American rights to property

> Regulation of international waters

There are also a number of passages that deal with legal theory, and "big picture" issues related to the legal system. Various passages have addressed how to interpret law, how to model legal reasoning on computers, and the basis for punishment within the legal system. These passages tend to be more theoretical in nature and focus less on real world examples.

The makers of the test also do not limit themselves to addressing just the U.S. system of law. A number of previous passages have addressed the legal systems of Canada and England, and even South Africa.

In short, the law is treated as the complicated, powerful system it is, and the test makers examine both the faults and benefits of the system, as well as the theoretical underpinnings. Given that the name of the company that produces the LSAT is LSAC, one would expect that they have a great deal of familiarity with law related elements.

Chapter Six—Regulation Passages

The legal system is used to correct possible damage and to regulate actions and industries. On the LSAT, passages occasionally appear that address the legal regulation of marketplaces and borders. In almost all cases the viewpoint presented by the authors is the same: regulation is either needed or should be expanded if already in place. Considering that LSAC is an organization that ultimately assists in producing lawyers, and it is the law which regulates our society, the consistency of this viewpoint should come as no surprise.

Science Passages

The spectrum of topics covered in the Reading Comprehension section is quite broad, but one topic that consistently appears is Science. On average, each Reading Comprehension section contains one passage based on Science.

Chapter Seven—Soft Science Passages

Up until the October 1991 LSAT, all LSAT Reading Comprehension Science passages addressed the topic in a social science environment. For example, a passage would discuss the effects of technology on society, and examine the social implications of the new technology. Passages of this type, which we term Soft Science passages, still appear on the LSAT today, and are presented in Chapter Seven. These passages are relatively easy because they focus more on social impact, or alternatively, they address scientific ideas that the average person is somewhat familiar with, such as oil drilling or renewable energy resources.

Chapter Eight—Hard Science Passages

Starting in October 1991 with the infamous "Waterbugs" passage (which is contained in this book), the makers of the LSAT began to introduce passages based on scientific topics that the average student had never previously encountered, or knew little about. These passages, which we term Hard Science passages, still appear on today's LSAT, and appear with greater frequency than Soft Science passages. These passages are presented in Chapter Eight.

The introduction of Hard Science often increases the difficulty of the section and includes a broader variety of subject matter on the test. Consider some of the Science passages that have appeared on the LSAT:

Embryos and the genetic mechanisms of early polarity

Brain neurotransmitter theory

Gravity, dark matter, and neutrinos

Max Planck and radiation wave theory

To most students, those topics appear at least a bit intimidating. However, you should not be overly concerned about any individual Science passage, because you are neither required nor expected to possess any degree of real scientific expertise.

Chapter Nine—Humanities Passages

Humanities passages appear frequently on the LSAT, often with topics drawn from the fields of history or economics or literature. Although Humanities passages as a whole have no consistent, definable structure or theme. The VIEWSTAMP analysis approach allows you to attack any humanities passage effectively.

Chapter Two:
Diversity I

Affirming Underrepresented Groups

Passage #1: June 1991 Questions 1-8

For the poet Phillis Wheatley, who was brought to colonial New England as a slave in 1761, the formal literary code of eighteenth-century English was thrice removed—by the initial barrier
(5) of the unfamiliar English language, by the discrepancy between spoken and literary forms of English, and by the African tradition of oral rather than written verbal art. Wheatley transcended these barriers—she learned the English language and
(10) English literary forms so quickly and well that she was composing good poetry in English within a few years of her arrival in New England.

Wheatley's experience exemplifies the meeting of oral and written literary cultures. The aesthetic
(15) principles of the African oral tradition were preserved in America by folk artists in work songs, dancing, field hollers, religious music, the use of the drum, and, after the drum was forbidden, in the perpetuation of drum effects in song. African
(20) languages and the functions of language in African societies not only contributed to the emergence of a distinctive Black English but also exerted demonstrable effects on the manner in which other Americans spoke English. Given her African
(25) heritage and her facility with English and the conventions of English poetry, Wheatley's work had the potential to apply the ideas of a written literature to an oral literary tradition in the creation of an African American literary language.
(30) But this was a potential that her poetry unfortunately did not exploit. The standards of eighteenth-century English poetry, which itself reflected little of the American language, led Wheatley to develop a notion of poetry as a closed
(35) system, derived from imitation of earlier written works. No place existed for the rough-and-ready Americanized English she heard in the streets, for the English spoken by Black people, or for Africanisms. The conventions of eighteenth-century
(40) neoclassical poetry ruled out casual talk; her voice and feelings had to be generalized according to rules of poetic diction and characterization; the particulars of her African past, if they were to be dealt with at all, had to be subordinated to the
(45) reigning conventions. African poetry did not count as poetry in her new situation, and African aesthetic canons were irrelevant to the new context because no linguistic or social framework existed to reinforce them. Wheatley adopted a foreign
(50) language and a foreign literary tradition; they were not extensions of her past experience, but replacements.

Thus limited by the eighteenth-century English literary code, Wheatley's poetry contributed little to
(55) the development of a distinctive African American literary language. Yet by the standards of the literary conventions in which she chose to work, Wheatley's poetry is undeniably accomplished, and she is justly celebrated as the first Black American
(60) poet.

1. Which one of the following best expresses the main idea of the passage?

(A) Folk artists employed more principles of African oral tradition in their works than did Phillis Wheatley in her poetry.
(B) Although Phillis Wheatley had to overcome significant barriers in learning English, she mastered the literary conventions of eighteenth century English as well as African aesthetic canons.
(C) Phillis Wheatley's poetry did not fulfill the potential inherent in her experience but did represent a significant accomplishment.
(D) The evolution of a distinctive African American literary language can be traced from the creations of African American folk artists to the poetry of Phillis Wheatley.
(E) Phillis Wheatley joined with African American folk artists in preserving the principles of the African oral tradition.

2. The approach to poetry taken by a modern day Italian immigrant in America would be most analogous to Phillis Wheatley's approach, as it is described in the passage, if the immigrant

(A) translated Italian literary forms into the American idiom
(B) combined Italian and American literary traditions into a new form of poetic expression
(C) contributed to the development of a distinctive Italian American literary style
(D) defined artistic expression in terms of eighteenth century Italian poetic conventions
(E) adopted the language and forms of modern American poetry

3. According to the passage, African languages had a notable influence on

(A)   the religious music of colonists in New England
(B)   the folk art of colonists in New England
(C)   formal written English
(D)   American speech patterns
(E)   eighteenth century aesthetic principles

4. By a "closed system" of poetry (lines 34-35), the author most probably means poetry that

(A)   cannot be written by those who are not raised knowing its conventions
(B)   has little influence on the way language is actually spoken
(C)   substitutes its own conventions for the aesthetic principles of the past
(D)   does not admit the use of street language and casual talk
(E)   is ultimately rejected because its conventions leave little room for further development

5. According to the passage, the standards of eighteenth-century English poetry permitted Wheatley to include which one of the following in her poetry?

(A)   generalized feelings
(B)   Americanized English
(C)   themes from folk art
(D)   casual talk
(E)   Black speech

6. Which one of the following, if true, would most weaken the author's argument concerning the role that Wheatley played in the evolution of an African American literary language?

(A)   Wheatley's poetry was admired in England for its faithfulness to the conventions of neoclassical poetry.
(B)   Wheatley compiled a history in English of her family's experiences in Africa and America.
(C)   The language barriers that Wheatley overcame were eventually transcended by all who were brought from Africa as slaves.
(D)   Several modern African American poets acknowledge the importance of Wheatley's poetry to American literature.
(E)   Scholars trace themes and expressions in African American poetry back to the poetry of Wheatley.

7. It can be inferred that the author of the passage would most probably have praised Phillis Wheatley's poetry more if it had

(A)   affected the manner in which slaves and freed Black people spoke English
(B)   defined African American artistic expression in terms of earlier works
(C)   adopted the standards of eighteenth century English poetry
(D)   combined elements of the English literary tradition with those of the African oral tradition
(E)   focused on the barriers that written English literary forms presented to Black artists

8. Which one of the following most accurately characterizes the author's attitude with respect to Phillis Wheatley's literary accomplishments?

(A)   enthusiastic advocacy
(B)   qualified admiration
(C)   dispassionate impartiality
(D)   detached ambivalence
(E)   perfunctory dismissal

Passage #2: October 1991 Questions 1-6

There is substantial evidence that by 1926, with
the publication of *The Weary Blues,* Langston
Hughes had broken with two well-established
traditions in African American literature. In *The*
(5) *Weary Blues*, Hughes chose to modify the traditions
that decreed that African American literature must
promote racial acceptance and integration, and that,
in order to do so, it must reflect an understanding
and mastery of Western European literary
(10) techniques and styles. Necessarily excluded by this
decree, linguistically and thematically, was the vast
amount of secular folk material in the oral tradition
that had been created by Black people in the years
of slavery and after. It might be pointed out that
(15) even the spirituals or "sorrow songs" of the slaves—
as distinct from their secular songs and stories—
had been Europeanized to make them acceptable
within these African American traditions after the
Civil War. In 1862 northern White writers had
(20) commented favorably on the unique and provocative
melodies of these "sorrow songs" when they first
heard them sung by slaves in the Carolina sea
islands. But by 1916, ten years before the publication
of *The Weary Blues,* Harry T. Burleigh, the Black
(25) baritone soloist at New York's ultra-fashionable
Saint George's Episcopal Church, had published
Jubilee Songs of the United States, with every
spiritual arranged so that a concert singer could
sing it "in the manner of an art song." Clearly, the
(30) artistic work of Black people could be used to
promote racial acceptance and integration only on
the condition that it became Europeanized.
    Even more than his rebellion against this
restrictive tradition in African American art,
(35) Hughes's expression of the vibrant folk culture of
Black people established his writing as a landmark
in the history of African American literature. Most
of his folk poems have the distinctive marks of this
folk culture's oral tradition: they contain many
(40) instances of naming and enumeration, considerable
hyperbole and understatement, and a strong infusion
of street-talk rhyming. There is a deceptive veil of
artlessness in these poems. Hughes prided himself
on being an impromptu and impressionistic writer
(45) of poetry. His, he insisted, was not an artfully
constructed poetry. Yet an analysis of his dramatic
monologues and other poems reveals that his poetry
was carefully and artfully crafted. In his folk poetry
we find features common to all folk literature, such
(50) as dramatic ellipsis, narrative compression, rhythmic
repetition, and monosyllabic emphasis. The peculiar
mixture of irony and humor we find in his writing
is a distinguishing feature of his folk poetry.
Together, these aspects of Hughes's writing helped
(55) to modify the previous restrictions on the techniques
and subject matter of Black writers and consequently
to broaden the linguistic and thematic range of
African American literature.

1. The author mentions which one of the following as
an example of the influence of Black folk culture
on Hughes's poetry?

(A) his exploitation of ambiguous and deceptive
meanings
(B) his care and craft in composing poems
(C) his use of naming and enumeration
(D) his use of first-person narrative
(E) his strong religious beliefs

2. The author suggests that the "deceptive veil" (line
42) in Hughes's poetry obscures

(A) evidence of his use of oral techniques in his
poetry
(B) evidence of his thoughtful deliberation in
composing his poems
(C) his scrupulous concern for representative
details in his poetry
(D) his incorporation of Western European
literary techniques in his poetry
(E) his engagement with social and political
issues rather than aesthetic ones

3. With which one of the following statements regarding *Jubilee Songs of the United States* would the author be most likely to agree?

   (A) Its publication marked an advance in the intrinsic quality of African American art.
   (B) It paved the way for publication of Hughes's *The Weary Blues* by making African American art fashionable.
   (C) It was an authentic replication of African American spirituals and "sorrow songs."
   (D) It demonstrated the extent to which spirituals were adapted in order to make them more broadly accepted.
   (E) It was to the spiritual what Hughes's *The Weary Blues* was to secular songs and stories.

4. The author most probably mentions the reactions of northern White writers to non-Europeanized "sorrow songs" in order to

   (A) indicate that modes of expression acceptable in the context of slavery in the South were acceptable only to a small number of White writers in the North after the Civil War
   (B) contrast White writers' earlier appreciation of these songs with the growing tendency after the Civil War to regard Europeanized versions of the songs as more acceptable
   (C) show that the requirement that such songs be Europeanized was internal to the African American tradition and was unrelated to the literary standards or attitudes of White writers
   (D) demonstrate that such songs in their non-Europeanized form were more imaginative than Europeanized versions of the same songs
   (E) suggest that White writers benefited more from exposure to African American art forms than Black writers did from exposure to European art forms

5. The passage suggests that the author would be most likely to agree with which one of the following statements about the requirement that Black writers employ Western European literary techniques?

   (A) The requirement was imposed more for social than for aesthetic reasons.
   (B) The requirement was a relatively unimportant aspect of the African American tradition.
   (C) The requirement was the chief reason for Hughes's success as a writer.
   (D) The requirement was appropriate for some forms of expression but not for others.
   (E) The requirement was never as strong as it may have appeared to be.

6. Which one of the following aspects of Hughes's poetry does the author appear to value most highly?

   (A) its novelty compared to other works of African American literature
   (B) its subtle understatement compared to that of other kinds of folk literature
   (C) its virtuosity in adapting musical forms to language
   (D) its expression of the folk culture of Black people
   (E) its universality of appeal achieved through the adoption of colloquial expressions

Women's participation in the revolutionary events in France between 1789 and 1795 has only recently been given nuanced treatment. Early twentieth century historians of the French Revolution are
(5) typified by Jaures, who, though sympathetic to the women's movement of his own time, never even mentions its antecedents in revolutionary France. Even today most general histories treat only cursorily a few individual women, like Marie Antoinette. The
(10) recent studies by Landes, Badinter, Godineau, and Roudinesco, however, should signal a much-needed reassessment of women's participation.

Godineau and Roudinesco point to three significant phases in that participation. The first, up
(15) to mid-1792, involved those women who wrote political tracts. Typical of their orientation to theoretical issues—in Godineau's view, without practical effect—is Marie Gouze's *Declaration of the Rights of Women*. The emergence of vocal middle-
(20) class women's political clubs marks the second phase. Formed in 1791 as adjuncts of middle-class male political clubs, and originally philanthropic in function, by late 1792 independent clubs of women began to advocate military participation for women.
(25) In the final phase, the famine of 1795 occasioned a mass women's movement: women seized food supplies, held officials hostage, and argued for the implementation of democratic politics. This phase ended in May of 1795 with the military suppression
(30) of this multiclass movement. In all three phases women's participation in politics contrasted markedly with their participation before 1789. Before that date some noblewomen participated indirectly in elections, but such participation by more
(35) than a narrow range of the population—women or men—came only with the Revolution.

What makes the recent studies particularly compelling, however, is not so much their organization of chronology as their unflinching
(40) willingness to confront the reasons for the collapse of the women's movement. For Landes and Badinter, the necessity of women's having to speak in the established vocabularies of certain intellectual and political traditions diminished the ability of the
(45) women's movement to resist suppression. Many women, and many men, they argue, located their vision within the confining tradition of Jean-Jacques Rousseau, who linked male and female roles with public and private spheres respectively. But, when
(50) women went on to make political alliances with radical Jacobin men, Badinter asserts, they adopted a vocabulary and a violently extremist viewpoint that unfortunately was even more damaging to their political interests.
(55) Each of these scholars has a different political

agenda and takes a different approach—Godineau, for example, works with police archives while Roudinesco uses explanatory schema from modern psychology. Yet, admirably, each gives center stage
(60) to a group that previously has been marginalized, or at best undifferentiated, by historians. And in the case of Landes and Badinter, the reader is left with a sobering awareness of the cost to the women of the Revolution of speaking in borrowed voices.

14. Which one of the following best states the main point of the passage?

(A) According to recent historical studies, the participation of women in the revolutionary events of 1789-1795 can most profitably be viewed in three successive stages.

(B) The findings of certain recent historical studies have resulted from an earlier general reassessment, by historians, of women's participation in the revolutionary events of 1789-1795.

(C) Adopting the vocabulary and viewpoint of certain intellectual and political traditions resulted in no political advantage for women in France in the years 1789-1795.

(D) Certain recent historical studies have provided a much-needed description and evaluation of the evolving roles of women in the revolutionary events of 1789-1795.

(E) Historical studies that seek to explain the limitations of the women's movement in France during the years 1789-1795 are much more convincing than are those that seek only to describe the general features of that movement.

15. The passage suggests that Godineau would be likely to agree with which one of the following statements about Marie Gouze's *Declaration of the Rights of Women*?

    (A) This work was not understood by many of Gouze's contemporaries.
    (B) This work indirectly inspired the formation of independent women's political clubs.
    (C) This work had little impact on the world of political action.
    (D) This work was the most compelling produced by a French woman between 1789 and 1792.
    (E) This work is typical of the kind of writing French women produced between 1793 and 1795.

16. According to the passage, which one of the following is a true statement about the purpose of the women's political clubs mentioned in line 20?

    (A) These clubs fostered a mass women's movement.
    (B) These clubs eventually developed a purpose different from their original purpose.
    (C) These clubs were founded to advocate military participation for women.
    (D) These clubs counteracted the original purpose of male political clubs.
    (E) These clubs lost their direction by the time of the famine of 1795.

17. The primary function of the first paragraph of the passage is to

    (A) outline the author's argument about women's roles in France between 1789 and 1795
    (B) anticipate possible challenges to the findings of the recent studies of women in France between 1789 and 1795
    (C) summarize some long-standing explanations of the role of individual women in France between 1789 and 1795
    (D) present a context for the discussion of recent studies of women in France between 1789 and 1795
    (E) characterize various eighteenth-century studies of women in France

18. The passage suggests that Landes and Badinter would be likely to agree with which one of the following statements about the women's movement in France in the 1790s?

    (A) The movement might have been more successful if women had developed their own political vocabularies.
    (B) The downfall of the movement was probably unrelated to its alliance with Jacobin men.
    (C) The movement had a great deal of choice about whether to adopt a Rousseauist political vocabulary.
    (D) The movement would have triumphed if it had not been suppressed by military means.
    (E) The movement viewed a Rousseauist political tradition, rather than a Jacobin political ideology, as detrimental to its interests.

19. In the context of the passage, the word "cost" in line 63 refers to the

    (A) dichotomy of private roles for women and public roles for men
    (B) almost nonexistent political participation of women before 1789
    (C) historians' lack of differentiation among various groups of women
    (D) political alliances women made with radical Jacobin men
    (E) collapse of the women's movement in the 1790s

20. The author of the passage is primarily concerned with

    (A) criticizing certain political and intellectual traditions
    (B) summarizing the main points of several recent historical studies and assessing their value
    (C) establishing a chronological sequence and arguing for its importance
    (D) comparing and contrasting women's political activities before and after the French Revolution
    (E) reexamining a long-held point of view and isolating its strengths and weaknesses

Passage #4: October 1992 Questions 7-12

In the late nineteenth century, the need for women physicians in missionary hospitals in Canton, China, led to expanded opportunities for both Western and Chinese women. The presence of
(5) Western women as medical missionaries in China was made possible by certain changes within the Western missionary movement. Beginning in the 1870s, increasingly large numbers of women were forming women's foreign mission societies
(10) dedicated to the support of women's foreign mission work. Beyond giving the women who organized the societies a formal activity outside their home circles, these organizations enabled an increasing number of single women missionaries (as
(15) opposed to women who were part of the more typical husband-wife missionary teams) to work abroad. Before the formation of these women's organizations, mission funds had been collected by ministers and other church leaders, most of whom
(20) emphasized local parish work. What money was spent on foreign missions was under the control of exclusively male foreign mission boards whose members were uniformly uneasy about the new idea of sending single women out into the mission field.
(25) But as women's groups began raising impressive amounts of money donated specifically in support of single women missionaries, the home churches bowed both to women's changing roles at home and to increasing numbers of single professional
(30) missionary women abroad.

Although the idea of employing a woman physician was a daring one for most Western missionaries in China, the advantages of a well-trained Western woman physician could not be
(35) ignored by Canton mission hospital administrators. A woman physician could attend women patients without offending any of the accepted conventions of female modesty. Eventually, some of these women were able to found and head separate
(40) women's medical institutions, thereby gaining access to professional responsibilities far beyond those available to them at home.

These developments also led to the attainment of valuable training and status by a significant number
(45) of Chinese women. The presence of women physicians in Canton mission hospitals led many Chinese women to avail themselves of Western medicine who might otherwise have failed to do so because of their culture's emphasis on physical
(50) modesty. In order to provide enough women physicians for these patients, growing numbers of young Chinese women were given instruction in medicine. This enabled them to earn an independent income, something that was then largely unavailable

(55) to women within traditional Chinese society. Many women graduates were eventually able to go out on their own into private practice, freeing themselves of dependence upon the mission community. The most important result of these opportunities was the
(60) establishment of clear evidence of women's abilities and strengths, clear reasons for affording women expanded opportunities, and clear role models for how these abilities and responsibilities might be exercised.

7. Which one of the following statements about Western women missionaries working abroad can be inferred from the passage?

(A) There were very few women involved in foreign missionary work before the 1870s.

(B) Most women working abroad as missionaries before the 1870s were financed by women's foreign mission societies.

(C) Most women employed in mission hospitals abroad before the 1870s were trained as nurses rather than as physicians.

(D) The majority of professional women missionaries working abroad before the 1870s were located in Canton, China.

(E) Most women missionaries working abroad before the 1870s were married to men who were also missionaries.

8. The author mentions that most foreign mission boards were exclusively male most probably in order to

(A) contrast foreign mission boards with the boards of secular organizations sending aid to China

(B) explain the policy of foreign mission boards toward training Chinese women in medicine

(C) justify the preference of foreign mission boards for professionally qualified missionaries

(D) help account for the attitude of foreign mission boards towards sending single women missionaries abroad

(E) differentiate foreign mission boards from boards directing parish work at home

9. Which one of the following best describes the organization of the passage?

(A) A situation is described, conditions that brought about the situation are explained, and results of the situation are enumerated.

(B) An assertion is made, statements supporting and refuting the assertion are examined, and a conclusion is drawn.

(C) An obstacle is identified, a variety of possible ways to overcome the obstacle are presented, and an opinion is ventured.

(D) A predicament is outlined, factors leading up to the predicament are scrutinized, and a tentative resolution of the predicament is recommended.

(E) A development is analyzed, the drawbacks and advantages accompanying the development are contrasted, and an eventual outcome is predicted.

10. Which one of the following, if true, would most undermine the author's analysis of the reason for the increasing number of single women missionaries sent abroad beginning in the 1870s?

(A) The Western church boards that sent the greatest number of single women missionaries abroad had not received any financial support from women's auxiliary groups.

(B) The women who were sent abroad as missionary physicians had been raised in families with a strong history of missionary commitment.

(C) Most of the single missionary women sent abroad were trained as teachers and translators rather than as medical practitioners.

(D) The Western church boards tended to send abroad single missionary women who had previously been active in local parish work.

(E) None of the single missionary women who were sent abroad were active members of foreign mission boards.

11. According to the passage, which one of the following was a factor in the acceptance of Western women as physicians in mission hospitals in Canton, China?

(A) the number of male physicians practicing in that region

(B) the specific women's foreign mission society that supplied the funding

(C) the specific home parishes from which the missionary women came

(D) the cultural conventions of the host society

(E) the relations between the foreign mission boards and the hospital administrators

12. The passage suggests which one of the following about medical practices in late-nineteenth-century Canton, China?

(A) There was great suspicion of non-Chinese medical practices.

(B) Medical care was more often administered in the home than in hospitals.

(C) It was customary for women physicians to donate a portion of their income for the maintenance of their extended family.

(D) It was not customary for female patients to be treated by male physicians.

(E) Young women tended to be afforded as many educational opportunities in medicine as young men were.

Passage #5: June 1994 Questions 22-27

Although surveys of medieval legislation, guild organization, and terminology used to designate different medical practitioners have demonstrated that numerous medical specialties were recognized
(5) in Europe during the Middle Ages, most historians continue to equate the term "woman medical practitioner" wherever they encounter it in medieval records, with "midwife." This common practice obscures the fact that, although women
(10) were not represented on all levels of medicine equally, they were represented in a variety of specialties throughout the broad medical community. A reliable study by Wickersheimer and Jacquart documents that, of 7,647 medical
(15) practitioners in France during the twelfth through fifteenth centuries, 121 were women; of these, only 44 were identified as midwives, while the rest practiced as physicians, surgeons, apothecaries, barbers, and other healers.
(20)   While preserving terminological distinctions somewhat increases the quality of the information extracted from medieval documents concerning women medical practitioners, scholars must also reopen the whole question of why documentary
(25) evidence for women medical practitioners comprises such a tiny fraction of the evidence historians of medieval medicine usually present. Is this due to the limitations of the historical record, as has been claimed, or does it also result from the methods
(30) historians use? Granted, apart from medical licenses, the principal sources of information regarding medical practitioners available to researchers are wills, property transfers, court records, and similar documents, all of which
(35) typically underrepresent women because of restrictive medieval legal traditions. Nonetheless, the parameters researchers choose when they define their investigations may contribute to the problem. Studies focusing on the upper echelons of "learned"
(40) medicine, for example, tend to exclude healers on the legal and social fringes of medical practice, where most women would have been found.
    The advantages of broadening the scope of such studies is immediately apparent in Pelling and
(45) Webster's study of sixteenth-century London. Instead of focusing solely on officially recognized and licensed practitioners, the researchers defined a medical practitioner as "any individual whose occupation is basically concerned with the care of
(50) the sick." Using this definition, they found primary source information suggesting that there were 60 women medical practitioners in the city of London in 1560. Although this figure may be slightly exaggerated, the evidence contrasts strikingly with

(55) that of Gottfried, whose earlier survey identified only 28 women medical practitioners in all of England between 1330 and 1530.
    Finally, such studies provide only statistical information about the variety and prevalence of
(60) women's medical practice in medieval Europe. Future studies might also make profitable use of analyses developed in other areas of women's history as a basis for exploring the social context of women's medical practice. Information about
(65) economic rivalry in medicine, women's literacy, and the control of medical knowledge could add much to our growing understanding of women medical practitioners' role in medieval society.

22. Which one of the following best expresses the main point of the passage?

(A) Recent studies demonstrate that women medical practitioners were more common in England than in the rest of Western Europe during the Middle Ages.

(B) The quantity and quality of the information historians uncover concerning women's medical practice in medieval Europe would be improved if they changed their methods of study.

(C) The sparse evidence for women medical practitioners in studies dealing with the Middle Ages is due primarily to the limitations of the historical record.

(D) Knowledge about the social issues that influenced the role women medical practitioners played in medieval society has been enhanced by several recent studies.

(E) Analyses developed in other areas of women's history could probably be used to provide more information about the social context of women's medical practice during the Middle Ages.

23. Which one of the following is most closely analogous to the error the author believes historians make when they equate the term "woman medical practitioner" with "midwife"?

(A) equating pear with apple
(B) equating science with biology
(C) equating supervisor with subordinate
(D) equating member with nonmember
(E) equating instructor with trainee

24. It can be inferred from the passage that the author would be most likely to agree with which one of the following assertions regarding Gottfried's study?

(A) Gottfried's study would have recorded a much larger number of women medical practitioners if the time frame covered by the study had included the late sixteenth century.

(B) The small number of women medical practitioners identified in Gottfried's study is due primarily to problems caused by inaccurate sources.

(C) The small number of women medical practitioners identified in Gottfried's study is due primarily to the loss of many medieval documents.

(D) The results of Gottfried's study need to be considered in light of the social changes occurring in Western Europe during the fourteenth and fifteenth centuries.

(E) In setting the parameters for his study, Gottfried appears to have defined the term "medical practitioner" very narrowly.

25. The passage suggests that a future study that would be more informative about medieval women medical practitioners might focus on which one of the following?

(A) the effect of social change on the political and economic structure of medieval society

(B) the effect of social constraints on medieval women's access to a medical education

(C) the types of medical specialties that developed during the Middle Ages

(D) the reasons why medieval historians tend to equate the term "woman medical practitioner" with midwife

(E) the historical developments responsible for the medieval legal tradition's restrictions on women

26. The author refers to the study by Wickersheimer and Jacquart in order to

(A) demonstrate that numerous medical specialties were recognized in Western Europe during the Middle Ages

(B) demonstrate that women are often underrepresented in studies of medieval medical practitioners

(C) prove that midwives were officially recognized as members of the medical community during the Middle Ages

(D) prove that midwives were only a part of a larger community of women medical practitioners during the Middle Ages

(E) prove that the existence of midwives can be documented in Western Europe as early as the twelfth century

27. In the passage, the author is primarily concerned with doing which one of the following?

(A) describing new methodological approaches
(B) revising the definitions of certain concepts
(C) comparing two different analyses
(D) arguing in favor of changes in method
(E) chronicling certain historical developments

Passage #6: September 1995 Questions 22-27

Historians have long accepted the notion that women of English descent who lived in the English colonies of North America during the seventeenth and eighteenth centuries were better off than either
(5) the contemporary women in England or the colonists' own nineteenth-century daughters and granddaughters. The "golden age" theory originated in the 1920s with the work of Elizabeth Dexter, who argued that there were relatively few
(10) women among the colonists, and that all hands—male and female—were needed to sustain the growing settlements. Rigid sex-role distinctions could not exist under such circumstances; female colonists could accordingly engage in whatever
(15) occupations they wished, encountering few legal or social constraints if they sought employment outside the home. The surplus of male colonists also gave women crucial bargaining power in the marriage market, since women's contributions were vital to
(20) the survival of colonial households.

Dexter's portrait of female colonists living under conditions of rough equality with their male counterparts was eventually incorporated into studies of nineteenth-century middle-class women.
(25) The contrast between the self-sufficient colonial woman and the oppressed nineteenth-century woman, confined to her home by stultifying ideologies of domesticity and by the fact that industrialization eliminated employment
(30) opportunities for middle-class women, gained an extraordinarily tenacious hold on historians. Even scholars who have questioned the "golden age" view of colonial women's status have continued to accept the paradigm of a nineteenth-century
(35) decline from a more desirable past. For example, Joan Hoff-Wilson asserted that there was no "golden age" and yet emphasized that the nineteenth century brought "increased loss of function and authentic status for" middle-class
(40) women.

Recent publications about colonial women have exposed the concept of a decline in status as simplistic and unsophisticated, a theory that based its assessment of colonial women's status solely on
(45) one factor (their economic function in society) and assumed all too readily that a relatively simple social system automatically brought higher standing to colonial women. The new scholarship presents a far more complicated picture, one in which
(50) definitions of gender roles, the colonial economy, demographic patterns, religion, the law, and household organization all contributed to defining the circumstances of colonial women's lives. Indeed, the primary concern of modern scholarship is not to
(55) generalize about women's status but to identify the

specific changes and continuities in women's lives during the colonial period. For example, whereas earlier historians suggested that there was little change for colonial women before 1800, the new
(60) scholarship suggests that a three-part chronological division more accurately reflects colonial women's experiences. First was the initial period of English colonization (from the 1620s to about 1660); then a period during which patterns of family and
(65) community were challenged and reshaped (roughly from 1660 to 1750); and finally the era of revolution (approximately 1750 to 1815), which brought other chances to women's lives.

22. Which one of the following best expresses the main idea of the passage?

(A) An earlier theory about the status of middle-class women in the nineteenth century has been supported by recent scholarship.
(B) Recent studies of middle-class nineteenth-century women have altered an earlier theory about the status of colonial women.
(C) Recent scholarship has exposed an earlier theory about the status of colonial women as too narrowly based and oversimplified.
(D) An earlier theory about colonial women has greatly influenced recent studies on middle-class women in the nineteenth century.
(E) An earlier study of middle-class women was based on insufficient research on the status of women in the nineteenth century.

23. The author discusses Hoff-Wilson primarily in order to

(A) describe how Dexter's theory was refuted by historians of nineteenth-century North America
(B) describe how the theory of middle-class women's nineteenth-century decline in status was developed
(C) describe an important influence on recent scholarship about the colonial period
(D) demonstrate the persistent influence of the "golden age" theory
(E) provide an example of current research on the colonial period

24. It can be inferred from the passage that the author would be most likely to describe the views of the scholars mentioned in line 32 as

(A) unassailable
(B) innovative
(C) paradoxical
(D) overly sophisticated
(E) without merit

25. It can be inferred from the passage that, in proposing the "three-part chronological division" (lines 60-61), scholars recognized which one of the following?

(A) The circumstances of colonial women's lives were defined by a broad variety of social and economic factors.

(B) Women's lives in the English colonies of North America were similar to women's lives in seventeenth- and eighteenth-century England.

(C) Colonial women's status was adversely affected when patterns of family and community were established in the late seventeenth century.

(D) Colonial women's status should be assessed primarily on the basis of their economic function in society.

(E) Colonial women's status was low when the colonies were settled but changed significantly during the era of revolution.

26. According to the author, the publications about colonial women mentioned in the third paragraph had which one of the following effects?

(A) They undermined Dexter's argument on the status of women colonists during the colonial period.

(B) They revealed the tenacity of the "golden age" theory in American history.

(C) They provided support for historians, such as Hoff-Wilson, who study the nineteenth century.

(D) They established that women's status did not change significantly from the colonial period to the nineteenth century.

(E) They provided support for earlier theories about women colonists in the English colonies of North America.

27. Practitioners of the new scholarship discussed in the last paragraph would be most likely to agree with which one of the following statements about Dexter's argument?

(A) It makes the assumption that women's status is determined primarily by their political power in society.

(B) It makes the assumption that a less complex social system necessarily confers higher status on women.

(C) It is based on inadequate research on women's economic role in the colonies.

(D) It places too much emphasis on the way definitions of gender roles affected women colonists in the colonial period.

(E) It accurately describes the way women's status declined in the nineteenth century.

Passage #7: December 1995 Questions 1-8

Many literary scholars believe that Zora Neale Hurston's *Their Eyes Were Watching God* (1937) has been the primary influence on some of the most accomplished Black women writing in the United
(5) States today. Indeed, Alice Walker, the author of the prize-winning novel *The Color Purple*, has said of *Their Eyes*, "There is no book more important to me than this one." Thus, it seems necessary to ask why *Their Eyes,* a work now viewed by a multitude
(10) of readers as remarkably successful in its complex depiction of a Black woman's search for self and community, was ever relegated to the margins of the literary canon.

The details of the novel's initial reception help
(15) answer this question. Unlike the recently rediscovered and reexamined work of Harriet Wilson, *Their Eyes* was not totally ignored by book reviewers upon its publication. In fact, it received a mixture of positive and negative reviews both from
(20) White book reviewers working for prominent periodicals and from important figures within Black literary circles. In the *Saturday Review of Literature*, George Stevens wrote that "the narration is exactly right, because most of it is dialogue and the
(25) dialogue gives us a constant sense of character in action." The negative criticism was partially a result of Hurston's ideological differences with other members of the Black literary community about the depiction of Black Americans in literature. Black
(30) writers of the 1940s believed that the Black artist's primary responsibility was to create protest fiction that explored the negative effects of racism in the United States. For example, Richard Wright, the author of the much acclaimed *Native Son* (1940),
(35) wrote that *Their Eyes* had "no theme" and "no message." Most critics' and readers' expectations of Black literature rendered them unable to appreciate Hurston's subtle delineation of the life of an ordinary Black woman in a Black community,
(40) and the novel went quietly out of print.

Recent acclaim for *Their Eyes* results from the emergence of feminist literary criticism and the development of standards of evaluation specific to the work of Black writers; these kinds of criticism
(45) changed readers' expectations of art and enabled them to appreciate Hurston's novel. The emergence of feminist criticism was crucial because such criticism brought new attention to neglected works such as Hurston's and alerted readers to Hurston's
(50) exploration of women's issues in her fiction. The Afrocentric standards of evaluation were equally important to the rediscovery of *Their Eyes,* for such standards provided readers with the tools to recognize and appreciate the Black folklore and
(55) oral storytelling traditions Hurston incorporated

within her work. In one of the most illuminating discussions of the novel to date, Henry Louis Gates, Jr., states that "Hurston's strategy seems to concern itself with the possibilities of representation of the
(60) speaking Black voice in writing."

1. The passage suggests which one of the following about Harriet Wilson's novel?

   (A) It was written at the same time as *Their Eyes Were Watching God,* but it did not receive as much critical attention.
   (B) It greatly influenced Black women writing after the 1940s.
   (C) It was widely read when it was published, but it has not received attention from literary critics until recently.
   (D) It was not formally published, and the manuscript has only recently been discovered by literary critics.
   (E) It did not receive critical attention when it was published, but it has recently become the subject of critical study.

2. The passage offers support for which one of the following statements about literary reviewers and *Their Eyes Were Watching God* ?

   (A) *Their Eyes* was widely acclaimed by reviewers upon its publication, even though it eventually went out of print.
   (B) The eventual obscurity of *Their Eyes* was not the result of complete neglect by reviewers.
   (C) Some early reviewers of *Their Eyes* interpreted the novel from a point of view that later became known as Afrocentric.
   (D) *Their Eyes* was more typical of the protest fiction of the 1940s than reviewers realized.
   (E) Most early reviewers of *Their Eyes* did not respond positively to the book.

3. Which one of the following best states the main idea of the passage?

   (A) Hurston's *Their Eyes Were Watching God* had little in common with novels written by Black authors during the 1940s.

   (B) Feminist critics and authors such as Alice Walker were instrumental in establishing Hurston's *Their Eyes Were Watching God* as an important part of the American literary canon.

   (C) Critics and readers were unable to appreciate fully Hurston's *Their Eyes Were Watching God* until critics applied new standards of evaluation to the novel.

   (D) Hurston's *Their Eyes Were Watching God* was an important influence on the protest fiction written by Black writers in the mid-twentieth century.

   (E) Afrocentric strategies of analysis have brought attention to the use of oral storytelling traditions in novels written by Black Americans, such as Hurston's *Their Eyes Were Watching God.*

4. According to the passage, which one of the following is true of Black folklore traditions as used in literature written in the United States?

   (A) They are an aspect of Black American literature first recognized and written about by Henry Louis Gates, Jr.

   (B) They were not widely incorporated into novels written by Black Americans until after the 1940s.

   (C) They were first used by a novelist in Zora Neale Hurston's *Their Eyes Were Watching God.*

   (D) They were not incorporated into novels published by Black Americans in the 1940s.

   (E) They are an aspect of Black literature that some readers did not fully appreciate until relatively recently.

5. The passage suggests that *Native Son* differs from *Their Eyes Were Watching God* in which one of the following ways?

   (A) It received fewer positive reviews at the time of its publication than did *Their Eyes.*

   (B) It is less typical of literature written by Black Americans during the 1940s than is *Their Eyes.*

   (C) It is less focused on an ordinary individual's search for self within a Black community than is *Their Eyes.*

   (D) It depicts more aspects of Black American folklore than does *Their Eyes.*

   (E) It has received more attention from feminist and Afrocentric literary critics than has *Their Eyes.*

6. Which one of the following provides the clearest example of the kind of fiction that many Black writers of the 1940s, as their views are described in the passage, believed should be written?

   (A) a novel that focuses on the interrelationships among four generations of Black women

   (B) a historical novel that re-creates actual events that occurred as Black people suffered from oppression and racial injustice in a small town

   (C) a novel, based on biographical stories orally relayed to the author as a child, that describes the development of traditions in a Black family

   (D) a novel that explores the psychological aspects of a relationship between a White man and a Black man as they work together to organize protests against unjust working conditions

   (E) a novel that examines the different ways in which three Black children experience their first day of school in a rural community

7. The author would be most likely to agree with which one of the following statements about the relationship between art and literary criticism?

   (A) The long-term reputation of a work of art is less dependent on the response of literary critics than on the response of readers and authors.

   (B) Experimental works of fiction are usually poorly received and misunderstood by literary critics when they are first published.

   (C) The response of literary critics to a work of art can be determined by certain ideological perspectives and assumptions about the purpose of art.

   (D) Literary critics do not significantly affect the way most people interpret and appreciate literature.

   (E) The ideological bases of a work of art are the first consideration of most literary critics.

8. The primary purpose of the passage is to

   (A) correct a misconception
   (B) explain a reassessment
   (C) reconcile two points of view
   (D) criticize a conventional approach
   (E) announce a new discovery

Passage #8: October 1996 Questions 1-6

The career of trumpeter Miles Davis was one of the most astonishingly productive that jazz music has ever seen. Yet his genius has never received its due. The impatience and artistic restlessness that
(5) characterized his work spawned one stylistic turn after another and made Davis anathema to many critics, who deplored his abandonment first of bebop and then of "cool" acoustic jazz for ever more innovative sounds.

(10) Having begun his career studying bebop, Davis pulled the first of many stylistic surprises when, in 1948, he became a member of an impromptu musical think tank that gathered in a New York City apartment. The work of this group not only
(15) slowed down tempos and featured ensemble playing as much as or even more than solos—in direct reaction to bebop—it also became the seedbed for the "West Coast cool" jazz style.

In what would become a characteristic zigzag,
(20) Davis didn't follow up on these innovations himself. Instead, in the late 1950s he formed a new band that broke free from jazz's restrictive pattern of chord changes. Soloists could determine the shapes of their melodies without referring back to
(25) the same unvarying repetition of chords. In this period, Davis attempted to join jazz phrasings, harmonies, and tonal qualities with a unified and integrated sound similar to that of a classical orchestral piece: in his recordings the rhythms, no
(30) matter how jazzlike, are always understated, and the instrumental voicings seem muted.

Davis's recordings from the late 1960s signal that, once again, his direction was changing. On *Filles de Kilimanjaro*, Davis's request that
(35) keyboardist Herbie Hancock play electric rather than acoustic piano caused consternation among jazz purists of the time. Other albums featured rock-style beats, heavily electronic instrumentation, a loose improvisational attack and a growing use of
(40) studio editing to create jagged soundscapes. By 1969 Davis's typical studio procedure was to have musicians improvise from a base script of material and then to build finished pieces out of tape, like a movie director. Rock groups had pioneered the
(45) process; to jazz lovers, raised on the ideal of live improvisation, that approach was a violation of the premise that recordings should simply document the musicians' thought processes in real time. Davis again became the target of fierce polemics by purist
(50) jazz critics, who have continued to belittle his contributions to jazz.

What probably underlies the intensity of the reactions against Davis is fear of the broadening of possibilities that he exemplified. Ironically, he was

(55) simply doing what jazz explorers have always done: reaching for something new that was his own. But because his career endured, because he didn't die young or record only sporadically, and because he refused to dwell in whatever niche he had
(60) previously carved out, critics find it difficult to definitively rank Davis in the aesthetic hierarchy to which they cling.

1. Which one of the following best states the main point of the passage?

(A) Because the career of Miles Davis was characterized by frequent shifts in styles, he never fulfilled his musical potential.

(B) Because the career of Miles Davis does not fit neatly into their preconceptions about the life and music of jazz musicians, jazz critics have not accorded him the appreciation he deserves.

(C) Because the career of Miles Davis was unusually long and productive, he never received the popular acclaim generally reserved for artists with more tragic life histories.

(D) The long and productive career of Miles Davis spawned most of the major stylistic changes affecting twentieth-century jazz.

(E) Miles Davis's versatility and openness have inspired the admiration of most jazz critics.

2. According to the passage, which one of the following is true of the "West Coast cool" jazz style?

(A) It was popularized by Miles Davis.
(B) It was characterized by a unified and integrated sound.
(C) It was played primarily by large ensembles.
(D) It introduced a wide variety of chord change patterns.
(E) It grew out of innovations developed in New York City.

3. The passage suggests which one of the following about the kind of jazz played by Miles Davis prior to 1948?

(A) It was characterized by rapid tempos and an emphasis on solo playing.
(B) It equally balanced ensemble and solo playing.
(C) It was a reaction against more restrictive jazz styles.
(D) It is regarded by purist jazz critics as the only authentic jazz style.
(E) It was played primarily in New York City jazz clubs.

4. Which one of the following best describes the author's attitude toward Miles Davis's music?

    (A)   uneasy ambivalence
    (B)   cautious neutrality
    (C)   grudging respect
    (D)   moderate commendation
    (E)   appreciative advocacy

5. Which one of the following creative processes is most similar to Miles Davis's typical studio procedure of the late 1960s, as described in the fourth paragraph of the passage?

    (A)   The producer of a television comedy show suggests a setting and general topic for a comedy sketch and then lets the comedians write their own script.
    (B)   An actor digresses from the written script and improvises during a monologue in order to introduce a feeling of spontaneity to the performance.
    (C)   A conductor rehearses each section of the orchestra separately before assembling them to rehearse the entire piece together.
    (D)   An artist has several photographers take pictures pertaining to a certain assigned theme and then assembles them into a pictorial collage.
    (E)   A teacher has each student in a writing class write an essay on an assigned topic and then submits the best essays to be considered for publication in a journal.

6. Which one of the following, if true, would most undermine the author's explanation for the way Miles Davis is regarded by jazz critics?

    (A)   Many jazz musicians who specialize in improvisational playing are greatly admired by Jazz critics.
    (B)   Many jazz musicians whose careers have been characterized by several radical changes in style are greatly admired by jazz critics.
    (C)   Several jazz musicians who perform exclusively on electronic instruments are very highly regarded by jazz critics.
    (D)   The jazz innovators who are held in the highest regard by jazz critics had brief yet brilliant careers.
    (E)   Jazz critics are known to have a higher regard for musicality than for mere technical virtuosity.

Chapter Three:
Diversity II

Undermining Overrepresented Groups

POWERSCORE
TEST PREPARATION

Passage #1: October 1991 Questions 7-13

Historians generally agree that, of the great modern innovations, the railroad had the most far-reaching impact on major events in the United States in the nineteenth and early twentieth
(5) centuries, particularly on the Industrial Revolution. There is, however, considerable disagreement among cultural historians regarding public attitudes toward the railroad, both at its inception in the 1830s and during the half century between 1880
(10) and 1930, when the national rail system was completed and reached the zenith of its popularity in the United States. In a recent book, John Stilgoe has addressed this issue by arguing that the "romantic-era distrust" of the railroad that he claims
(15) was present during the 1830s vanished in the decades after 1880. But the argument he provides in support of this position is unconvincing.
    What Stilgoe calls "romantic-era distrust" was in fact the reaction of a minority of writers, artists,
(20) and intellectuals who distrusted the railroad not so much for what it was as for what it signified. Thoreau and Hawthorne appreciated, even admired, an improved means of moving things and people from one place to another. What these writers and
(25) others were concerned about was not the new machinery as such, but the new kind of economy, social order, and culture that it prefigured. In addition, Stilgoe is wrong to imply that the critical attitude of these writers was typical of the period;
(30) their distrust was largely a reaction against the prevailing attitude in the 1830s that the railroad was an unqualified improvement.
    Stilgoe's assertion that the ambivalence toward the railroad exhibited by writers like Hawthorne and
(35) Thoreau disappeared after the 1880s is also misleading. In support of this thesis, Stilgoe has unearthed an impressive volume of material, the work of hitherto unknown illustrators, journalists, and novelists, all devotees of the railroad; but it is
(40) not clear what this new material proves except perhaps that the works of popular culture greatly expanded at the time. The volume of the material proves nothing if Stilgoe's point is that the earlier distrust of a minority of intellectuals did not endure
(45) beyond the 1880s, and, oddly, much of Stilgoe's other evidence indicates that it did. When he glances at the treatment of railroads by writers like Henry James, Sinclair Lewis, or F. Scott Fitzgerald, what comes through in spite of Stilgoe's analysis is
(50) remarkably like Thoreau's feeling of contrariety and ambivalence. (Had he looked at the work of Frank Norris, Eugene O'Neill, or Henry Adams, Stilgoe's case would have been much stronger.) The point is that the sharp contrast between the enthusiastic
(55) supporters of the railroad in the 1830s and the minority of intellectual dissenters during that period extended into the 1880s and beyond.

7. The passage provides information to answer all of the following questions EXCEPT:

(A) During what period did the railroad reach the zenith of its popularity in the United States?
(B) How extensive was the impact of the railroad on the Industrial Revolution in the United States, relative to that of other modern innovations?
(C) Who are some of the writers of the 1830s who expressed ambivalence toward the railroad?
(D) In what way could Stilgoe have strengthened his argument regarding intellectuals' attitudes toward the railroad in the years after the 1880s?
(E) What arguments did the writers after the 1880s, as cited by Stilgoe, offer to justify their support for the railroad?

8. According to the author of the passage, Stilgoe uses the phrase "romantic-era distrust" (line 14) to imply that the view he is referring to was

(A) the attitude of a minority of intellectuals toward technological innovation that began after 1830
(B) a commonly held attitude toward the railroad during the 1830s
(C) an ambivalent view of the railroad expressed by many poets and novelists between 1880 and 1930
(D) a critique of social and economic developments during the 1830s by a minority of intellectuals
(E) an attitude toward the railroad that was disseminated by works of popular culture after 1880

9. According to the author, the attitude toward the railroad that was reflected in writings of Henry James, Sinclair Lewis, and F. Scott Fitzgerald was

(A) influenced by the writings of Frank Norris, Eugene O'Neill, and Henry Adams
(B) similar to that of the minority of writers who had expressed ambivalence toward the railroad prior to the 1880s
(C) consistent with the public attitudes toward the railroad that were reflected in works of popular culture after the 1880s
(D) largely a reaction to the works of writers who had been severely critical of the railroad in the 1830s
(E) consistent with the prevailing attitude toward the railroad during the 1830s

10. It can be inferred from the passage that the author uses the phrase "works of popular culture" (line 41) primarily to refer to the

(A) work of a large group of writers that was published between 1880 and 1930 and that in Stilgoe's view was highly critical of the railroad

(B) work of writers who were heavily influenced by Hawthorne and Thoreau

(C) large volume of writing produced by Henry Adams, Sinclair Lewis, and Eugene O'Neill

(D) work of journalists, novelists, and illustrators who were responsible for creating enthusiasm for the railroad during the 1830s

(E) work of journalists, novelists, and illustrators that was published after 1880 and that has received little attention from scholars other than Stilgoe

11. Which one of the following can be inferred from the passage regarding the work of Frank Norris, Eugene O'Neill, and Henry Adams?

(A) Their work never achieved broad popular appeal.

(B) Their ideas were disseminated to a large audience by the popular culture of the early 1800s.

(C) Their work expressed a more positive attitude toward the railroad than did that of Henry James, Sinclair Lewis, and F. Scott Fitzgerald.

(D) Although they were primarily novelists, some of their work could be classified as journalism.

(E) Although they were influenced by Thoreau, their attitude toward the railroad was significantly different from his.

12. It can be inferred from the passage that Stilgoe would be most likely to agree with which one of the following statements regarding the study of cultural history?

(A) It is impossible to know exactly what period historians are referring to when they use the term "romantic era."

(B) The writing of intellectuals often anticipates ideas and movements that are later embraced by popular culture.

(C) Writers who were not popular in their own time tell us little about the age in which they lived.

(D) The works of popular culture can serve as a reliable indicator of public attitudes toward modern innovations like the railroad.

(E) The best source of information concerning the impact of an event as large as the Industrial Revolution is the private letters and journals of individuals.

13. The primary purpose of the passage is to

(A) evaluate one scholar's view of public attitudes toward the railroad in the United States from the early nineteenth to the early twentieth century

(B) review the treatment of the railroad in American literature of the nineteenth and twentieth centuries

(C) survey the views of cultural historians regarding the railroad's impact on major events in United States history

(D) explore the origins of the public support for the railroad that existed after the completion of a national rail system in the United States

(E) define what historians mean when they refer to the "romantic-era distrust" of the railroad

Passage #2: December 1991 Questions 21-28

Amsden has divided Navajo weaving into four distinct styles. He argues that three of them can be identified by the type of design used to form horizontal bands: colored stripes, zigzags, or
(5) diamonds. The fourth, or bordered, style he identifies by a distinct border surrounding centrally placed, dominating figures.

Amsden believes that the diamond style appeared after 1869 when, under Anglo influence
(10) and encouragement, the blanket became a rug with larger designs and bolder lines. The bordered style appeared about 1890, and, Amsden argues, it reflects the greatest number of Anglo influences on the newly emerging rug business. The Anglo desire
(15) that anything with graphic designs have a top, bottom, and border is a cultural preference that the Navajo abhorred, as evidenced, he suggests, by the fact that in early bordered specimens strips of color unexpectedly break through the enclosing pattern.

(20) Amsden argues that the bordered rug represents a radical break with previous styles. He asserts that the border changed the artistic problem facing weavers: a blank area suggests the use of isolated figures, while traditional, banded Navajo designs
(25) were continuous and did not use isolated figures. The old patterns alternated horizontal decorative zones in a regular order.

Amsden's view raises several questions. First, what is involved in altering artistic styles? Some
(30) studies suggest that artisans' motor habits and thought processes must be revised when a style changes precipitously. In the evolution of Navajo weaving, however, no radical revisions in the way articles are produced need be assumed. After all, all
(35) weaving subordinates design to the physical limitations created by the process of weaving, which includes creating an edge or border. The habits required to make decorative borders are, therefore, latent and easily brought to the surface.

(40) Second, is the relationship between the banded and bordered styles as simple as Amsden suggests? He assumes that a break in style is a break in psychology. But if style results from constant quests for invention, such stylistic breaks are inevitable.
(45) When a style has exhausted the possibilities inherent in its principles, artists cast about for new, but not necessarily alien, principles. Navajo weaving may have reached this turning point prior to 1890.

(50) Third, is there really a significant stylistic gap? Two other styles lie between the banded styles and the bordered style. They suggest that disintegration of the bands may have altered visual and motor habits and prepared the way for a border filled with
(55) separate units. In the Chief White Antelope blanket, dated prior to 1865, ten years before the first Anglo trading post on the Navajo reservation, whole and partial diamonds interrupt the flowing design and become separate forms. Parts of diamonds
(60) arranged vertically at each side may be seen to anticipate the border.

21. The author's central thesis is that

(A) the Navajo rejected the stylistic influences of Anglo culture
(B) Navajo weaving cannot be classified by Amsden's categories
(C) the Navajo changed their style of weaving because they sought the challenge of new artistic problems
(D) original motor habits and thought processes limit the extent to which a style can be revised
(E) the causal factors leading to the emergence of the bordered style are not as clear-cut as Amsden suggests

22. It can be inferred from the passage that Amsden views the use of "strips of color" (line 18) in the early bordered style as

(A) a sign of resistance to a change in style
(B) an echo of the diamond style
(C) a feature derived from Anglo culture
(D) an attempt to disintegrate the rigid form of the banded style
(E) a means of differentiating the top of the weaving from the bottom

23. The author's view of Navajo weaving suggests which one of the following?

(A) The appearance of the first trading post on the Navajo reservation coincided with the appearance of the diamond style.
(B) Traces of thought processes and motor habits of one culture can generally be found in the art of another culture occupying the same period and region.
(C) The bordered style may have developed gradually from the banded style as a result of Navajo experiments with design.
(D) The influence of Anglo culture was not the only non-Native American influence on Navajo weaving.
(E) Horizontal and vertical rows of diamond forms were transformed by the Navajos into solid lines to create the bordered style.

24. According to the passage, Navajo weavings made prior to 1890 typically were characterized by all of the following EXCEPT

(A) repetition of forms
(B) overall patterns
(C) horizontal bands
(D) isolated figures
(E) use of color

25. The author would most probably agree with which one of the following conclusions about the stylistic development of Navajo weaving?

(A) The styles of Navajo weaving changed in response to changes in Navajo motor habits and thought processes.
(B) The zigzag style was the result of stylistic influences from Anglo culture.
(C) Navajo weaving used isolated figures in the beginning, but combined naturalistic and abstract designs in later styles.
(D) Navajo weaving changed gradually from a style in which the entire surface was covered by horizontal bands to one in which central figures dominated the surface.
(E) The styles of Navajo weaving always contained some type of isolated figure.

26. The author suggests that Amsden's claim that borders in Navajo weaving were inspired by Anglo culture could be

(A) conceived as a response to imagined correspondences between Anglo and Navajo art
(B) biased by Amsden's feelings about Anglo culture
(C) a result of Amsden's failing to take into account certain aspects of Navajo weaving
(D) based on a limited number of specimens of the styles of Navajo weaving
(E) based on a confusion between the stylistic features of the zigzag and diamond styles

27. The author most probably mentions the Chief White Antelope blanket in order to

(A) establish the direct influence of Anglo culture on the bordered style
(B) cast doubts on the claim that the bordered style arose primarily from Anglo influence
(C) cite an example of a blanket with a central design and no border
(D) suggest that the Anglo influence produced significant changes in the two earliest styles of Navajo weaving
(E) illustrate how the Navajo had exhausted the stylistic possibilities of the diamond style

28. The passage is primarily concerned with

(A) comparing and contrasting different styles
(B) questioning a view of how a style came into being
(C) proposing alternate methods of investigating the evolution of styles
(D) discussing the influence of one culture on another
(E) analyzing the effect of the interaction between two different cultures

Art historians' approach to French Impressionism has changed significantly in recent years. While a decade ago Rewald's *History of Impressionism*, which emphasizes Impressionist
(5) painters' stylistic innovations, was unchallenged, the literature on Impressionism has now become a kind of ideological battlefield, in which more attention is paid to the subject matter of the paintings, and to the social and moral issues raised by it, than to their
(10) style. Recently, politically charged discussions that address the Impressionists' unequal treatment of men and women and the exclusion of modern industry and labor from their pictures have tended to crowd out the stylistic analysis favored by
(15) Rewald and his followers. In a new work illustrating this trend, Robert L. Herbert dissociates himself from formalists whose preoccupation with the stylistic features of Impressionist painting has, in Herbert's view, left the history out of art history;
(20) his aim is to restore Impressionist paintings "to their sociocultural context." However, his arguments are not, finally, persuasive.

In attempting to place Impressionist painting in its proper historical context, Herbert has redrawn
(25) the traditional boundaries of Impressionism. Limiting himself to the two decades between 1860 and 1880, he assembles under the Impressionist banner what can only be described as a somewhat eccentric grouping of painters. Cezanne, Pisarro,
(30) and Sisley are almost entirely ignored, largely because their paintings do not suit Herbert's emphasis on themes of urban life and suburban leisure, while Manet, Degas, and Caillebotte—who paint scenes of urban life but whom many would
(35) hardly characterize as Impressionists—dominate the first half of the book. Although this new description of Impressionist painting provides a more unified conception of nineteenth-century French painting by grouping quite disparate modernist painters together
(40) and emphasizing their common concerns rather than their stylistic differences, it also forces Herbert to overlook some of the most important genres of Impressionist painting—portraiture, pure landscape, and still-life painting.
(45) Moreover, the rationale for Herbert's emphasis on the social and political realities that Impressionist paintings can be said to communicate rather than on their style is finally undermined by what even Herbert concedes was the failure of impressionist
(50) painters to serve as particularly conscientious illustrators of their social milieu. They left much ordinary experience—work and poverty, for example—out of their paintings, and what they did put in was transformed by a style that had only an
(55) indirect relationship to the social realities of the world they depicted. Not only were their pictures inventions rather than photographs, they were inventions in which style to some degree disrupted description. Their paintings in effect have two
(60) levels of "subject": what is represented and how it is represented, and no art historian can afford to emphasize one at the expense of the other.

21. Which one of the following best expresses the main point of the passage?

(A) The style of Impressionist paintings has only an indirect relation to their subject matter.
(B) The approach to Impressionism that is illustrated by Herbert's recent book is inadequate.
(C) The historical context of Impressionist paintings is not relevant to their interpretation.
(D) Impressionism emerged from a historical context of ideological conflict and change.
(E) Any adequate future interpretation of Impressionism will have to come to terms with Herbert's view of this art movement.

22. According to the passage, Rewald's book on Impressionism was characterized by which one of the following?

(A) evenhanded objectivity about the achievements of Impressionism
(B) bias in favor of certain Impressionist painters
(C) an emphasis on the stylistic features of Impressionist painting
(D) an idiosyncratic view of which painters were to be classified as Impressionists
(E) a refusal to enter into the ideological debates that had characterized earlier discussions of Impressionism

23. The author implies that Herbert's redefinition of the boundaries of Impressionism resulted from which one of the following?

(A) an exclusive emphasis on form and style
(B) a bias in favor of the representation of modern industry
(C) an attempt to place Impressionism within a specific sociocultural context
(D) a broadening of the term "Impressionism" to include all of nineteenth-century French painting
(E) an insufficient familiarity with earlier interpretations of Impressionism

24. The author states which one of the following about modern industry and labor as subjects for painting?

(A) The Impressionists neglected these subjects in their paintings.
(B) Herbert's book on Impressionism fails to give adequate treatment of these subjects.
(C) The Impressionists' treatment of these subjects was idealized.
(D) Rewald's treatment of Impressionist painters focused inordinately on their representations of these subjects.
(E) Modernist painters presented a distorted picture of these subjects.

25. Which one of the following most accurately describes the structure of the author's argument in the passage?

(A) The first two paragraphs each present independent arguments for a conclusion that is drawn in the third paragraph.
(B) A thesis is stated in the first paragraph and revised in the second paragraph, and the revised thesis is supported with an argument in the third paragraph.
(C) The first two paragraphs discuss and criticize a thesis, and the third paragraph presents an alternative thesis.
(D) A claim is made in the first paragraph, and the next two paragraphs each present reasons for accepting that claim.
(E) An argument is presented in the first paragraph, a counterargument is presented in the second paragraph, and the third paragraph suggests a way to resolve the dispute.

26. The author's statement that Impressionist paintings "were inventions in which style to some degree disrupted description" (lines 57-59) serves to

(A) strengthen the claim that Impressionists sought to emphasize the differences between painting and photography
(B) weaken the argument that style is the only important feature of Impressionist paintings
(C) indicate that Impressionists recognized that they had been strongly influenced by photography
(D) support the argument that an exclusive emphasis on the Impressionists' subject matter is mistaken
(E) undermine the claim that Impressionists neglected certain kinds of subject matter

27. The author would most likely regard a book on the Impressionists that focused entirely on their style as

(A) a product of the recent confusion caused by Herbert's book on Impressionism
(B) emphasizing what Impressionists themselves took to be their primary artistic concern
(C) an overreaction against the traditional interpretation of Impressionism
(D) neglecting the most innovative aspects of Impressionism
(E) addressing only part of what an adequate treatment should cover

The labor force is often organized as if workers had no family responsibilities. Preschool age children need full time care; children in primary school need care after school and during school
(5) vacations. Although day care services can resolve some scheduling conflicts between home and office, workers cannot always find or afford suitable care. Even when they obtain such care, parents must still cope with emergencies, such as illnesses, that keep
(10) children at home. Moreover, children need more than tending; they also need meaningful time with their parents. Conventional full time workdays, especially when combined with unavoidable household duties, are too inflexible for parents
(15) with primary child care responsibility.

Although a small but increasing number of working men are single parents, those barriers against successful participation in the labor market that are related to primary child care
(20) responsibilities mainly disadvantage women. Even in families where both parents work, cultural pressures are traditionally much greater on mothers than on fathers to bear the primary child rearing responsibilities.

(25) In reconciling child rearing responsibilities with participation in the labor market, many working mothers are forced to make compromises. For example, approximately one-third of all working mothers are employed only part-time, even though
(30) part-time jobs are dramatically underpaid and often less desirable in comparison to full-time employment. Even though part-time work is usually available only in occupations offering minimal employee responsibility and little
(35) opportunity for advancement or self-enrichment, such employment does allow many women the time and flexibility to fulfill their family duties, but only at the expense of the advantages associated with full-time employment.

(40) Moreover, even mothers with full time employment must compromise opportunities in order to adjust to barriers against parents in the labor market. Many choose jobs entailing little challenge or responsibility or those offering flexible
(45) scheduling, often available only in poorly paid positions, while other working mothers, although willing and able to assume as much responsibility as people without children, find that their need to spend regular and predictable time with their
(50) children inevitably causes them to lose career opportunities to those without such demands. Thus, women in education are more likely to become teachers than school administrators, whose more conventional full time work schedules do not

(55) correspond to the schedules of school age children, while female lawyers are more likely to practice law in trusts and estates, where they can control their work schedules, than in litigation, where they cannot. Nonprofessional women are concentrated
(60) in secretarial work and department store sales, where their absences can be covered easily by substitutes and where they can enter and leave the work force with little loss, since the jobs offer so little personal gain. Indeed, as long as the labor
(65) market remains hostile to parents, and family roles continue to be allocated on the basis of gender, women will be seriously disadvantaged in that labor market.

1. Which one of the following best summarizes the main idea of the passage?

(A) Current trends in the labor force indicate that working parents, especially women, may not always need to choose between occupational and child care responsibilities.

(B) In order for mothers to have an equal opportunity for advancement in the labor force, traditional family roles have to be reexamined and revised.

(C) Although single parents who work have to balance parental and career demands, single mothers suffer resulting employment disadvantages that single fathers can almost always avoid.

(D) Although child care responsibilities disadvantage many women in the labor force, professional women (such as teachers and lawyers) are better able to overcome this problem than are nonprofessional women.

(E) Traditional work schedules are too inflexible to accommodate the child care responsibilities of many parents, a fact that severely disadvantages women in the labor force.

2. Which one of the following statements about part-time work can be inferred from the information presented in the passage?

   (A) One third of all part time workers are working mothers.
   (B) Part time work generally offers fewer opportunities for advancement to working mothers than to women generally.
   (C) Part time work, in addition to having relatively poor wages, often requires that employees work during holidays, when their children are out of school.
   (D) Part time employment, despite its disadvantages, provides working mothers with an opportunity to address some of the demands of caring for children.
   (E) Many mothers with primary child care responsibility choose part time jobs in order to better exploit full time career opportunities after their children are grown.

3. It can be inferred from the passage that the author would be most likely to agree with which one of the following statements about working fathers in two-parent families?

   (A) They are equally burdened by the employment disadvantages placed upon all parents—male and female—in the labor market.
   (B) They are so absorbed in their jobs that they often do not see the injustice going on around them.
   (C) They are shielded by the traditional allocation of family roles from many of the pressures associated with child rearing responsibilities.
   (D) They help compound the inequities in the labor market by keeping women from competing with men for career opportunities.
   (E) They are responsible for many of the problems of working mothers because of their insistence on traditional roles in the family.

4. Of the following, which one would the author most likely say is the most troublesome barrier facing working parents with primary child-care responsibility?

   (A) the lack of full time jobs open to women
   (B) the inflexibility of work schedules
   (C) the low wages of part time employment
   (D) the limited advancement opportunities for nonprofessional employees
   (E) the practice of allocating responsibilities in the workplace on the basis of gender

5. The passage suggests that day care is at best a limited solution to the pressures associated with child rearing for all of the following reasons EXCEPT:

   (A) Even the best day care available cannot guarantee that children will have meaningful time with their parents.
   (B) Some parents cannot afford day-care services.
   (C) Working parents sometimes have difficulty finding suitable day care for their children.
   (D) Parents who send their children to day care still need to provide care for their children during vacations.
   (E) Even children who are in day care may have to stay home when they are sick.

6. According to the passage, many working parents may be forced to make any of the following types of career decisions EXCEPT

   (A) declining professional positions for nonprofessional ones, which typically have less conventional work schedules
   (B) accepting part time employment rather than full-time employment
   (C) taking jobs with limited responsibility, and thus more limited career opportunities, in order to have a more flexible schedule
   (D) pursuing career specializations that allow them to control their work schedules instead of pursuing a more desirable specialization in the same field
   (E) limiting the career potential of one parent, often the mother, who assumes greater child-care responsibility

7. Which one of the following statements would most appropriately continue the discussion at the end of the passage?

   (A) At the same time, most men will remain better able to enjoy the career and salary opportunities offered by the labor market.
   (B) Of course, men who are married to working mothers know of these employment barriers but seem unwilling to do anything about them.
   (C) On the other hand, salary levels may become more equitable between men and women even if the other career opportunities remain more accessible to men than to women.
   (D) On the contrary, men with primary child rearing responsibilities will continue to enjoy more advantages in the workplace than their female counterparts.
   (E) Thus, institutions in society that favor men over women will continue to widen the gap between the career opportunities available for men and for women.

Passage #5: February 1993 Questions 21-27

In 1887 the Dawes Act legislated wide scale private ownership of reservation lands in the United States for Native Americans. The act allotted plots of 80 acres to each Native American adult.
(5)   However, the Native Americans were not granted outright title to their lands. The act defined each grant as a "trust patent," meaning that the Bureau of Indian Affairs (BIA), the governmental agency in charge of administering policy regarding Native
(10)   Americans, would hold the allotted land in trust for 25 years, during which time the Native American owners could use, but not alienate (sell) the land. After the 25-year period, the Native American allottee would receive a "fee patent" awarding full
(15)   legal ownership of the land.
         Two main reasons were advanced for the restriction on the Native Americans' ability to sell their lands. First, it was claimed that free alienability would lead to immediate transfer of
(20)   large amounts of former reservation land to non-Native Americans, consequently threatening the traditional way of life on those reservations. A second objection to free alienation was that Native Americans were unaccustomed to, and did not
(25)   desire, a system of private landownership. Their custom, it was said, favored communal use of land.
         However, both of these arguments bear only on the transfer of Native American lands to non-Native Americans; neither offers a reason for prohibiting
(30)   Native Americans from transferring land among themselves. Selling land to each other would not threaten the Native American culture. Additionally, if communal land use remained preferable to Native Americans after allotment, free alienability would
(35)   have allowed allottees to sell their lands back to the tribe.
         When stated rationales for government policies prove empty, using an interest-group model often provides an explanation. While neither Native
(40)   Americans nor the potential non-Native American purchasers benefited from the restraint on alienation contained in the Dawes Act, one clearly defined group did benefit: the BIA bureaucrats. It has been convincingly demonstrated that bureaucrats seek to
(45)   maximize the size of their staffs and their budgets in order to compensate for the lack of other sources of fulfillment, such as power and prestige. Additionally, politicians tend to favor the growth of governmental bureaucracy because such growth
(50)   provides increased opportunity for the exercise of political patronage. The restraint on alienation vastly increased the amount of work, and hence the budgets, necessary to implement the statute. Until allotment was ended in 1934, granting fee patents

(55)   and leasing Native American lands were among the principal activities of the United States government. One hypothesis, then, for the temporary restriction on alienation in the Dawes Act is that it reflected a compromise between non-Native Americans
(60)   favoring immediate alienability so they could purchase land and the BIA bureaucrats who administered the privatization system.

21. Which one of the following best summarizes the main idea of the passage?

   (A)   United States government policy toward Native Americans has tended to disregard their needs and consider instead the needs of non-Native American purchasers of land.
   (B)   In order to preserve the unique way of life on Native American reservations, use of Native American lands must be communal rather than individual.
   (C)   The Dawes Act's restriction on the right of Native Americans to sell their land may have been implemented primarily to serve the interests of politicians and bureaucrats.
   (D)   The clause restricting free alienability in the Dawes Act greatly expanded United States governmental activity in the area of land administration.
   (E)   Since passage of the Dawes Act in 1887, Native Americans have not been able to sell or transfer their former reservation land freely.

22. Which one of the following statements concerning the reason for the end of allotment, if true, would provide the most support for the author's view of politicians?

   (A)   Politicians realized that allotment was damaging the Native American way of life.
   (B)   Politicians decided that allotment would be more congruent with the Native American custom of communal land use.
   (C)   Politicians believed that allotment's continuation would not enhance their opportunities to exercise patronage.
   (D)   Politicians felt that the staff and budgets of the BIA had grown too large.
   (E)   Politicians were concerned that too much Native American land was falling into the hands of non-Native Americans.

23. Which one of the following best describes the organization of the passage?

   (A) The passage of a law is analyzed in detail, the benefits and drawbacks of one of its clauses are studied, and a final assessment of the law is offered.

   (B) The history of a law is narrated, the effects of one of its clauses on various populations are studied, and repeal of the law is advocated.

   (C) A law is examined, the political and social backgrounds of one of its clauses are characterized, and the permanent effects of the law are studied.

   (D) A law is described, the rationale put forward for one of its clauses is outlined and dismissed, and a different rationale for the clause is presented.

   (E) The legal status of an ethnic group is examined with respect to issues of landownership and commercial autonomy, and the benefits to rival groups due to that status are explained.

24. The author's attitude toward the reasons advanced for the restriction on alienability in the Dawes Act at the time of its passage can best be described as

   (A) completely credulous
   (B) partially approving
   (C) basically indecisive
   (D) mildly questioning
   (E) highly skeptical

25. It can be inferred from the passage that which one of the following was true of Native American life immediately before passage of the Dawes Act?

   (A) Most Native Americans supported themselves through farming.

   (B) Not many Native Americans personally owned the land on which they lived.

   (C) The land on which most Native Americans lived had been bought from their tribes.

   (D) Few Native Americans had much contact with their non-Native American neighbors.

   (E) Few Native Americans were willing to sell their land to non-Native Americans.

26. According to the passage, the type of landownership initially obtainable by Native Americans under the Dawes Act differed from the type of ownership obtainable after a 25-year period in that only the latter allowed

   (A) owners of land to farm it
   (B) owners of land to sell it
   (C) government some control over how owners disposed of land
   (D) owners of land to build on it with relatively minor governmental restrictions
   (E) government to charge owners a fee for developing their land

27. Which one of the following, if true, would most strengthen the author's argument regarding the true motivation for the passage of the Dawes Act?

   (A) The legislators who voted in favor of the Dawes Act owned land adjacent to Native American reservations.

   (B) The majority of Native Americans who were granted fee patents did not sell their land back to their tribes.

   (C) Native Americans managed to preserve their traditional culture even when they were geographically dispersed.

   (D) The legislators who voted in favor of the Dawes Act were heavily influenced by BIA bureaucrats.

   (E) Non-Native Americans who purchased the majority of Native American lands consolidated them into larger farm holdings.

Passage #6: June 1993 Questions 14-20

Any study of autobiographical narratives that appeared under the ostensible authorship of African American writers between 1760 and 1865 inevitably raises concerns about authenticity and interpretation.
(5) Should an autobiography whose written composition was literally out of the hands of its narrator be considered as the literary equivalent of those autobiographies that were authored independently by their subjects?

(10) In many cases, the so-called edited narrative of an ex-slave ought to be treated as a ghostwritten account insofar as literary analysis is concerned, especially when it was composed by its editor from "a statement of facts" provided by an African
(15) American subject. Blassingame has taken pains to show that the editors of several of the more famous antebellum slave narratives were "noted for their integrity" and thus were unlikely to distort the facts given them by slave narrators. From a literary
(20) standpoint, however, it is not the moral integrity of these editors that is at issue but the linguistic, structural, and tonal integrity of the narratives they produced. Even if an editor faithfully reproduced the facts of a narrator's life, it was still the editor
(25) who decided what to make of these facts, how they should be emphasized, in what order they ought to be presented, and what was extraneous or germane. Readers of African American autobiography then and now have too readily accepted the presumption
(30) of these eighteenth- and nineteenth-century editors that experiential facts recounted orally could be recorded and sorted by an amanuensis-editor, taken out of their original contexts, and then published with editorial prefaces, footnotes, and appended
(35) commentary, all without compromising the validity of the narrative as a product of an African American consciousness.

Transcribed narratives in which an editor explicitly delimits his or her role undoubtedly may
(40) be regarded as more authentic and reflective of the narrator's thought in action than those edited works that flesh out a statement of facts in ways unaccounted for. Still, it would be naive to accord dictated oral narratives the same status as
(45) autobiographies composed and written by the subjects of the stories themselves. This point is illustrated by an analysis of Works Progress Administration interviews with ex-slaves in the 1930s that suggests that narrators often told
(50) interviewers what they seemed to want to hear. If it seemed impolitic for former slaves to tell all they knew and thought about the past to interviewers in the 1930s, the same could be said of escaped slaves on the run in the antebellum era. Dictated

(55) narratives, therefore, are literary texts whose authenticity is difficult to determine. Analysts should reserve close analytic readings for independently authored texts. Discussion of collaborative texts should take into account the
(60) conditions that governed their production.

14. Which one of the following best summarizes the main point of the passage?

(A) The personal integrity of an autobiography's editor has little relevance to its value as a literary work.
(B) Autobiographies dictated to editors are less valuable as literature than are autobiographies authored by their subjects.
(C) The facts that are recorded in an autobiography are less important than the personal impressions of its author.
(D) The circumstances under which an autobiography was written should affect the way it is interpreted as literature.
(E) The autobiographies of African Americans written between 1760 and 1865 deserve more careful study than they have so far received.

15. The information in the passage suggests that the role of the "editor" (lines 23-24) is most like that of

(A) an artist who wishes to invent a unique method of conveying the emotional impact of a scene in a painting
(B) a worker who must interpret the instructions of an employer
(C) a critic who must provide evidence to support opinions about a play being reviewed
(D) an architect who must make the best use of a natural setting in designing a public building
(E) a historian who must decide how to direct the reenactment of a historical event

16. Which one of the following best describes the author's opinion about applying literary analysis to edited autobiographies?

   (A)   The author is adamantly opposed to the application of literary analysis to edited autobiographies.
   (B)   The author is skeptical of the value of close analytical reading in the case of edited autobiographies.
   (C)   The author believes that literary analysis of the prefaces, footnotes, and commentaries that accompany edited autobiographies would be more useful than an analysis of the text of the autobiographies.
   (D)   The author believes that an exclusively literary analysis of edited autobiographies is more valuable than a reading that emphasizes their historical import.
   (E)   The author believes that the literary analysis of edited autobiographies would enhance their linguistic, structural, and tonal integrity.

17. The passage supports which one of the following statements about the readers of autobiographies of African Americans that were published between 1760 and 1865?

   (A)   They were more concerned with the personal details in the autobiographies than with their historical significance.
   (B)   They were unable to distinguish between ghostwritten and edited autobiographies.
   (C)   They were less naive about the facts of slave life than are readers today.
   (D)   They presumed that the editing of the autobiographies did not affect their authenticity.
   (E)   They had little interest in the moral integrity of the editors of the autobiographies.

18. Which one of the following words, as it is used in the passage, best serves to underscore the author's concerns about the authenticity of the autobiographies discussed?

   (A)   "ostensible" (line 2)
   (B)   "integrity" (line 18)
   (C)   "extraneous" (line 27)
   (D)   "delimits" (line 39)
   (E)   "impolitic" (line 51)

19. According to the passage, close analytic reading of an autobiography is appropriate only when the

   (A)   autobiography has been dictated to an experienced amanuensis-editor
   (B)   autobiography attempts to reflect the narrator's thought in action
   (C)   autobiography was authored independently by its subject
   (D)   moral integrity of the autobiography's editor is well established
   (E)   editor of the autobiography collaborated closely with its subject in its editing

20. It can be inferred that the discussion in the passage of Blassingame's work primarily serves which one of the following purposes?

   (A)   It adds an authority's endorsement to the author's view that edited narratives ought to be treated as ghostwritten accounts.
   (B)   It provides an example of a mistaken emphasis in the study of autobiography.
   (C)   It presents an account of a new method of literary analysis to be applied to autobiography.
   (D)   It illustrates the inadequacy of traditional approaches to the analysis of autobiography.
   (E)   It emphasizes the importance of the relationship between editor and narrator.

During the 1940s and 1950s the United States government developed a new policy toward Native Americans, often known as "readjustment." Because the increased awareness of civil rights in
(5) these decades helped reinforce the belief that life on reservations prevented Native Americans from exercising the rights guaranteed to citizens under the United States Constitution. the readjustment movement advocated the end of the federal
(10) government's involvement in Native American affairs and encouraged the assimilation of Native Americans as individuals into mainstream society. However, the same years also saw the emergence of a Native American leadership and efforts to develop
(15) tribal institutions and reaffirm tribal identity. The clash of these two trends may be traced in the attempts on the part of the Bureau of Indian Affairs (BIA) to convince the Oneida tribe of Wisconsin to accept readjustment.
(20)   The culmination of BIA efforts to sway the Oneida occurred at a meeting that took place in the fall of 1956. The BIA suggested that it would be to the Oneida's benefit to own their own property and, like other homeowners, pay real estate taxes
(25) on it. The BIA also emphasized that, after readjustment, the government would not attempt to restrict Native Americans' ability to sell their individually owned lands. The Oneida were then offered a one-time lump-sum payment of $60,000 in
(30) lieu of the $0.52 annuity guaranteed in perpetuity to each member of the tribe under the Canandaigua Treaty.
   The efforts of the BIA to "sell" readjustment to the tribe failed because the Oneida realized that
(35) they had heard similar offers before. The Oneida delegates reacted negatively to the BIA's first suggestion because taxation of Native American lands had been one past vehicle for dispossessing the Oneida: after the distribution of some tribal
(40) lands to individual Native Americans in the late nineteenth century. Native American lands became subject to taxation, resulting in new and impossible financial burdens, foreclosures, and subsequent tax sales of property. The Oneida delegates were
(45) equally suspicious of the BIA's emphasis on the rights of individual landowners, since in the late nineteenth century many individual Native Americans had been convinced by unscrupulous speculators to sell their lands. Finally, the offer of a
(50) lump-sum payment was unanimously opposed by the Oneida delegates, who saw that changing the terms of a treaty might jeopardize the many pending land claims based upon the treaty.
   As a result of the 1956 meeting, the Oneida
(55) rejected readjustment. Instead, they determined to

improve tribal life by lobbying for federal monies for postsecondary education, for the improvement of drainage on tribal lands, and for the building of a convalescent home for tribal members. Thus, by
(60) learning the lessons of history, the Oneida were able to survive as a tribe in their homeland.

7.   Which one of the following would be most consistent with the policy of readjustment described in the passage?

   (A)   the establishment among Native Americans of a tribal system of elected government
   (B)   the creation of a national project to preserve Native American language and oral history
   (C)   the establishment of programs to encourage Native Americans to move from reservations to urban areas
   (D)   the development of a large-scale effort to restore Native American lands to their original tribes
   (E)   the reaffirmation of federal treaty obligations to Native American tribes

8.   According to the passage, after the 1956 meeting the Oneida resolved to

   (A)   obtain improved social services and living conditions for members of the tribe
   (B)   pursue litigation designed to reclaim tribal lands
   (C)   secure recognition of their unique status as a self-governing Native American nation within the United States
   (D)   establish new kinds of tribal institutions
   (E)   cultivate a life-style similar to that of other United States citizens

9.   Which one of the following best describes the function of the first paragraph in the context of the passage as a whole?

   (A)   It summarizes the basis of a conflict underlying negotiations described elsewhere in the passage.
   (B)   It presents two positions, one of which is defended by evidence provided in succeeding paragraphs.
   (C)   It compares competing interpretations of a historical conflict.
   (D)   It analyzes the causes of a specific historical event and predicts a future development.
   (E)   It outlines the history of a government agency.

10. The author refers to the increased awareness of civil rights during the 1940s and 1950s most probably in order to

   (A) contrast the readjustment movement with other social phenomena
   (B) account for the stance of the Native American leadership
   (C) help explain the impetus for the readjustment movement
   (D) explain the motives of BIA bureaucrats
   (E) foster support for the policy of readjustment

11. The passage suggests that advocates of readjustment would most likely agree with which one of the following statements regarding the relationship between the federal government and Native Americans?

   (A) The federal government should work with individual Native Americans to improve life on reservations.
   (B) The federal government should be no more involved in the affairs of Native Americans than in the affairs of other citizens.
   (C) The federal government should assume more responsibility for providing social services to Native Americans.
   (D) The federal government should share its responsibility for maintaining Native American territories with tribal leaders.
   (E) The federal government should observe all provisions of treaties made in the past with Native Americans.

12. The passage suggests that the Oneida delegates viewed the Canandaigua Treaty as

   (A) a valuable safeguard of certain Oneida rights and privileges
   (B) the source of many past problems for the Oneida tribe
   (C) a model for the type of agreement they hoped to reach with the federal government
   (D) an important step toward recognition of their status as an independent Native American nation
   (E) an obsolete agreement without relevance for their current condition

13. Which one of the following situations most closely parallels that of the Oneida delegates in refusing to accept a lump-sum payment of $60,000?

   (A) A university offers a student a four-year scholarship with the stipulation that the student not accept any outside employment; the student refuses the offer and attends a different school because the amount of the scholarship would not have covered living expenses.
   (B) A company seeking to reduce its payroll obligations offers an employee a large bonus if he will accept early retirement; the employee refuses because he does not want to compromise an outstanding worker's compensation suit.
   (C) Parents of a teenager offer to pay her at the end of the month for performing weekly chores rather than paying her on a weekly basis; the teenager refuses because she has a number of financial obligations that she must meet early in the month.
   (D) A car dealer offers a customer a $500 cash payment for buying a new car; the customer refuses because she does not want to pay taxes on the amount, and requests instead that her monthly payments be reduced by a proportionate amount.
   (E) A landlord offers a tenant several months rent-free in exchange for the tenant's agreeing not to demand that her apartment be painted every two years, as is required by the lease; the tenant refuses because she would have to spend her own time painting the apartment.

In 1964 the United States federal government began attempts to eliminate racial discrimination in employment and wages: the United States Congress enacted Title VII of the Civil Rights Act,
(5) prohibiting employers from making employment decisions on the basis of race. In 1965 President Johnson issued Executive Order 11,246, which prohibited discrimination by United States government contractors and emphasized direct
(10) monitoring of minority representation in contractors' work forces.

Nonetheless, proponents of the "continuous change" hypothesis believe that United States federal law had a marginal impact on the economic
(15) progress made by black people in the United States between 1940 and 1975. Instead they emphasize slowly evolving historical forces, such as long-term trends in education that improved segregated schools for black students during the 1940s and
(20) were operative during and after the 1960s. They argue that as the quality of black schools improved relative to that of white schools, the earning potential of those attending black schools increased relative to the earning potential of those attending
(25) white schools.

However, there is no direct evidence linking increased quality of underfunded segregated black schools to these improvements in earning potential. In fact, even the evidence on relative schooling
(30) quality is ambiguous. Although in the mid-1940s term length at black schools was approaching that in white schools, the rapid growth in another important measure of school quality, school expenditures, may be explained by increases in
(35) teachers' salaries, and, historically, such increases have not necessarily increased school quality. Finally, black individuals in all age groups, even those who had been educated at segregated schools before the 1940s, experienced post-1960 increases
(40) in their earning potential. If improvements in the quality of schooling were an important determinant of increased returns, only those workers who could have benefited from enhanced school quality should have received higher returns. The relative
(45) improvement in the earning potential of educated black people of all age groups in the United States is more consistent with a decline in employment discrimination.

An additional problem for continuity theorists is
(50) how to explain the rapid acceleration of black economic progress in the United States after 1964. Education alone cannot account for the rate of change. Rather, the coincidence of increased United States government antidiscrimination pressure in the
(55) mid-1960s with the acceleration in the rate of black economic progress beginning in 1965 argues against the continuity theorists' view. True, correlating federal intervention and the acceleration of black economic progress might be incorrect. One could
(60) argue that changing attitudes about employment discrimination sparked both the adoption of new federal policies and the rapid acceleration in black economic progress. Indeed, the shift in national attitude that made possible the enactment of Title
(65) VII was in part produced by the persistence of racial discrimination in the southern United States. However, the fact that the law had its greatest effect in the South, in spite of the vigorous resistance of many Southern leaders, suggests its importance for
(70) black economic progress.

22. According to the passage, Title VII of the 1964 Civil Rights Act differs from Executive Order 11,246 in that Title VII

(A) monitors employers to ensure minority representation
(B) assesses the work forces of government contractors
(C) eliminates discriminatory disparities in wages
(D) focuses on determining minority representation in government
(E) governs hiring practices in a wider variety of workplaces

23. Which one of the following statements about schooling in the United States during the mid 1940s can be inferred from the passage?

(A) School expenditures decreased for white schools.
(B) The teachers in white schools had more time to cover material during a school year than did teachers in black schools.
(C) The basic curriculum of white schools was similar to the curriculum at black schools.
(D) White schools did not change substantially in quality.
(E) Although the salaries of teachers in black schools increased, they did not keep pace with the salaries of teachers in white schools.

24. The primary purpose of the passage is to

(A) explain why an argument about black economic progress is incomplete
(B) describe the impact of education on black economic progress
(C) refute an argument about the factors influencing black economic progress
(D) describe black economic progress before and after the 1960s
(E) clarify the current view about the factors influencing black economic progress

25. Which one of the following best states the position of proponents of the "continuous change" hypothesis regarding the relationship between law and racial discrimination?

(A) Individuals cannot be forced by legal means to behave in nondiscriminatory ways.
(B) Discriminatory practices in education have been effectively altered by legal means.
(C) Legislation alone has had little effect on racially discriminatory behavior.
(D) Legislation is necessary, but not sufficient, to achieve changes in racial attitudes.
(E) Legislation can only exacerbate conflicts about racially discriminatory behavior.

26. The author concedes that "correlating federal intervention and the acceleration of black economic progress might be incorrect" (lines 57-59) primarily in order to

(A) strengthen the overall argument by anticipating an objection
(B) introduce another factor that may have influenced black economic progress
(C) concede a point to the continuity theorists
(D) change the overall argument in light of the views of the continuity theorists
(E) introduce a discussion about the impact of federal intervention on discrimination

27. The "continuous change" hypothesis, as it is presented in the passage, can best be applied to which one of the following situations?

(A) Homes are found for many low income families because the government funds a project to build subsidized housing in an economically depressed area.
(B) A depressed economy does not cause the closing of small businesses in a local community because the government provides special grants to aid these businesses.
(C) Unemployed people are able to obtain jobs because private contractors receive tax incentives for constructing office buildings in an area with a high unemployment rate.
(D) A housing shortage is remedied because the changing state of the economy permits private investors to finance construction in a depressed area.
(E) A community's sanitation needs are met because neighborhood organizations lobby aggressively for government assistance.

Chapter Four: Diversity III

Mixed Group Passages

POWERSCORE
TEST PREPARATION

Anthropologist David Mandelbaum makes a distinction between life-passage studies and life-history studies which emerged primarily out of research concerning Native Americans. Life-
(5) passage studies, he says, "emphasize the requirements of society, showing how groups socialize and enculturate their young in order to make them into viable members of society." Life histories, however, "emphasize the experiences and
(10) requirements of the individual, how the person copes with society rather than how society copes with the stream of individuals." Life-passage studies bring out the general cultural characteristics and commonalities that broadly define a culture, but are
(15) unconcerned with an individual's choices or how the individual perceives and responds to the demands and expectations imposed by the constraints of his or her culture. This distinction can clearly be seen in the autobiographies of Native American women.
(20) For example, some early recorded autobiographies, such as *The Autobiography of a Fox Indian Woman*, a life passage recorded by anthropologist Truman Michelson, emphasizes prescribed roles. The narrator presents her story in
(25) a way that conforms with tribal expectations. Michelson's work is valuable as ethnography, as a reflection of the day-to-day responsibilities of Mesquakie women, yet as is often the case with life-passage studies, it presents little of the central
(30) character's psychological motivation. The Fox woman's life story focuses on her tribal education and integration into the ways of her people, and relates only what Michelson ultimately decided was worth preserving. The difference between the two
(35) types of studies is often the result of the amount of control the narrator maintains over the material; autobiographies in which there are no recorder editors are far more reflective of the life-history category, for there are no outsiders shaping the
(40) story to reflect their preconceived notions of what the general cultural patterns are.
For example, in Maria Campbell's account of growing up as a Canadian Metis who was influenced strongly, and often negatively, by the non-Native
(45) American world around her, one learns a great deal about the life of Native American women, but Campbell's individual story, which is told to us directly, is always the center of her narrative. Clearly it is important to her to communicate
(50) to the audience what her experiences as a Native American have been. Through Campbell's story of her family the reader learns of the effect of poverty and prejudice on a people. The reader becomes an intimate of Campbell the writer, sharing her pain
(55) and celebrating her small victories. Although

Campbell's book is written as a life history (the dramatic moments, the frustrations, and the fears are clearly hers), it reveals much about ethnic relations in Canada while reflecting the period in
(60) which it was written.

22. Which one of the following is the most accurate expression of the main point of the passage?

(A)   The contributions of life-history studies to anthropology have made life-passage studies obsolete.

(B)   Despite their dissimilar approaches to the study of culture, life-history and life-passage studies have similar goals.

(C)   The autobiographies of Native American women illustrate the differences between life-history and life-passage studies.

(D)   The roots of Maria Campbell's autobiography can be traced to earlier narratives such as *The Autobiography of a Fox Indian Woman*.

(E)   Despite its shortcomings, the life-passage study is a more effective tool than the life-history study for identifying important cultural patterns.

23. The term "prescribed roles" in line 24 of the passage refers to the

(A)   function of life-passage studies in helping ethnologists to understand cultural tradition

(B)   function of life-history studies in helping ethnologists to gather information

(C)   way in which a subject of a life passage views himself or herself

(D)   roles clearly distinguishing the narrator of an autobiography from the recorder of an autobiography

(E)   roles generally adopted by individuals in order to comply with cultural demands

24. The reference to the "psychological motivation" (line 30) of the subject of *The Autobiography of a Fox Indian Woman* serves primarily to

(A)   dismiss as irrelevant the personal perspective in the life-history study

(B)   identify an aspect of experience that is not commonly a major focus of life-passage studies

(C)   clarify the narrator's self-acknowledged purpose in relating a life passage

(D)   suggest a common conflict between the goals of the narrator and those of the recorder in most life-passage studies

(E)   assert that developing an understanding of an individual's psychological motivation usually undermines objective ethnography

25. Which one of the following statements about Maria Campbell can be inferred from material in the passage?

(A)   She was familiar with the very early history of her tribe but lacked insight into the motivations of non-Native Americans.

(B)   She was unfamiliar with Michelson's work but had probably read a number of life-passage studies about Native Americans.

(C)   She had training as a historian but was not qualified as an anthropologist.

(D)   Her family influenced her beliefs and opinions more than the events of her time did.

(E)   Her life history provides more than a record of her personal experience.

26. According to the passage, one way in which life-history studies differ from life-passage studies is that life-history studies are

(A)   usually told in the subject's native language

(B)   less reliable because they rely solely on the subject's recall

(C)   more likely to be told without the influence of an intermediary

(D)   more creative in the way they interpret the subject's cultural legacy

(E)   more representative of the historian's point of view than of the ethnographer's

27. Which one of the following pairings best illustrates the contrast between life passages and life histories?

(A)   a study of the attitudes of a society toward a mainstream religion and an analysis of techniques used to instruct members of that religious group

(B)   a study of how a preindustrial society maintains peace with neighboring societies and a study of how a postindustrial society does the same

(C)   a study of the way a military organization establishes and maintains discipline and a newly enlisted soldier's narrative describing his initial responses to the military environment

(D)   an analysis of a society's means of subsistence and a study of how its members celebrate religious holidays

(E)   a political history of a society focussing on leaders and parties and a study of how the electorate shaped the political landscape of the society

For too many years scholars of African American history focused on the harm done by slaveholders and by the institution of slavery, rather than on what Africans in the United States were
(5) able to accomplish despite the effects of that institution. In *Myne Owne Ground*, T.H. Breen and Stephen Innes contribute significantly to a recent, welcome shift from a white centered to a black-centered inquiry into the role of African Americans
(10) in the American colonial period. Breen and Innes focus not on slaves, but on a small group of freed indentured servants in Northampton County (in the Chesapeake Bay region of Virginia) who, according to the authors, maintained their freedom, secured
(15) property, and interacted with persons of different races and economic standing from 1620 through the 1670s. African Americans living on the Chesapeake were to some extent disadvantaged, say Breen and Innes, but this did not preclude the attainment of
(20) status roughly equal to that of certain white planters of the area. Continuously acting within black social networks, and forming economic relationships with white planters, local Native Americans, indentured servants, and white settlers outside the gentry class,
(25) the free African Americans of Northampton County held their own in the rough-hewn world of Chesapeake Bay.

The authors emphasize that in this early period, when the percentage of African Americans in any
(30) given Chesapeake county was still no more than 10 percent of the population, very little was predetermined so far as racial status or race relations were concerned. By schooling themselves in the local legal process and by working
(35) prodigiously on the land, African Americans acquired property, established families, and warded off contentious white neighbors. Breen and Innes do acknowledge that political power on the Chesapeake was asymmetrically distributed among black and
(40) white residents. However, they underemphasize much evidence that customary law, only gradually embodied in statutory law, was closing in on free African Americans well before the 1670s: during the 1660s, when the proportion of African
(45) Americans in Virginia increased dramatically, Virginia tightened a law regulating interracial relations (1662) and enacted a statute prohibiting baptism from altering slave status (1667). Anthony Johnson, a leader in the community of free African
(50) Americans in the Chesapeake Bay region, sold the land he had cultivated for more than twenty years and moved north with his family around 1665, an action that the authors attribute to a search for "fresh, more productive land." But the answer to

(55) why the Johnsons left that area where they had labored so long may lie in their realization that their white neighbors were already beginning the transition from a largely white indentured labor force to reliance on a largely black slave labor
(60) force, and that the institution of slavery was threatening their descendants' chances for freedom and success in Virginia.

9. The author of the passage objects to many scholarly studies of African American history for which one of the following reasons?

(A) Their emphases have been on statutory law rather than on customary law.

(B) They have ignored specific historical situations and personages in favor of broad interpretations.

(C) They have focused on the least eventful periods in African American history.

(D) They have underemphasized the economic system that was the basis of the institution of slavery.

(E) They have failed to focus to a sufficient extent on the achievements of African Americans.

10. Which one of the following can be inferred from the passage concerning the relationship between the African American population and the law in the Chesapeake Bay region of Virginia between 1650 and 1670?

(A) The laws affecting black citizens were embodied in statutes much more gradually than were laws affecting white citizens.

(B) As the percentage of black citizens in the population grew, the legal restrictions placed on them also increased.

(C) Because of discriminatory laws, black farmers suffered more economic setbacks than did white farmers.

(D) Because of legal constraints on hiring indentured servants, black farmers faced a chronic labor shortage on their farms.

(E) The adherence to customary law was more rigid in regions with relatively large numbers of free black citizens.

11. The author of the passage most probably refers to Anthony Johnson and his family in order to

   (A) provide a specific example of the potential shortcomings of Breen and Innes's interpretation of historical events
   (B) provide a specific example of relevant data overlooked by Breen and Innes in their discussion of historical events
   (C) provide a specific example of data that Breen and Innes might profitably have used in proving their thesis
   (D) argue that the standard interpretation of historical events is superior to Breen and Innes's revisionist interpretation
   (E) argue that a new historiographical method is needed to provide a full and coherent reading of historical events

12. The attitude of the author of the passage toward Breen and Innes's study can best be described as one of

   (A) condescending dismissal
   (B) wholehearted acceptance
   (C) contentious challenge
   (D) qualified approval
   (E) sincere puzzlement

13. The primary purpose of the passage is to

   (A) summarize previous interpretations
   (B) advocate a new approach
   (C) propose and then illustrate a thesis
   (D) present and evaluate an interpretation
   (E) describe a historical event

It has become something of a truism in folklore studies that until recently the lore was more often studied than the folk. That is, folklorists concentrated on the folklore—the songs, tales, and
(5) proverbs themselves—and ignored the people who transmitted that lore as part of their oral culture. However, since the early 1970s, folklore studies have begun to regard folk performers as people of creativity who are as worthy of attention as are
(10) artists who transmit their ideas in writing. This shift of emphasis has also encouraged a growing interest in women folk performers.

Until recently, folklorists tended to collect folklore from women on only a few topics such as
(15) health and games. In other areas, as Weigle and Farrer have noted, if folklorists "had a choice between a story as told by a man or as told by a woman, the man's version was chosen." It is still too early to tell how profoundly this situation has
(20) changed, but one can point to several recent studies in which women performers play central roles. Perhaps more telling is the focus of the most recently published major folklore textbook, *The Dynamics of Folklore*. Whereas earlier textbooks
(25) gave little attention to women and their folklore, this book devotes many pages to women folk performers.

Recognition of women as important bearers of folklore is not entirely a recent phenomenon. As
(30) early as 1903, a few outstanding women folk performers were the focus of scholarly attention. But the scholarship devoted to these women tended to focus primarily on presenting the performer's repertoire. Recent works about women folk artists,
(35) however, have been more biographically oriented. Juha Pentikäinen's study of Marina Tokalo, a Finnish healer and narrator of folktales, is especially extensive and probing. Though interested in the problems of repertoire analysis, Pentikäinen
(40) gives considerable attention to the details of Tokalo's life and cultural background, so that a full picture of a woman and her folklore emerges. Another notable work is Roger Abraham's book, which presents a very clear picture of the
(45) significance of traditional singing in the life of noted ballad singer Almeda Riddle. Unfortunately, unlike Pentikäinen's study, Abraham's study contains little repertoire analysis.

These recent books reflect the current interest of
(50) folklorists in viewing folklore in context and thus answering questions about what folklore means to the people who use it. One unexpected result of this line of study has been the discovery that women may use the same folklore that men use, but for
(55) very different purposes. This realization has potential importance for future folklore studies in calling greater attention to the type of study required if a folklorist wants truly to understand the role folklore plays in a particular culture.

8. Which one of the following best describes the main point of the passage?

(A) It is only since the early 1970s that folklore studies have begun to recognize women as important bearers of folklore.

(B) A careful analysis of the repertoires of women folk performers has led to a new discovery with important implications for future folklore studies.

(C) Recent studies of women folk performers have focused primarily on the problems of repertoire analysis to the exclusion of a discussion of the culture within which the folklore was developed.

(D) The emphasis in folklore studies has shifted from a focus on the life and the cultural background of the folk performers themselves to a broader understanding of the role folklore plays in a culture.

(E) A change in the focus of folklore studies has led to increased interest in women folk performers and to a new understanding of the importance of the context in which folklore is produced.

9. The author of the passage refers to *The Dynamics of Folklore* primarily in order to

(A) support the idea that it is too soon to tell whether or not folklorists are giving greater attention to women's folklore

(B) refute Weigle and Farrer's contention that folklorists prefer to collect folklore from men rather than from women

(C) support the assertion that scholarship devoted to women folk performers tends to focus primarily on repertoire

(D) present an example of the new emphasis in folklore studies on the performer rather than on the folklore

(E) suggest that there are some signs that women folk performers are gaining increased critical attention in the field of folklore

10. The focus of which one of the following books would most clearly reflect the current interest of the folklorists mentioned in the last paragraph?

   (A) an anthology of tales and songs collected exclusively from women in different cultures
   (B) a compilation of tales and songs from both men and women covering a great variety of traditional and nontraditional topics
   (C) a study of the purpose and meaning of a tale or song for the men and women in a particular culture
   (D) an analysis of one particular tale or song that documents changes in the text of the folklore over a period of time
   (E) a comparison of the creative process of performers who transmit folklore with that of artists who transmit their ideas in writing

11. According to the passage, which one of the following changes has occurred in the field of folklore since the early 1970s?

   (A) increased recognition of the similar ways in which men and women use folklore
   (B) increased recognition of folk performers as creative individuals
   (C) increased emphasis on the need for repertoire analysis
   (D) less emphasis on the relationship between cultural influences and folklore
   (E) less emphasis on the individual performers and more emphasis on the meaning of folklore to a culture

12. It can be inferred from the passage that early folklorists assumed that which one of the following was true?

   (A) The people who transmitted the folklore did not play a creative role in the development of that folklore.
   (B) The people who transmitted the folklore were not consciously aware of the way in which they creatively shaped that folklore.
   (C) The text of a song or tale did not change as the folklore was transmitted from one generation to another.
   (D) Women were not involved in transmitting folklore except for songs or tales dealing with a few traditional topics.
   (E) The meaning of a piece of folklore could differ depending on whether the tale or song was transmitted by a man or by a woman.

13. Based on the information in the passage, which one of the following is most closely analogous to the type of folklore studies produced before the early 1970s?

   (A) An anthropologist studies the implements currently used by an isolated culture, but does not investigate how the people of that culture designed and used those implements.
   (B) A manufacturer hires a consultant to determine how existing equipment in a plant might be modified to improve efficiency, but does not ask employees for their suggestions on how to improve efficiency.
   (C) A historian studies different types of documents dealing with a particular historical event, but decides not to review newspaper accounts written by journalists who lived through that event.
   (D) An archaeologist studies the artifacts of an ancient culture to reconstruct the life-style of that culture, but does not actually visit the site where those artifacts were unearthed.
   (E) An architect designs a private home for a client, but ignores many of the client's suggestions concerning minor details about the final design of the home.

14. The author of the passage uses the term "context" (line 50) to refer to

   (A) a holistic assessment of a piece of folklore rather than a critical analysis of its parts
   (B) a study that examines a piece of folklore in light of earlier interpretations provided by other folklorists
   (C) the parts of a piece of folklore that can shed light on the meaning of the entire piece
   (D) the environment and circumstances in which a particular piece of folklore is used
   (E) the location in which the story line of a piece of folklore is set

15. The author's attitude toward Roger Abraham's book can best be described as one of

   (A) wholehearted approval
   (B) qualified admiration
   (C) uneasy ambivalence
   (D) extreme skepticism
   (E) trenchant criticism

Until recently, it was thought that the Cherokee, a Native American tribe, were compelled to assimilate Euro American culture during the 1820s. During that decade, it was supposed, White
(5) missionaries arrived and, together with their part-Cherokee intermediaries, imposed the benefits of "civilization" on Cherokee tribes while the United States government actively promoted acculturalization by encouraging the Cherokee to
(10) switch from hunting to settled agriculture. This view was based on the assumption that the end of a Native American group's economic and political autonomy would automatically mean the end of its cultural autonomy as well.
(15) William G. McLoughlin has recently argued that not only did Cherokee culture flourish during and after the 1820s, but the Cherokee themselves actively and continually reshaped their culture. Missionaries did have a decisive impact during
(20) these years, he argues, but that impact was far from what it was intended to be. The missionaries' tendency to cater to the interests of an acculturating part-Cherokee elite (who comprised the bulk of their converts) at the expense of the more
(25) traditionalist full-Cherokee majority created great intratribal tensions. As the elite initiated reforms designed to legitimize their own and the Cherokee Nation's place in the new republic of the United States, antimission Cherokee reacted by fostering
(30) revivals of traditional religious beliefs and practices. However, these revivals did not, according to McLoughlin, undermine the elitist reforms, but supplemented them with popular, traditionalist counterparts.
(35) Traditionalist Cherokee did not reject the elitist reforms outright, McLoughlin argues, simply because they recognized that there was more than one way to use the skills the missionaries could provide them. As he quotes one group as saying,
(40) "We want our children to learn English so that the White man cannot cheat us." Many traditionalist Cherokee welcomed the missionaries for another reason: they perceived that it would be useful to have White allies. In the end, McLoughlin asserts,
(45) most members of the Cherokee council, including traditionalists, supported a move which preserved many of the reforms of the part Cherokee elite but limited the activities and influence of the missionaries and other White settlers. According to
(50) McLoughlin, the identity and culture that resulted were distinctively Cherokee, yet reflected the larger political and social setting in which they flourished.
Because his work concentrates on the nineteenth century, McLoughlin unfortunately overlooks
(55) earlier sources of influence, such as eighteenth-century White resident traders and

neighbors, thus obscuring the relative impact of the missionaries of the 1820s in contributing to both acculturalization and resistance to it among the
(60) Cherokee. However, McLoughlin is undoubtedly correct in recognizing that culture is an ongoing process rather than a static entity, and he has made a significant contribution to our understanding of how Cherokee culture changed while retaining its
(65) essential identity after confronting the missionaries.

16. Which one of the following best states the main idea of the passage?

(A) McLoughlin's studies of the impact of missionaries on Cherokee culture during the 1820s are fundamentally flawed, since McLoughlin ignores the greater impact of White resident traders in the eighteenth century.

(B) Though his work is limited in perspective, McLoughlin is substantially correct that changes in Cherokee culture in the 1820s were mediated by the Cherokee themselves rather than simply imposed by the missionaries.

(C) Although McLoughlin is correct in asserting that cultural changes among the Cherokee were autonomous and so not a result of the presence of missionaries, he overemphasizes the role of intratribal conflicts.

(D) McLoughlin has shown that Cherokee culture not only flourished during and after the 1820s, but that changes in Cherokee culture during this time developed naturally from elements already present in Cherokee culture.

(E) Although McLoughlin overlooks a number of relevant factors in Cherokee cultural change in the 1820s, he convincingly demonstrates that these changes were fostered primarily by missionaries.

17. It can be inferred from the author's discussion of McLoughlin's views that the author thinks that Cherokee acculturalization in the 1820s

(A) was reversed in the decades following the 1820s

(B) may have been part of an already existing process of acculturalization

(C) could have been the result of earlier contacts with missionaries

(D) would not have occurred without the encouragement of the United States government

(E) was primarily a result of the influence of White traders living near the Cherokee

18. Which one of the following statements regarding the Cherokee council in the 1820s can be inferred from the passage?

(A) Members of the Cherokee council were elected democratically by the entire Cherokee Nation.

(B) In order for a policy to come into effect for the Cherokee Nation, it had to have been approved by a unanimous vote of the Cherokee council.

(C) Despite the fact that the Cherokee were dominated politically and economically by the United States in the 1820s, the Cherokee council was able to override policies set by the United States government.

(D) Though it did not have complete autonomy in governing the Cherokee Nation, it was able to set some policies affecting the activities of White people living in tribal areas.

(E) The proportions of traditionalist and acculturating Cherokee in the Cherokee council were determined by the proportions of traditionalist and acculturating Cherokee in the Cherokee population.

19. Which one of the following statements regarding the attitudes of traditionalist Cherokee toward the reforms that were instituted in the 1820s can be inferred from the passage?

(A) They supported the reforms merely as a way of placating the increasingly vocal acculturating elite.

(B) They thought that the reforms would lead to the destruction of traditional Cherokee culture but felt powerless to stop the reforms.

(C) They supported the reforms only because they thought that they were inevitable and it was better that the reforms appear to have been initiated by the Cherokee themselves.

(D) They believed that the reforms were a natural extension of already existing Cherokee traditions.

(E) They viewed the reforms as a means of preserving the Cherokee Nation and protecting it against exploitation.

20. According to the passage, McLoughlin cites which one of the following as a contributing factor in the revival of traditional religious beliefs among the Cherokee in the 1820s?

(A) Missionaries were gaining converts at an increasing rate as the 1820s progressed.

(B) The traditionalist Cherokee majority thought that most of the reforms initiated by the missionaries' converts would corrupt Cherokee culture.

(C) Missionaries unintentionally created conflict among the Cherokee by favoring the interests of the acculturating elite at the expense of the more traditionalist majority.

(D) Traditionalist Cherokee recognized that only some of the reforms instituted by a small Cherokee elite would be beneficial to all Cherokee.

(E) A small group of Cherokee converted by missionaries attempted to institute reforms designed to acquire political supremacy for themselves in the Cherokee council.

21. Which one of the following, if true, would most seriously undermine McLoughlin's account of the course of reform among the Cherokee during the 1820s?

(A) Traditionalist Cherokee gained control over the majority of seats on the Cherokee council during the 1820s.

(B) The United States government took an active interest in political and cultural developments within Native American tribes.

(C) The missionaries living among the Cherokee in the 1820s were strongly in favor of the cultural reforms initiated by the acculturating elite.

(D) Revivals of traditional Cherokee religious beliefs and practices began late in the eighteenth century, before the missionaries arrived.

(E) The acculturating Cherokee elite of the 1820s did not view the reforms they initiated as beneficial to all Cherokee.

In *The Dynamics of Apocalypse*, John Lowe attempts to solve the mystery of the collapse of the Classic Mayan civilization. Lowe bases his study on a detailed examination of the known archaeological

(5) record. Like previous investigators, Lowe relies on dated monuments to construct a step-by-step account of the actual collapse. Using the erection of new monuments as a means to determine a site's occupation span, Lowe assumes that once new

(10) monuments ceased to be built, a site had been abandoned. Lowe's analysis of the evidence suggests that construction of new monuments continued to increase between A.D. 672 and 751, but that the civilization stopped expanding

(15) geographically; new construction took place almost exclusively in established settlements. The first signs of trouble followed. Monument inscriptions indicate that between 751 and 790, long-standing alliances started to break down. Evidence also

(20) indicates that between 790 and 830, the death rate in Classic Mayan cities outstripped the birthrate. After approximately 830, construction stopped throughout the area, and within a hundred years, the Classic Mayan civilization all but vanished.

(25) Having established this chronology, Lowe sets forth a plausible explanation of the collapse that accommodates the available archaeological evidence. He theorizes that Classic Mayan civilization was brought down by the interaction of

(30) several factors, set in motion by population growth. An increase in population, particularly within the elite segment of society, necessitated ever more intense farming. Agricultural intensification exerted stress on the soil and led to a decline in

(35) productivity (the amount of food produced through each unit of labor invested). At the same time, the growth of the elite class created increasing demands for ceremonial monuments and luxuries, diverting needed labor from the fields. The theory holds that

(40) these stresses were communicated—and amplified—throughout the area as Mayan states engaged in warfare to acquire laborers and food, and refugees fled impoverished areas. The most vulnerable states thus began to break down, and

(45) each downfall triggered others, until the entire civilization collapsed.

If there is a central flaw in Lowe's explanation, it is that the entire edifice rests on the assumption that the available evidence paints a true picture of

(50) how the collapse proceeded. However, it is difficult to know how accurately the archaeological record reflects historic activity, especially of a complex civilization such as the Mayans', and a hypothesis can be tested only against the best available data.

(55) It is quite possible that our understanding of the collapse might be radically altered by better data. For example, Lowe's assumption about monument construction and the occupation span of a site might well be disproved if further investigations of Classic

(60) Mayan sites established that some remained heavily settled long after the custom of carving dynastic monuments had ceased.

22. Which one of the following best describes the organization of the passage?

(A) A method used to analyze evidence is described, an explanation of the evidence is suggested, and then a conclusion is drawn from the evidence.

(B) A hypothesis is presented, evidence supporting the hypothesis is provided, and then the hypothesis is affirmed.

(C) An analysis of a study is presented, contradictory evidence is examined, and then a direction for future studies is suggested.

(D) The basis of a study is described, a theory that explains the available evidence is presented, and a possible flaw in the study is pointed out.

(E) An observation is made, evidence supporting the observation is presented, and then contradictions in the evidence are discussed.

23. Which one of the following best expresses the main idea of the passage?

(A) In *The Dynamics of Apocalypse*, John Lowe successfully proves that the collapse of Classic Mayan civilization was set in motion by increasing population and decreasing productivity.

(B) In *The Dynamics of Apocalypse*, John Lowe breaks new ground in solving the mystery of the collapse of Classic Mayan civilization through his use of dated monuments to create a step-by-step account of the collapse.

(C) In *The Dynamics of Apocalypse*, John Lowe successfully uses existing data to document the reduction and then cessation of new construction throughout Classic Mayan civilization.

(D) Although John Lowe's study is based on a careful examination of the historical record, it does not accurately reflect the circumstances surrounding the collapse of Classic Mayan civilization.

(E) While John Lowe's theory about the collapse of Classic Mayan civilization appears credible, it is based on an assumption that cannot be verified using the archaeological record.

24. Which one of the following is most closely analogous to the assumption Lowe makes about the relationship between monument construction and Classic Mayan cities?

(A) A person assumes that the shortage of fresh produce on the shelves of a grocery store is due to the effects of poor weather conditions during the growing season.

(B) A person assumes that a movie theater only shows foreign films because the titles of the films shown there are not familiar to the person.

(C) A person assumes that a restaurant is under new ownership because the restaurant's menu has changed drastically since the last time the person ate there.

(D) A person assumes that a corporation has been sold because there is a new name for the corporation on the sign outside the building where the company is located.

(E) A person assumes a friend has sold her stamp collection because the friend has stopped purchasing new stamps.

25. It can be inferred from the passage that the author would describe the method Lowe used to construct a step-by-step chronology of the actual collapse of Classic Mayan civilization as

(A) daringly innovative but flawed
(B) generally accepted but questionable
(C) very reliable but outdated
(D) unscientific but effective
(E) unconventional but brilliant

26. The author of the passage would most likely agree with which one of the following statements about the use of the archaeological record to reconstruct historic activity?

(A) With careful analysis, archaeological evidence can be used to reconstruct accurately the historic activity of a past civilization.

(B) Archaeological evidence is more useful for reconstructing the day-to-day activities of a culture than its long-term trends.

(C) The accuracy of the archaeological record for reconstructing historic activity is dependent on the duration of the particular civilization.

(D) The archaeological record is not an appropriate source of data for reconstructing historic activity.

(E) Historic activity can be reconstructed from archaeological evidence, but it is ultimately impossible to confirm the accuracy of the reconstruction.

Chapter Five:
Law

Law Passages

There are two major systems of criminal procedure in the modern world—the adversarial and the inquisitorial. Both systems were historically preceded by the system of private vengeance in
(5) which the victim of a crime fashioned a remedy and administered it privately, either personally or through an agent.

The modern adversarial system is only one historical step removed from the private vengeance
(10) system and still retains some of its characteristic features. For example, even though the right to initiate legal action against a criminal has now been extended to all members of society (as represented by the office of the public prosecutor), and even
(15) though the police department has effectively assumed the pretrial investigative functions on behalf of the prosecution, the adversarial system still leaves the defendant to conduct his or her own pretrial investigation. The trial is viewed as a
(20) forensic duel between two adversaries, presided over by a judge who, at the start, has no knowledge of the investigative background of the case. In the final analysis the adversarial system of criminal procedure symbolizes and regularizes punitive
(25) combat.

By contrast, the inquisitorial system begins historically where the adversarial system stopped its development. It is two historical steps removed from the system of private vengeance. From the
(30) standpoint of legal anthropology, then, it is historically superior to the adversarial system. Under the inquisitorial system, the public prosecutor has the duty to investigate not just on behalf of society but also on behalf of the defendant.
(35) Additionally, the public prosecutor has the duty to present the court not only evidence that would convict the defendant, but also evidence that could prove the defendant's innocence. The system mandates that both parties permit full pretrial
(40) discovery of the evidence in their possession. Finally, an aspect of the system that makes the trial less like a duel between two adversarial parties is that the inquisitorial system mandates that the judge take an active part in the conduct of the trial, with a
(45) role that is both directive and protective.

Fact-finding is at the heart of the inquisitorial system. This system operates on the philosophical premise that in a criminal action the crucial factor is the body of facts, not the legal rule (in contrast to
(50) the adversarial system), and the goal of the entire procedure is to attempt to recreate, in the mind of the court, the commission of the alleged crime.

Because of the inquisitorial system's thoroughness in conducting its pretrial investigation,

(55) it can be concluded that, if given the choice, a defendant who is innocent would prefer to be tried under the inquisitorial system, whereas a defendant who is guilty would prefer to be tried under the adversarial system.

17. It can be inferred from the passage that the crucial factor in a trial under the adversarial system is

(A) rules of legality
(B) dramatic reenactments of the crime
(C) the search for relevant facts
(D) the victim's personal pursuit of revenge
(E) police testimony about the crime

18. The author sees the judge's primary role in a trial under the inquisitorial system as that of

(A) passive observer
(B) biased referee
(C) uninvolved administrator
(D) aggressive investigator
(E) involved manager

19. According to the passage, a central distinction between the system of private vengeance and the two modern criminal procedure systems was the shift in responsibility for initiating legal action against a criminal from the

(A) defendant to the courts
(B) victim to society
(C) defendant to the prosecutor
(D) courts to a law enforcement agency
(E) victim to the judge

20. All of the following are characteristics of the inquisitorial system that the author cites EXCEPT:

   (A) It is based on cooperation rather than conflict.
   (B) It encourages full disclosure of evidence.
   (C) It requires that the judge play an active role in the conduct of the trial.
   (D) It places the defendant in charge of his or her defense.
   (E) It favors the innocent.

21. The author's attitude toward the inquisitorial system can best be described as

   (A) doubtful that its judges can be both directive and protective
   (B) satisfied that it has potential for uncovering the relevant facts in a case
   (C) optimistic that it will replace the adversarial system
   (D) wary about its downplaying of legal rules
   (E) critical of its close relationship with the private vengeance system

Passage #2: October 1991 Questions 22-28

The Constitution of the United States does not explicitly define the extent of the President's authority to involve United States troops in conflicts with other nations in the absence of a declaration of
(5) war. Instead, the question of the President's authority in this matter falls in the hazy area of concurrent power, where authority is not expressly allocated to either the President or the Congress. The Constitution gives Congress the basic power to
(10) declare war, as well as the authority to raise and support armies and a navy, enact regulations for the control of the military, and provide for the common defense. The President, on the other hand, in addition to being obligated to execute the laws of
(15) the land, including commitments negotiated by defense treaties, is named commander in chief of the armed forces and is empowered to appoint envoys and make treaties with the consent of the Senate. Although this allocation of powers does not
(20) expressly address the use of armed forces short of a declared war, the spirit of the Constitution at least requires that Congress should be involved in the decision to deploy troops, and in passing the War Powers Resolution of 1973, Congress has at last
(25) reclaimed a role in such decisions.
        Historically, United States Presidents have not waited for the approval of Congress before involving United States troops in conflicts in which a state of war was not declared. One scholar has
(30) identified 199 military engagements that occurred without the consent of Congress, ranging from Jefferson's conflict with the Barbary pirates to Nixon's invasion of Cambodia during the Vietnam conflict, which President Nixon argued was justified
(35) because his role as commander in chief allowed him almost unlimited discretion over the deployment of troops. However, the Vietnam conflict, never a declared war, represented a turning point in Congress's tolerance of presidential discretion
(40) in the deployment of troops in undeclared wars. Galvanized by the human and monetary cost of those hostilities and showing a new determination to fulfill its proper role, Congress enacted the War Powers Resolution of 1973, a statute designed
(45) to ensure that the collective judgment of both Congress and the President would be applied to the involvement of United States troops in foreign conflicts.
        The resolution required the President, in the
(50) absence of a declaration of war, to consult with Congress "in every possible instance" before introducing forces and to report to Congress within 48 hours after the forces have actually been deployed. Most important, the resolution allows

(55) Congress to veto the involvement once it begins, and requires the President, in most cases, to end the involvement within 60 days unless Congress specifically authorizes the military operation to continue. In its final section, by declaring that the
(60) resolution is not intended to alter the constitutional authority of either Congress or the President, the resolution asserts that congressional involvement in decisions to use armed force is in accord with the intent and spirit of the Constitution.

22. In the passage, the author is primarily concerned with

(A)   showing how the Vietnam conflict led to a new interpretation of the Constitution's provisions for use of the military
(B)   arguing that the War Powers Resolution of 1973 is an attempt to reclaim a share of constitutionally concurrent power that had been usurped by the President
(C)   outlining the history of the struggle between the President and Congress for control of the military
(D)   providing examples of conflicts inherent in the Constitution's approach to a balance of powers
(E)   explaining how the War Powers Resolution of 1973 alters the Constitution to eliminate an overlap of authority

23. With regard to the use of United States troops in a foreign conflict without a formal declaration of war by the United States, the author believes that the United States Constitution does which one of the following?

(A)   assumes that the President and Congress will agree on whether troops should be used
(B)   provides a clear-cut division of authority between the President and Congress in the decision to use troops
(C)   assigns a greater role to the Congress than to the President in deciding whether troops should be used
(D)   grants final authority to the President to decide whether to use troops
(E)   intends that both the President and Congress should be involved in the decision to use troops

24. The passage suggests that each of the following contributed to Congress's enacting the War Powers Resolution of 1973 EXCEPT

    (A)   a change in the attitude in Congress toward exercising its role in the use of armed forces

    (B)   the failure of Presidents to uphold commitments specified in defense treaties

    (C)   Congress's desire to be consulted concerning United States military actions instigated by the President

    (D)   the amount of money spent on recent conflicts waged without a declaration of war

    (E)   the number of lives lost in Vietnam

25. It can be inferred from the passage that the War Powers Resolution of 1973 is applicable only in "the absence of a declaration of war" (lines 49-50) because

    (A)   Congress has enacted other laws that already set out presidential requirements for situations in which war has been declared

    (B)   by virtue of declaring war, Congress already implicitly participates in the decision to deploy troops

    (C)   the President generally receives broad public support during wars that have been formally declared by Congress

    (D)   Congress felt that the President should be allowed unlimited discretion in cases in which war has been declared

    (E)   the United States Constitution already explicitly defines the reporting and consulting requirements of the President in cases in which war has been declared

26. It can be inferred from the passage that the author believes that the War Powers Resolution of 1973

    (A)   is not in accord with the explicit roles of the President and Congress as defined in the Constitution

    (B)   interferes with the role of the President as commander in chief of the armed forces

    (C)   signals Congress's commitment to fulfill a role intended for it by the Constitution

    (D)   fails explicitly to address the use of armed forces in the absence of a declaration of war

    (E)   confirms the role historically assumed by Presidents

27. It can be inferred from the passage that the author would be most likely to agree with which one of the following statements regarding the invasion of Cambodia?

    (A)   Because it was undertaken without the consent of Congress, it violated the intent and spirit of the Constitution.

    (B)   Because it galvanized support for the War Powers Resolution, it contributed indirectly to the expansion of presidential authority.

    (C)   Because it was necessitated by a defense treaty, it required the consent of Congress.

    (D)   It served as a precedent for a new interpretation of the constitutional limits on the President's authority to deploy troops.

    (E)   It differed from the actions of past Presidents in deploying United States troops in conflicts without a declaration of war by Congress.

28. According to the provisions of the War Powers Resolution of 1973 as described in the passage, if the President perceives that an international conflict warrants the immediate involvement of United States armed forces, the President is compelled in every instance to

    (A)   request that Congress consider a formal declaration of war

    (B)   consult with the leaders of both houses of Congress before deploying armed forces

    (C)   desist from deploying any troops unless expressly approved by Congress

    (D)   report to Congress within 48 hours of the deployment of armed forces

    (E)   withdraw any armed forces deployed in such a conflict within 60 days unless war is declared

Governments of developing countries occasionally enter into economic development agreements with foreign investors who provide capital and technological expertise that may not be
(5) readily available in such countries. Besides the normal economic risk that accompanies such enterprises, investors face the additional risk that the host government may attempt unilaterally to change in its favor the terms of the agreement or
(10) even to terminate the agreement altogether and appropriate the project for itself. In order to make economic development agreements more attractive to investors, some developing countries have attempted to strengthen the security of such agree-
(15) ments with clauses specifying that the agreements will be governed by "general principles of law recognized by civilized nations"—a set of legal principles or rules shared by the world's major legal systems. However, advocates of governments'
(20) freedom to modify or terminate such agreements argue that these agreements fall within a special class of contracts known as administrative contracts, a concept that originated in French law. They assert that under the theory of administrative contracts, a
(25) government retains inherent power to modify or terminate its own contract, and that this power indeed constitutes a general principle of law. However, their argument is flawed on at least two counts.
(30) First, in French law not all government contracts are treated as administrative contracts. Some contracts are designated as administrative by specific statute, in which case the contractor is made aware of the applicable legal rules upon
(35) entering into agreement with the government. Alternatively, the contracting government agency can itself designate a contract as administrative by including certain terms not found in private civil contracts. Moreover, even in the case of adminis-
(40) trative contracts, French law requires that in the event that the government unilaterally modifies the terms of the contract, it must compensate the contractor for any increased burden resulting from the government's action. In effect, the government
(45) is thus prevented from modifying those contractual terms that define the financial balance of the contract.
Second, the French law of administrative contracts, although adopted by several countries, is
(50) not so universally accepted that it can be embraced as a general principle of law. In both the United States and the United Kingdom, government contracts are governed by the ordinary law of contracts, with the result that the government can
(55) reserve the power to modify or terminate a contract unilaterally only by writing such power into the contract as a specific provision. Indeed, the very fact that termination and modification clauses are commonly found in government contracts suggests
(60) that a government's capacity to modify or terminate

agreements unilaterally derives from specific contract provisions, not from inherent state power.

1. In the passage, the author is primarily concerned with doing which one of the following?

(A) pointing out flaws in an argument provided in support of a position
(B) analyzing the weaknesses inherent in the proposed solution to a problem
(C) marshaling evidence in support of a new explanation of a phenomenon
(D) analyzing the risks inherent in adopting a certain course of action
(E) advocating a new approach to a problem that has not been solved by traditional means

2. It can be inferred from the passage that the author would be most likely to agree with which one of the following assertions regarding the "general principles of law" mentioned in line 16 of the passage?

(A) They fail to take into account the special needs and interests of developing countries that enter into agreements with foreign investors.
(B) They have only recently been invoked as criteria for adjudicating disputes between governments and foreign investors.
(C) They are more compatible with the laws of France and the United States than with those of the United Kingdom.
(D) They do not assert that governments have an inherent right to modify unilaterally the terms of agreements that they have entered into with foreign investors.
(E) They are not useful in adjudicating disputes between developing countries and foreign investors.

3. The author implies that which one of the following is true of economic development agreements?

(A) They provide greater economic benefits to the governments that are parties to such agreements than to foreign investors.
(B) They are interpreted differently by courts in the United Kingdom than they are by courts in the United States.
(C) They have proliferated in recent years as a result of governments' attempts to make them more legally secure.
(D) They entail greater risk to investors when the governments that enter into such agreements reserve the right to modify unilaterally the terms of the agreements.
(E) They have become less attractive to foreign investors as an increasing number of governments that enter into such agreements consider them governed by the law of ordinary contracts.

4. According to the author, which one of the following is true of a contract that is designated by a French government agency as an administrative contract?

(A) It requires the government agency to pay for unanticipated increases in the cost of delivering the goods and services specified in the contract.

(B) It provides the contractor with certain guarantees that are not normally provided in private civil contracts.

(C) It must be ratified by the passage of a statute.

(D) It discourages foreign companies from bidding on the contract.

(E) It contains terms that distinguish it from a private civil contract.

5. It can be inferred from the passage that under the "ordinary law of contracts" (lines 53-54), a government would have the right to modify unilaterally the terms of a contract that it had entered into with a foreign investor if which one of the following were true?

(A) The government undertook a greater economic risk by entering into the contract than did the foreign investor.

(B) The cost to the foreign investor of abiding by the terms of the contract exceeded the original estimates of such costs.

(C) The modification of the contract did not result in any increased financial burden for the investor.

(D) Both the government and the investor had agreed to abide by the general principles of law recognized by civilized nations.

(E) The contract contains a specific provision allowing the government to modify the contract.

6. In the last paragraph, the author refers to government contracts in the United States and the United Kingdom primarily in order to

(A) cite two governments that often reserve the right to modify unilaterally contracts that they enter into with foreign investors

(B) support the assertion that there is no general principle of law governing contracts between private individuals and governments

(C) cast doubt on the alleged universality of the concept of administrative contracts

(D) provide examples of legal systems that might benefit from the concept of administrative contracts

(E) provide examples of characteristics that typically distinguish government contracts from private civil contracts

7. Which one of the following best states the author's main conclusion in the passage?

(A) Providing that an international agreement be governed by general principles of law is not a viable method of guaranteeing the legal security of such an agreement.

(B) French law regarding contracts is significantly different from those in the United States and the United Kingdom.

(C) Contracts between governments and private investors in most nations are governed by ordinary contract law.

(D) An inherent power of a government to modify or terminate a contract cannot be considered a general principle of law.

(E) Contracts between governments and private investors can be secured only by reliance on general principles of law.

8. The author's argument in lines 57-62 would be most weakened if which one of the following were true?

(A) The specific provisions of government contracts often contain explicit statements of what all parties to the contracts already agree are inherent state powers.

(B) Governments are more frequently put in the position of having to modify or terminate contracts than are private individuals.

(C) Modification clauses in economic development agreements have frequently been challenged in international tribunals by foreign investors who were a party to such agreements.

(D) The general principles of law provide that modification clauses cannot allow the terms of a contract to be modified in such a way that the financial balance of the contract is affected.

(E) Termination and modification agreements are often interpreted differently by national courts than they are by international tribunals.

Currently, legal scholars agree that in some cases legal rules do not specify a definite outcome. These scholars believe that such indeterminacy results from the vagueness of language: the
(5) boundaries of the application of a term are often unclear. Nevertheless, they maintain that the system of legal rules by and large rests on clear core meanings that do determine definite outcomes for most cases. Contrary to this view, an earlier group
(10) of legal philosophers, called "realists," argued that indeterminacy pervades every part of the law.

The realists held that there is always a cluster of rules relevant to the decision in any litigated case. For example, deciding whether an aunt's promise to
(15) pay her niece a sum of money if she refrained from smoking is enforceable would involve a number of rules regarding such issues as offer, acceptance, and revocation. Linguistic vagueness in any one of these rules would affect the outcome of the case, making
(20) possible multiple points of indeterminacy, not just one or two, in any legal case.

For the realists, an even more damaging kind of indeterminacy stems from the fact that in a common-law system based on precedent, a judge's
(25) decision is held to be binding on judges in subsequent similar cases. Judicial decisions are expressed in written opinions, commonly held to consist of two parts: the holding (the decision for or against the plaintiff and the essential grounds or
(30) legal reasons for it, that is, what subsequent judges are bound by), and the dicta (everything in an opinion not essential to the decision, for example, comments about points of law not treated as the basis of the outcome). The realists argued that in
(35) practice the common-law system treats the "holding/dicta" distinction loosely. They pointed out that even when the judge writing an opinion characterizes part of it as "the holding," judges writing subsequent opinions, although unlikely to
(40) dispute the decision itself, are not bound by the original judge's perception of what was essential to the decision. Later judges have tremendous leeway in being able to redefine the holding and the dicta in a precedential case. This leeway enables judges
(45) to choose which rules of law formed the basis of the decision in the earlier case. When judging almost any case, then, a judge can find a relevant precedential case which, in subsequent opinions, has been read by one judge as stating one legal rule,
(50) and by another judge as stating another, possibly contradictory one. A judge thus faces an indeterminate legal situation in which he or she has to choose which rules are to govern the case at hand.

15. According to the passage, the realists argued that which one of the following is true of a common-law system?

(A) It gives rise to numerous situations in which the decisions of earlier judges are found to be in error by later judges.

(B) It possesses a clear set of legal rules in theory, but in practice most judges are unaware of the strict meaning of those rules.

(C) Its strength lies in the requirement that judges decide cases according to precedent rather than according to a set of abstract principles.

(D) It would be improved judges refrained from willfully misinterpreting the written opinions of prior judges.

(E) It treats the difference between the holding and the dicta in a written opinion rather loosely in practice.

16. According to the passage, which one of the following best describes the relationship between a judicial holding and a judicial decision?

(A) The holding is not commonly considered binding on subsequent judges, but the decision is.

(B) The holding formally states the outcome of the case, while the decision explains it.

(C) The holding explains the decision but does not include it.

(D) The holding consists of the decision and the dicta.

(E) The holding sets forth and justifies a decision.

17. The information in the passage suggests that the realists would most likely have agreed with which one of the following statements about the reaction of judges to past interpretations of a precedential case, each of which states a different legal rule?

(A) The judges would most likely disagree with one or more of the interpretations and overturn the earlier judges' decisions.

(B) The judges might differ from each other concerning which of the interpretations would apply in a given case.

(C) The judges probably would consider themselves bound by all the legal rules stated in the interpretations.

(D) The judges would regard the lack of unanimity among interpretations as evidence that no precedents existed.

(E) The judges would point out in their holdings the inherent contradictions arising from the earlier judges' differing interpretations.

18. It can be inferred from the passage that most legal scholars today would agree with the realists that

(A) linguistic vagueness can cause indeterminacy regarding the outcome of a litigated case

(B) in any litigated case, several different and possibly contradictory legal rules are relevant to the decision of the case

(C) the distinction between holding and dicta in a written opinion is usually difficult to determine in practice

(D) the boundaries of applicability of terms may sometimes be difficult to determine, but the core meanings of the terms are well established

(E) a common-law system gives judges tremendous leeway in interpreting precedents, and contradictory readings of precedential cases can usually be found

19. The passage suggests that the realists believed which one of the following to be true of the dicta in a judge's written opinion?

(A) The judge writing the opinion is usually careful to specify those parts of the opinion he or she considers part of the dicta.

(B) The appropriateness of the judge's decision would be disputed by subsequent judges on the basis of legal rules expressed in the dicta.

(C) A consensus concerning what constitutes the dicta in a judge's opinion comes to be fixed over time as subsequent similar cases are decided.

(D) Subsequent judges can consider parts of what the original judge saw as the dicta to be essential to the original opinion.

(E) The judge's decision and the grounds for it are usually easily distinguishable from the dicta.

20. Which one of the following best describes the overall organization of the passage?

(A) A traditional point of view is explained and problems arising from it are described.

(B) Two conflicting systems of thought are compared point for point and then evaluated.

(C) A legal concept is defined and arguments justifying that definition are refuted.

(D) Two viewpoints on an issue are briefly described and one of those viewpoints is discussed at greater length.

(E) A theoretical description of how a system develops is contrasted with the actual practices characterizing the system.

21. Which one of the following titles best reflects the content of the passage?

(A) Legal Indeterminacy: The Debate Continues

(B) Holding Versus Dicta: A Distinction Without a Difference

(C) Linguistic Vagueness: Is It Circumscribed in Legal Terminology?

(D) Legal Indeterminacy: The Realist's View of Its Scope

(E) Legal Rules and the Precedential System: How Judges Interpret the Precedents

Although the legal systems of England and the United States are superficially similar, they differ profoundly in their approaches to and uses of legal reasons: substantive reasons are more common than (5) formal reasons in the United States, whereas in England the reverse is true. This distinction reflects a difference in the visions of law that prevail in the two countries. In England the law has traditionally been viewed as a system of rules; the United States (10) favors a vision of law as an outward expression of the community's sense of right and justice.

Substantive reasons, as applied to law, are based on moral, economic, political, and other considerations. These reasons are found both "in the (15) law" and "outside the law," so to speak. Substantive reasons inform the content of a large part of the law: constitutions, statutes, contracts, verdicts, and the like. Consider, for example, a statute providing that "no vehicles shall be taken into public parks." (20) Suppose that no specific rationales or purposes were explicitly written into this statute, but that it was clear (from its legislative history) that the substantive purpose of the statute was to ensure quiet and safety in the park. Now suppose that a (25) veterans' group mounts a World War II jeep (in running order but without a battery) as a war memorial on a concrete slab in the park, and charges are brought against its members. Most judges in the United States would find the (30) defendants not guilty because what they did had no adverse effect on park quiet and safety.

Formal reasons are different in that they frequently prevent substantive reasons from coming into play, even when substantive reasons are (35) explicitly incorporated into the law at hand. For example, when a document fails to comply with stipulated requirements, the court may render the document legally ineffective. A will requiring written witness may be declared null and void and, (40) therefore, unenforceable for the formal reason that the requirement was not observed. Once the legal rule—that a will is invalid for lack of proper witnessing—has been clearly established, and the legality of the rule is not in question, application of (45) that rule precludes from consideration substantive arguments in favor of the will's validity or enforcement.

Legal scholars in England and the United States have long bemused themselves with extreme (50) examples of formal and substantive reasoning. On the one hand, formal reasoning in England has led to wooden interpretations of statutes and an unwillingness to develop the common law through judicial activism. On the other hand, freewheeling

(55) substantive reasoning in the United States has resulted in statutory interpretations so liberal that the texts of some statutes have been ignored altogether.

14. Which one of the following best describes the content of the passage as a whole?

(A) an analysis of similarities and differences between the legal systems of England and the United States

(B) a reevaluation of two legal systems with the use of examples

(C) a contrast between the types of reasons embodied in the United States and English legal systems

(D) an explanation of how two distinct visions of the law shaped the development of legal reasoning

(E) a presentation of two types of legal reasons that shows the characteristics they have in common

15. It can be inferred from the passage that English judges would be likely to find the veterans' group discussed in the second paragraph guilty of violating the statute because

(A) not to do so would encourage others to act as the group did

(B) not to do so would be to violate the substantive reasons underlying the law

(C) the veterans failed to comply with the substantive purpose of the statute

(D) the veterans failed to demonstrate that their activities had no adverse effect on the public

(E) the veterans failed to comply with the stipulated requirements of the statute

16. From the discussion of wills in the third paragraph it can be inferred that substantive arguments as to the validity of a will might be considered under which one of the following circumstances?

   (A) The legal rule requiring that a will be witnessed in writing does not stipulate the format of the will.
   (B) The legal rule requiring that a will be witnessed stipulates that the will must be witnessed in writing by two people.
   (C) The legal ruling requiring that a will be witnessed in writing stipulates that the witnessing must be done in the presence of a judge.
   (D) A judge rules that the law requires a will to be witnessed in writing regardless of extenuating circumstances.
   (E) A judge rules that the law can be interpreted to allow for a verbal witness to a will in a case involving a medical emergency.

17. The author of the passage makes use of all of the following in presenting the discussion of the English and the United States legal systems EXCEPT

   (A) comparison and contrast
   (B) generalization
   (C) explication of terms
   (D) a chronology of historical developments
   (E) a hypothetical case

18. Which one of the following best describes the function of the last paragraph of the passage?

   (A) It presents the consequences of extreme interpretations of the two types of legal reasons discussed by the author.
   (B) It shows how legal scholars can incorrectly use extreme examples to support their views.
   (C) It corrects inaccuracies in legal scholars' views of the nature of the two types of legal systems.
   (D) It suggests how characterizations of the two types of legal reasons can become convoluted and inaccurate.
   (E) It presents scholars' characterizations of both legal systems that are only partially correct.

19. The author of the passage suggests that in English law a substantive interpretation of a legal rule might be warranted under which one of the following circumstances?

   (A) Social conditions have changed to the extent that to continue to enforce the rule would be to decide contrary to present-day social norms.
   (B) The composition of the legislature has changed to the extent that to enforce the rule would be contrary to the views of the majority in the present legislative assembly.
   (C) The legality of the rule is in question and its enforcement is open to judicial interpretation.
   (D) Individuals who have violated the legal rule argue that application of the rule would lead to unfair judicial interpretations.
   (E) Superior court judges have consistently ruled in decisions regarding the interpretation of the legal rule.

20. According to the passage, which one of the following statements about substantive reasons is true?

   (A) They may be written into laws, but they may also exert an external influence on the law.
   (B) They must be explicitly written into the law in order to be relevant to the application of the law.
   (C) They are legal in nature and determine particular applications of most laws.
   (D) They often provide judges with specific rationales for disregarding the laws of the land.
   (E) They are peripheral to the law, whereas formal reasons are central to the law.

Faced with the problems of insufficient evidence, of conflicting evidence, and of evidence relayed through the flawed perceptual, retentive, and narrative abilities of witnesses, a jury is forced to
(5) draw inferences in its attempt to ascertain the truth. By applying the same cognitive tools they have developed and used over a lifetime, jurors engage in the inferential exercise that lawyers call fact-finding. In certain decision-making contexts
(10) that are relevant to the trial of lawsuits, however, these normally reliable cognitive tools may cause jurors to commit inferential errors that distort rather than reveal the truth.

Although juries can make a variety of inferential
(15) errors, most of these mistakes in judgment involve the drawing of an unwarranted conclusion from the evidence, that is, deciding that the evidence proves something that, in reality, it does not prove. For example, evidence that the defendant in a criminal
(20) prosecution has a prior conviction may encourage jurors to presume the defendant's guilt, because of their preconception that a person previously convicted of a crime must be inclined toward repeated criminal behavior. That commonly held
(25) belief is at least a partial distortion of reality; not all former convicts engage in repeated criminal behavior. Also, a jury may give more probative weight than objective analysis would allow to vivid photographic evidence depicting a shooting victim's
(30) wounds, or may underestimate the weight of defense testimony that is not delivered in a sufficiently forceful or persuasive manner. Finally, complex or voluminous evidence might be so confusing to a jury that its members would draw
(35) totally unwarranted conclusions or even ignore the evidence entirely.

Recent empirical research in cognitive psychology suggests that people tend to commit inferential errors like these under certain predictable
(40) circumstances. By examining the available information, the situation, and the type of decision being made, cognitive psychologists can describe the kinds of inferential errors a person or group is likely to make. These patterns of human
(45) decision-making may provide the courts with a guide to evaluating the effect of evidence on the reliability of the jury's inferential processes in certain situations.

The notion that juries can commit inferential
(50) errors that jeopardize the accuracy of the fact finding process is not unknown to the courts. In fact, one of a presiding judge's duties is to minimize jury inferential error through explanation and clarification. Nonetheless, most judges now
(55) employ only a limited and primitive concept of jury inferential error: limited because it fails to recognize the potential for error outside certain traditional situations, primitive because it ignores the research and conclusions of psychologists in favor of notions
(60) about human cognition held by lawyers.

21. Which one of the following best expresses the main idea of the passage?

(A) When making decisions in certain predictable situations, juries may commit inferential errors that obscure rather than reveal the truth.

(B) The views of human cognition taken by cognitive psychologists on the one hand and by the legal profession on the other are demonstrably dissimilar.

(C) When confronting powerful preconceptions, particularly shocking evidence, or complex situations, jurors make errors in judgment.

(D) The problem of inferential error by juries is typical of the difficulties with cognitive processes that people face in their everyday lives.

(E) Juries would probably make more reliable decisions if cognitive psychologists, rather than judges, instructed them about the problems inherent in drawing unwarranted conclusions.

22. Of the following hypothetical reforms in trial procedure, which one would the author be most likely to support as the best way to address the problem of jury inferential error?

(A) a move away from jury trials

(B) the institution of minimum formal educational requirements for jurors

(C) the development of strict guidelines for defense testimony

(D) specific training for judges in the area of jury instruction

(E) restrictions on lawyers' use of psychological research

LAW

23. In the second paragraph, the author's primary purpose is to

(A)   refute the idea that the fact-finding process is a complicated exercise
(B)   emphasize how carefully evidence must be presented in order to avoid jury inferential error
(C)   explain how commonly held beliefs affect the jury's ability to ascertain the truth
(D)   provide examples of situations that may precipitate jury errors
(E)   recommend a method for minimizing mistakes by juries

24. Which one of the following best describes the author's attitude toward the majority of judges today?

(A)   apprehensive about whether they are consistent in their instruction of juries
(B)   doubtful of their ability to draw consistently correct conclusions based on the evidence
(C)   critical of their failure to take into account potentially helpful research
(D)   pessimistic about their willingness to make significant changes in trial procedure
(E)   concerned about their allowing the presentation of complex and voluminous evidence in the courtroom

25. Which one of the following statements, if true, would most seriously undermine the author's suggestion about the use of current psychological research in the courtroom?

(A)   All guidelines about human behavior must take account of variations in the patterns of human decision-making.
(B)   Current models of how humans make decisions apply reliably to individuals but do not hold for decisions made by groups.
(C)   The current conception of jury inferential error employed by judges has been in use for nearly a century.
(D)   Inferential errors can be more easily predicted in controlled situations such as the trial of lawsuits than in other kinds of decision-making processes.
(E)   In certain predictable circumstances, juries are less susceptible to inferential errors than they are in other circumstances.

26. It can be inferred from the passage that the author would be most likely to agree with which one of the following generalizations about lawyers?

(A)   They have a less sophisticated understanding of human cognition than do psychologists.
(B)   They often present complex or voluminous information merely in order to confuse a jury.
(C)   They are no better at making logical inferences from the testimony at a trial than are most judges.
(D)   They have worked to help judges minimize jury inferential error.
(E)   They are unrealistic about the ability of jurors to ascertain the truth.

27. The author would be most likely to agree with which one of the following generalizations about a jury's decision-making process?

(A)   The more evidence that a jury has, the more likely it is that the jury will reach a reliable verdict.
(B)   Juries usually overestimate the value of visual evidence such as photographs.
(C)   Jurors have preconceptions about the behavior of defendants that prevent them from making an objective analysis of the evidence in a criminal trial.
(D)   Most of the jurors who make inferential errors during a trial do so because they are unaccustomed to having to make difficult decisions based on inferences.
(E)   The manner in which evidence is presented to a jury may influence the jury either to overestimate or to underestimate the value of that evidence.

The United States Supreme Court has not
always resolved legal issues of concern to Native
Americans in a manner that has pleased the Indian
nations. Many of the Court's decisions have been
(5)   products of political compromise that looked more
to the temper of the times than to enduring
principles of law. But accommodation is part of the
judicial system in the United States, and judicial
decisions must be assessed with this fact in mind.
(10)   Despite the "accommodating" nature of the
judicial system, it is worth noting that the power of
the Supreme Court has been exercised in a manner
that has usually been beneficial to Native
Americans, at least on minor issues, and has not
(15)   been wholly detrimental on the larger, more
important issues. Certainly there have been
decisions that cast doubt on the validity of this
assertion. Some critics point to the patronizing tone
of many Court opinions and the apparent rejection
(20)   of Native American values as important points to
consider when reviewing a case. However, the
validity of the assertion can be illustrated by
reference to two important contributions that have
resulted from the exercise of judicial power.
(25)   First, the Court has created rules of judicial
construction that, in general, favor the rights of
Native American litigants. The Court's attitude has
been conditioned by recognition of the distinct
disadvantages Native Americans faced when
(30)   dealing with settlers in the past. Treaties were
inevitably written in English for the benefit of their
authors, whereas tribal leaders were accustomed to
making treaties without any written account, on the
strength of mutual promises sealed by religious
(35)   commitment and individual integrity. The written
treaties were often broken, and Native Americans
were confronted with fraud and political and
military aggression. The Court recognizes that past
unfairness to Native Americans cannot be
(40)   sanctioned by the force of law. Therefore,
ambiguities in treaties are to be interpreted in favor
of the Native American claimants, treaties are to be
interpreted as the Native Americans would have
understood them, and, under the reserved rights
(45)   doctrine, treaties reserve to Native Americans all
rights that have not been specifically granted away
in other treaties.
A second achievement of the judicial system is
the protection that has been provided against
(50)   encroachment by the states into tribal affairs.
Federal judges are not inclined to view favorably
efforts to extend states' powers and jurisdictions
because of the direct threat that such expansion
poses to the exercise of federal powers. In the
(55)   absence of a federal statute directly and clearly
allocating a function to the states, federal judges are
inclined to reserve for the federal government—and

the tribal governments under its charge—all those
powers and rights they can be said to have
(60)   possessed historically.

9. According to the passage, one reason why the
    United States Supreme Court "has not always
    resolved legal issues of concern to Native
    Americans in a manner that has pleased the Indian
    nations" (lines 1-4) is that

    (A) Native Americans have been prevented from
         presenting their concerns persuasively
    (B) the Court has failed to recognize that the
         Indian nations' concerns are different from
         those of other groups or from those of the
         federal government
    (C) the Court has been reluctant to curtail the
         powers of the federal government
    (D) Native Americans faced distinct
         disadvantages in dealing with settlers in the
         past
    (E) the Court has made political compromises in
         deciding some cases

10. It can be inferred that the objections raised by
    the critics mentioned in line 18 would be most
    clearly answered by a United States Supreme Court
    decision that

    (A) demonstrated respect for Native Americans
         and the principles and qualities they
         consider important
    (B) protected the rights of the states in conflicts
         with the federal government
    (C) demonstrated recognition of the unfair
         treatment Native Americans received in the
         past
    (D) reflected consideration of the hardships
         suffered by Native Americans because of
         unfair treaties
    (E) prevented repetition of inequities
         experienced by Native Americans in the
         past

11. It can be inferred that the author calls the judicial system of the United States "accommodating" (line 10) primarily in order to

    (A)   suggest that the decisions of the United States Supreme Court have been less favorable to Native Americans than most people believe
    (B)   suggest that the United States Supreme Court should be more supportive of the goals of Native Americans
    (C)   suggest a reason why the decisions of the United States Supreme Court have not always favored Native Americans
    (D)   indicate that the United States Supreme Court has made creditable efforts to recognize the values of Native Americans
    (E)   indicate that the United States Supreme Court attempts to be fair to all parties to a case

12. The author's attitude toward the United States Supreme Court's resolution of legal issues of concern to Native Americans can best be described as one of

    (A)   wholehearted endorsement
    (B)   restrained appreciation
    (C)   detached objectivity
    (D)   cautious opposition
    (E)   suppressed exasperation

13. It can be inferred that the author believes that the extension of the states' powers and jurisdictions with respect to Native American affairs would be

    (A)   possible only with the consent of the Indian nations
    (B)   favorably viewed by the United States Supreme Court
    (C)   in the best interests of both state and federal governments
    (D)   detrimental to the interests of Native Americans
    (E)   discouraged by most federal judges in spite of legal precedents supporting the extension

14. The author's primary purpose is to

    (A)   contrast opposing views
    (B)   reevaluate traditional beliefs
    (C)   reconcile divergent opinions
    (D)   assess the claims made by disputants
    (E)   provide evidence to support a contention

15. It can be inferred that the author believes the United States Supreme Court's treatment of Native Americans to have been

    (A)   irreproachable on legal grounds
    (B)   reasonably supportive in most situations
    (C)   guided by enduring principles of law
    (D)   misguided but generally harmless
    (E)   harmful only in a few minor cases

LAW

Legal cases can be termed "hard" cases if they raise issues that are highly controversial, issues about which people with legal training disagree. The ongoing debate over the completeness of the
(5) law usually concerns the extent to which such hard cases are legally determinate, or decidable according to existing law.

H. L. A. Hart's *The Concept of Law* is still the clearest and most persuasive statement of both the
(10) standard theory of hard cases and the standard theory of law on which it rests. For Hart, the law consists of legal rules formulated in general terms; these terms he calls "open textured," which means that they contain a "core" of settled meaning and a
(15) "penumbra" or "periphery" where their meaning is not determinate. For example, suppose an ordinance prohibits the use of vehicles in a park. "Vehicle" has a core of meaning which includes cars and motorcycles. But, Hart claims, other
(20) vehicles, such as bicycles, fall within the peripheral meaning of "vehicle," so that the law does not establish whether they are prohibited. There will always be cases not covered by the core meaning of legal terms within existing laws; Hart considers
(25) these cases to be legally indeterminate. Since courts cannot decide such cases on legal grounds, they must consider nonlegal (for example, moral and political) grounds, and thereby exercise judicial discretion to make, rather than apply, law.
(30) In Ronald Dworkin's view the law is richer than Hart would grant; he denies that the law consists solely of explicit rules. The law also includes principles that do not depend for their legal status on any prior official recognition or enactment.
(35) Dworkin claims that many cases illustrate the existence of legal principles that are different from legal rules and that Hart's "model of rules" cannot accommodate. For Dworkin, legal rules apply in an all-or-nothing fashion, whereas legal principles do
(40) not: they provide the rationale for applying legal rules. Thus, because Dworkin thinks there is law in addition to legal rules, he thinks that legal indeterminacy and the need for judicial discretion do not follow from the existence of open texture in
(45) legal rules.

It would be a mistake, though, to dispute Hart's theory of hard cases on this basis alone. If Hart's claim about the "open texture" of general terms is true, then we should expect to find legal
(50) indeterminacies even if the law consists of principles in addition to rules. Legal principles, as well as legal rules, contain general terms that have open texture. And it would be absurd to suppose that wherever the meaning of a legal rule is unclear,
(55) there is a legal principle with a clear meaning. Most interesting and controversial cases will occur in the penumbra of both rules and principles.

9. Which one of the following best expresses the main idea of the passage?

(A) The law will never be complete because new situations will always arise which will require new laws to resolve them.

(B) The most difficult legal cases are those concerning controversial issues about which trained legal minds have differing opinions.

(C) The concept of legal principles does not diminish the usefulness of the concept of the open texture of general terms in deciding whether hard cases are legally determinate.

(D) The concept of legal principles is a deleterious addition to the theory of law since any flaws exhibited by legal rules could also be shared by legal principles.

(E) The inherent inconsistency of terms used in laws provides a continuing opportunity for judges to exercise their discretion to correct defects and gaps in the law.

10. According to the passage, the term "legal principles" as used by Dworkin refers to

(A) a comprehensive code of ethics that governs the behavior of professionals in the legal system

(B) explicit analyses of the terms used in legal rules, indicating what meanings the terms do and do not cover

(C) legal doctrines that underlie and guide the use of accepted legal rules

(D) legal rules that have not yet passed through the entire legislative procedure necessary for them to become law

(E) the body of legal decisions regarding cases that required judicial discretion for their resolution

11. Which one of the following expresses a view that the author of the passage would most probably hold concerning legal principles and legal rules?

   (A)   Legal rules are applied more often than legal principles when a case involves issues about which legal professionals disagree.
   (B)   Both legal rules and legal principles are officially recognized as valid parts of the law.
   (C)   Hart's "model of rules" has been superseded by a "model of principles" that sheds light on legal determinacy.
   (D)   Legal principles are just as likely as legal rules to have terms that have both core and peripheral meanings.
   (E)   Legal principles eliminate the need for judicial discretion in resolving the problems generated by the open texture of legal rules.

12. In the passage, the author uses the example of the word "vehicle" to

   (A)   illustrate a legal rule that necessarily has exceptions
   (B)   show how legal principles are applied in the construction of legal rules
   (C)   represent the core of settled meaning of a legal term
   (D)   serve as an example of a legal term with both a core and a periphery of meaning
   (E)   provide a counterexample to Hart's concept of the open texture of legal terms

13. It can be inferred that the author of the passage regards Hart's theory of hard cases and the theory of standard law as

   (A)   exhaustive
   (B)   worthy of respect
   (C)   interesting but impractical
   (D)   plausible but unwieldy
   (E)   hopelessly outmoded

14. Which one of the following is true of the term "legally determinate" (line 6) as it is used in the passage?

   (A)   It represents the idea that every crime should have a fixed penalty rather than a range of penalties within which a judge can make an arbitrary choice.
   (B)   It refers to a legal case that can be definitively resolved in favor of one side or the other according to the law in effect at the time.
   (C)   It describes a legal rule that requires judges to limit their actions to applying written law when deciding cases over which people with legal training disagree.
   (D)   It refers to any legal case that involves terms with imprecise meanings and thus relies for its resolution only on the determination of judges.
   (E)   It refers to procedures for determining the legal outcome of complex issues in difficult cases.

15. In the passage, the author is primarily concerned with

   (A)   outlining the problems that might be faced by a legislature attempting to create a complete body of law that would prevent judges from making rather than applying the law
   (B)   justifying the idea that "hard" cases will always exist in the practice of law, no matter what laws are written or how they are applied
   (C)   presenting evidence to support Dworkin's idea that legal rules apply in an all-or-nothing fashion, whereas legal principles apply in more sophisticated ways
   (D)   critiquing the concept of the open texture of legal terms as a conceptual flaw in Hart's otherwise well-regarded book
   (E)   demonstrating that Dworkin's concept of legal principles does not form the basis for a successful attack on Hart's theory of legally indeterminate cases

The law-and-literature movement claims to have introduced a valuable pedagogical innovation into legal study: instructing students in techniques of literary analysis for the purpose of interpreting laws
(5) and in the reciprocal use of legal analysis for the purpose of interpreting literary texts. The results, according to advocates, are not only conceptual breakthroughs in both law and literature but also more sensitive and humane lawyers. Whatever the
(10) truth of this last claim, there can be no doubt that the movement is a success: law-and-literature is an accepted subject in law journals and in leading law schools. Indeed, one indication of the movement's strength is the fact that its most distinguished critic,
(15) Richard A. Posner, paradoxically ends up expressing qualified support for the movement in a recent study in which he systematically refutes the writings of its leading legal scholars and cooperating literary critics.
(20) Critiquing the movement's assumption that lawyers can offer special insights into literature that deals with legal matters, Posner points out that writers of literature use the law loosely to convey a particular idea, or as a metaphor for the workings
(25) of the society envisioned in their fiction. Legal questions per se, about which a lawyer might instruct readers, are seldom at issue in literature. This is why practitioners of law-and-literature end up discussing the law itself far less than one might
(30) suppose. Movement leader James White, for example, in his discussion of arguments in the *Iliad*, barely touches on law, and then so generally as to render himself vulnerable to Posner's devastating remark that "any argument can be analogized to a
(35) legal dispute."
Similarly, the notion that literary criticism can be helpful in interpreting law is problematic. Posner argues that literary criticism in general aims at exploring richness and variety of meaning in texts,
(40) whereas legal interpretation aims at discovering a single meaning. A literary approach can thus only confuse the task of interpreting the law, especially if one adopts current fashions like deconstruction, which holds that all texts are inherently
(45) uninterpretable.
Nevertheless, Posner writes that law-and-literature is a field with "promise." Why? Perhaps, recognizing the success of a movement that, in the past, has singled him out for abuse, he is
(50) attempting to appease his detractors, paying obeisance to the movement's institutional success by declaring that it "deserves a place in legal research" while leaving it to others to draw the conclusion from his cogent analysis that it is an
(55) entirely factitious undertaking, deserving of no

intellectual respect whatsoever. As a result, his work stands both as a rebuttal of law-and-literature and as a tribute to the power it has come to exercise in academic circles.

1. The primary purpose of the passage is to

   (A) assess the law-and-literature movement by examining the position of one of its most prominent critics
   (B) assert that a mutually beneficial relationship exists between the study of law and the study of literature
   (C) provide examples of the law-and-literature movement in practice by discussing the work of its proponents
   (D) dismiss a prominent critic's recent study of the law-and-literature movement
   (E) describe the role played by literary scholars in providing a broader context for legal issues

2. Posner's stated position with regard to the law-and-literature movement is most analogous to which one of the following?

   (A) a musician who is trained in the classics but frequently plays modern music while performing on stage
   (B) a partisan who transfers allegiance to a new political party that demonstrates more promise but has fewer documented accomplishments
   (C) a sports fan who wholeheartedly supports the team most likely to win rather than his or her personal favorite
   (D) an ideologue who remains committed to his or her own view of a subject in spite of compelling evidence to the contrary
   (E) a salesperson who describes the faults in a fashionable product while conceding that it may have some value

3. The passage suggests that Posner regards legal practitioners as using an approach to interpreting law that

   (A) eschews discovery of multiple meanings
   (B) employs techniques like deconstruction
   (C) interprets laws in light of varying community standards
   (D) is informed by the positions of literary critics
   (E) de-emphasizes the social relevance of the legal tradition

4. The passage suggests that Posner might find legal training useful in the interpretation of a literary text in which

   (A) a legal dispute symbolizes the relationship between two characters
   (B) an oppressive law is used to symbolize an oppressive culture
   (C) one of the key issues involves the answer to a legal question
   (D) a legal controversy is used to represent a moral conflict
   (E) the working of the legal system suggests something about the political character of a society

5. The author uses the word "success" in line 11 to refer to the law-and-literature movement's

   (A) positive effect on the sensitivity of lawyers
   (B) widespread acceptance by law schools and law journals
   (C) ability to offer fresh insights into literary texts
   (D) ability to encourage innovative approaches in two disciplines
   (E) response to recent criticism in law journals

6. According to the passage, Posner argues that legal analysis is not generally useful in interpreting literature because

   (A) use of the law in literature is generally of a quite different nature than use of the law in legal practice
   (B) law is rarely used to convey important ideas in literature
   (C) lawyers do not have enough literary training to analyze literature competently
   (D) legal interpretations of literature tend to focus on legal issues to the exclusion of other important elements
   (E) legal interpretations are only relevant to contemporary literature

7. According to Posner, the primary difficulty in using literary criticism to interpret law is that

   (A) the goals of the two disciplines are incompatible
   (B) there are few advocates for the law-and-literature movement in the literary profession
   (C) the task of interpreting law is too complex for the techniques of literary criticism
   (D) the interpretation of law relies heavily on legal precedent
   (E) legal scholars are reluctant to adopt the practice in the classroom

Passage #10: June 1996 Questions 9-14

Many Native Americans view the archaeological excavation and museum display of ancestral skeletal remains and items buried with them as a spiritual desecration. A number of legal remedies that either
(5) prohibit or regulate such activities may be available to Native American communities, if they can establish standing in such cases. In disinterment cases, courts have traditionally affirmed the standing of three classes of plaintiffs: the deceased's heirs, the owner of the
(10) property on which the grave is located, and parties, including organizations or distant relatives of the deceased, that have a clear interest in the preservation of a particular grave. If an archaeologically discovered grave is of recent historical origin and associated with
(15) an identifiable Native American community, Native Americans are likely to establish standing in a suit to prevent disinterment of the remains, but in cases where the grave is ancient and located in an area where the community of Native Americans associated with the
(20) grave has not recently lived, they are less likely to be successful in this regard. Indeed, in most cases involving ancient graves, to recognize that Native Americans have standing would represent a significant expansion of common law. In cases where standing can
(25) be achieved, however, common law may provide a basis for some Native American claims against archaeologists and museums.

Property law, for example, can be useful in establishing Native American claims to artifacts that
(30) are retrieved in the excavation of ancient graves and can be considered the communal property of Native American tribes or communities. In *Charrier v. Bell*, a United States appellate court ruled that the common law doctrine of abandonment, which allows the finder
(35) of abandoned property to claim ownership, does not apply to objects buried with the deceased. The court ruled that the practice of burying items with the body of the deceased "is not intended as a means of relinquishing ownership to a stranger," and that to
(40) interpret it as such "would render a grave subject to despoliation either immediately after interment or . . . after removal of the descendants of the deceased from the neighborhood of the cemetery." This ruling suggests that artifacts excavated from Native American
(45) ancestral graves should be returned to representatives of tribal groups who can establish standing in such cases.

More generally, United States courts have upheld the distinction between individual and communal
(50) property, holding that an individual Native American does not have title to communal property owned and held for common use by his or her tribe. As a result, museums cannot assume that they have valid title to cultural property merely because they purchased in
(55) good faith an item that was originally sold in good faith by an individual member of a Native American community.

9. The primary purpose of the passage is to provide an answer to which one of the following questions?

(A) How should the legal protection of Native American burial grounds be enhanced?

(B) What characteristics of Native American burial grounds enhance their chances for protection by the law?

(C) In what ways does the law protect the rights of Native Americans in regard to the contents of ancestral graves?

(D) Why are the courts concerned with protecting Native American burial grounds from desecration?

(E) By what means can Native Americans establish their rights to land on which their ancestors are buried?

10. It can be inferred that a court would be most likely to deny standing in a disinterment case to which one of the following Native American plaintiffs?

(A) one who seeks, as one of several beneficiaries of his father's estate, to protect the father's burial site

(B) one who seeks to prevent tenants on her land from taking artifacts from a grave located on the property

(C) one who represents a tribe whose members hope to prevent the disinterment of remains from a distant location from which the tribe recently moved

(D) one who seeks to have artifacts that have been removed from a grave determined to be that of her second cousin returned to the grave

(E) one who seeks the return of artifacts taken from the ancient burial grounds of disparate tribes and now displayed in a museum

11. According to the passage, which one of the following is true of cases involving ancient graves?

(A) Once a plaintiff's standing has been established, such cases are usually more difficult to resolve than are cases involving more recent graves.

(B) The distinction between individual and communal property is usually an issue in such cases.

(C) Even when a plaintiff's standing has been established, property law cannot be used as a basis for the claims of Native Americans in most such cases.

(D) In most such cases, common law does not currently provide a clear basis for establishing that Native Americans have standing.

(E) Common law is rarely used as a basis for the claims of Native Americans who have established standing in such cases.

12. The passage suggests that in making the ruling in *Charrier v. Bell* the court is most likely to have considered the answer to which one of the following questions?

(A) Are the descendants of the deceased still alive?

(B) What was the reason for burying the objects in question?

(C) How long after interment had buried objects been claimed by a stranger?

(D) Did the descendants of the deceased remain in the neighborhood of the cemetery?

(E) Could the property on which buried objects were found be legally considered to be abandoned property?

13. The author uses the second paragraph to

(A) illustrate the contention that common law may support the claims of Native Americans to the contents of ancestral graves

(B) exemplify the difficulties that Native Americans are likely to encounter in claiming ancestral remains

(C) introduce a discussion of the distinction between individual and communal property

(D) confirm the contention that cases involving ancient graves present unresolved legal problems

(E) suggest that property law is applicable in most disinterment cases

14. Which one of the following best expresses the main idea of the passage?

(A) Prior to an appellate court's ruling in *Charrier v. Bell*, Native Americans had no legal grounds for demanding the return of artifacts excavated from ancient graves.

(B) Property law offers the most promising remedies to Native Americans seeking to recover communally owned artifacts that were sold to museums without tribal authorization.

(C) The older the grave, the more difficult it is for Native Americans to establish standing in cases concerning the disposition of archaeologically excavated ancestral remains.

(D) In cases in which Native Americans can establish standing, common law can be useful in protecting ancestral remains and the artifacts buried with them.

(E) Native Americans are unlikely to make significant progress in the recovery of cultural property until common law is significantly expanded to provide them with standing in cases involving the excavation of ancient graves.

By the mid-fourteenth century, professional associations of canon lawyers (legal advocates in Christian ecclesiastical courts, which dealt with cases involving marriage, inheritance, and other issues) had (5) appeared in most of Western Europe, and a body of professional standards had been defined for them. One might expect that the professional associations would play a prominent role in enforcing these standards of conduct, as other guilds often did, and as modern (10) professional associations do, but that seems not to have happened. Advocates' professional organizations showed little fervor for disciplining their erring members. Some even attempted to hobble efforts at enforcement. The Florentine guild of lawyers, for (15) example, forbade its members to play any role in disciplinary proceedings against other guild members. In the few recorded episodes of disciplinary enforcement, the initiative for disciplinary action apparently came from a dissatisfied client, not from (20) fellow lawyers.

At first glance, there seem to be two possible explanations for the rarity of disciplinary proceedings. Medieval canon lawyers may have generally observed the standards of professional conduct scrupulously. (25) Alternatively, it is possible that deviations from the established standards of behavior were not uncommon, but that canonical disciplinary mechanisms were so inefficient that most delinquents escaped detection and punishment.

(30) Two considerations make it clear that the second of these explanations is more plausible. First, the English civil law courts, whose ethical standards were similar to those of ecclesiastical courts, show many more examples of disciplinary actions against legal (35) practitioners than do the records of church courts. This discrepancy could well indicate that the disciplinary mechanisms of the civil courts functioned more efficiently than those of the church courts. The alternative inference, namely, that ecclesiastical (40) advocates were less prone to ethical lapses than their counterparts in the civil courts, seems inherently weak, especially since there was some overlap of personnel between the civil bar and the ecclesiastical bar.

Second, church authorities themselves complained (45) about the failure of advocates to measure up to ethical standards and deplored the shortcomings of the disciplinary system. Thus the Council of Basel declared that canon lawyers failed to adhere to the ethical prescriptions laid down in numerous papal (50) constitutions and directed Cardinal Cesarini to address the problem. In England, where medieval church records are extraordinarily rich, similar complaints about the failure of the disciplinary system to reform unethical practices were very common.

(55) Such criticisms seem to have had a paradoxical result, for they apparently reinforced the professional solidarity of lawyers at the expense of the enforcement of ethical standards. Thus the profession's critics may actually have induced advocates to organize (60) professional associations for self-defense. The critics' attacks may also have persuaded lawyers to assign a higher priority to defending themselves against attacks by nonprofessionals than to disciplining wayward members within their own ranks.

7. Which one of the following best states the main conclusion of the passage?

(A) Professional organizations of medieval canon lawyers probably only enforced ethical standards among their own members when provoked to do so by outside criticisms.

(B) Professional organizations of medieval civil lawyers seem to have maintained stricter ethical standards for their own members than did professional organizations of medieval canon lawyers.

(C) Professional organizations of medieval canon lawyers apparently served to defend their members against critics' attacks rather than to enforce ethical standards.

(D) The ethical standards maintained by professional associations of medieval canon lawyers were chiefly laid down in papal constitutions.

(E) Ethical standards for medieval canon lawyers were not laid down until professional organizations for these lawyers had been formed.

8. According to the passage, which one of the following statements about law courts in medieval England is true?

(A) Some English lawyers who practiced in civil courts also practiced in church courts, but others served exclusively in one court or the other.

(B) English canon lawyers were more likely to initiate disciplinary proceedings against their colleagues than were English civil lawyers.

(C) English civil lawyers maintained more stringent ethical standards than did civil lawyers in the rest of Europe.

(D) English ecclesiastical courts had originally been modeled upon English civil courts.

(E) English ecclesiastical courts kept richer and more thorough records than did English civil courts.

9. The author refers to the Florentine guild of lawyers in the first paragraph most probably in order to

(A) introduce a theory about to be promoted
(B) illustrate the type of action referred to in the previous sentence
(C) underline the universality of a method discussed throughout the paragraph
(D) point out a flaw in an argument presented earlier in the paragraph
(E) rebut an anticipated objection to a thesis just proposed

10. The author refers to the Council of Basel (line 47) primarily in order to

(A) provide an example of the type of action needed to establish professional standards for canon lawyers
(B) contrast the reactions of English church authorities with the reactions of other bodies to violations of professional standards by canon lawyers
(C) bolster the argument that violations of professional standards by canon lawyers did take place
(D) explain how rules of conduct for canon lawyers were established
(E) describe the development of a disciplinary system to enforce professional standards among canon lawyers

11. According to the information in the passage, for which one of the following ethical violations would documentation of disciplinary action against a canon lawyer be most likely to exist?

(A) betraying a client's secrets to the opposing party
(B) bribing the judge to rule in favor of a client
(C) misrepresenting credentials in order to gain admission to the lawyers' guild
(D) spreading rumors in order to discredit an opposing lawyer
(E) knowingly helping a client to misrepresent the truth

12. Which one of the following is most analogous to the "professional solidarity" referred to in lines 56-57?

(A) Members of a teachers' union go on strike when they believe one of their colleagues to be falsely accused of using an inappropriate textbook.
(B) In order to protect the reputation of the press in the face of a largely hostile public, a journalist conceals distortions in a colleague's news article.
(C) Several dozen recording artists agree to participate in a concert to benefit an endangered environmental habitat.
(D) In order to expedite governmental approval of a drug, a government official is persuaded to look the other way when a pharmaceutical manufacturer conceals evidence that the drug may have minor side effects.
(E) A popular politician agrees to campaign for another, less popular politician belonging to the same political party.

13. The passage suggests that which one of the following is most likely to have been true of medieval guilds?

(A) Few guilds of any importance existed before the mid-fourteenth century.
(B) Many medieval guilds exercised influence over the actions of their members.
(C) Most medieval guilds maintained more exacting ethical standards than did the associations of canon lawyers.
(D) Medieval guilds found it difficult to enforce discipline among their members.
(E) The ethical standards of medieval guilds varied from one city to another.

14. The author would be most likely to agree with which one of the following regarding the hypothesis that medieval canon lawyers observed standards of professional conduct scrupulously?

(A) It is untrue because it is contradicted by documents obtained from the ecclesiastical courts.
(B) It is unlikely because it describes behavior markedly different from behavior observed in the same situation in modem society.
(C) It is unlikely because it describes behavior markedly different from behavior observed in a similar area of medieval society.
(D) It is impossible to assess intelligently because of the dearth of civil and ecclesiastical documents.
(E) It is directly supported by documents obtained from civil and ecclesiastical courts.

Chapter Six:
Law-Regulation

Law-Regulation Passages

POWERSCORE
TEST PREPARATION

The extent of a nation's power over its coastal ecosystems and the natural resources in its coastal waters has been defined by two international law doctrines: freedom of the seas and adjacent state
(5)   sovereignty. Until the mid-twentieth century, most nations favored application of broad open-seas freedoms and limited sovereign rights over coastal waters. A nation had the right to include within its territorial dominion only a very narrow band of
(10)   coastal waters (generally extending three miles from the shoreline), within which it had the authority, but not the responsibility, to regulate all activities. But, because this area of territorial dominion was so limited, most nations did not establish rules for
(15)   management or protection of their territorial waters.

        Regardless of whether or not nations enforced regulations in their territorial waters, large ocean areas remained free of controls or restrictions. The citizens of all nations had the right to use these
(20)   unrestricted ocean areas for any innocent purpose, including navigation and fishing. Except for controls over its own citizens, no nation had the responsibility, let alone the unilateral authority, to control such activities in international waters. And, since there
(25)   were few standards of conduct that applied on the "open seas," there were few jurisdictional conflicts between nations.

        The lack of standards is traceable to popular perceptions held before the middle of this century.
(30)   By and large, marine pollution was not perceived as a significant problem, in part because the adverse effect of coastal activities on ocean ecosystems was not widely recognized, and pollution caused by human activities was generally believed to be limited
(35)   to that caused by navigation. Moreover, the freedom to fish, or overfish, was an essential element of the traditional legal doctrine of freedom of the seas that no maritime country wished to see limited. And finally, the technology that later allowed exploitation
(40)   of other ocean resources, such as oil, did not yet exist.

        To date, controlling pollution and regulating ocean resources have still not been comprehensively addressed by law, but international law—established through the customs and practices of nations—does
(45)   not preclude such efforts. And two recent developments may actually lead to future international rules providing for ecosystem management. First, the establishment of extensive fishery zones, extending territorial authority as far as
(50)   200 miles out from a country's coast, has provided the opportunity for nations individually to manage larger ecosystems. This opportunity, combined with national self-interest in maintaining fish populations, could lead nations to reevaluate policies for
(55)   management of their fisheries and to address the problem of pollution in territorial waters. Second, the international community is beginning to understand the importance of preserving the resources and ecology of international waters and to show signs of
(60)   accepting responsibility for doing so. As an international consensus regarding the need for comprehensive management of ocean resources develops, it will become more likely that international standards and policies for broader
(65)   regulation of human activities that affect ocean ecosystems will be adopted and implemented.

1. According to the passage, until the mid-twentieth century there were few jurisdictional disputes over international waters because

    (A)   the nearest coastal nation regulated activities
    (B)   few controls or restrictions applied to ocean areas
    (C)   the ocean areas were used for only innocent purposes
    (D)   the freedom of the seas doctrine settled all claims concerning navigation and fishing
    (E)   broad authority over international waters was shared equally among all nations

2. According to the international law doctrines applicable before the mid-twentieth century, if commercial activity within a particular nation's territorial waters threatened all marine life in those waters, the nation would have been

   (A) formally censured by an international organization for not properly regulating marine activities
   (B) called upon by other nations to establish rules to protect its territorial waters
   (C) able but not required to place legal limits on such commercial activities
   (D) allowed to resolve the problem at its own discretion providing it could contain the threat to its own territorial waters
   (E) permitted to hold the commercial offenders liable only if they were citizens of that particular nation

3. The author suggests that, before the mid-twentieth century, most nations' actions with respect to territorial and international waters indicated that

   (A) managing ecosystems in either territorial or international waters was given low priority
   (B) unlimited resources in international waters resulted in little interest in territorial waters
   (C) nations considered it their responsibility to protect territorial but not international waters
   (D) a nation's authority over its citizenry ended at territorial lines
   (E) although nations could extend their territorial dominion beyond three miles from their shoreline, most chose not to do so

4. The author cites which one of the following as an effect of the extension of territorial waters beyond the three-mile limit?

   (A) increased political pressure on individual nations to establish comprehensive laws regulating ocean resources
   (B) a greater number of jurisdictional disputes among nations over the regulation of fishing on the open seas
   (C) the opportunity for some nations to manage large ocean ecosystems
   (D) a new awareness of the need to minimize pollution caused by navigation
   (E) a political incentive for smaller nations to solve the problems of pollution in their coastal waters

5. According to the passage, before the middle of the twentieth century, nations failed to establish rules protecting their territorial waters because

   (A) the waters appeared to be unpolluted and to contain unlimited resources
   (B) the fishing industry would be adversely affected by such rules
   (C) the size of the area that would be subject to such rules was insignificant
   (D) the technology needed for pollution control and resource management did not exist
   (E) there were few jurisdictional conflicts over nations' territorial waters

6. The passage as a whole can best be described as

   (A) a chronology of the events that have led up to a present-day crisis
   (B) a legal inquiry into the abuse of existing laws and the likelihood of reform
   (C) a political analysis of the problems inherent in directing national attention to an international issue
   (D) a historical analysis of a problem that requires international attention
   (E) a proposal for adopting and implementing international standards to solve an ecological problem

The Taft-Hartley Act, passed by the United
States Congress in 1947, gave states the power to
enact "right-to-work" legislation that prohibits
union shop agreements. According to such an
(5)   agreement, a labor union negotiates wages and
working conditions for all workers in a business,
and all workers are required to belong to the union.
Since 1947, 20 states have adopted right-to-work
laws. Much of the literature concerning
(10)   right-to-work laws implies that such legislation has
not actually had a significant impact. This point of
view, however, has not gone uncriticized. Thomas
M. Carroll has proposed that the conclusions
drawn by previous researchers are attributable to
(15)   their myopic focus on the premise that, unless
right-to-work laws significantly reduce union
membership within a state, they have no effect.
Carroll argues that the right-to-work laws "do
matter" in that such laws generate differences in
(20)   real wages across states. Specifically, Carroll
indicates that while right-to-work laws may not
"destroy" unions by reducing the absolute number
of unionized workers, they do impede the spread
of unions and thereby reduce wages within
(25)   right-to-work states. Because the countervailing
power of unions is weakened in right-to-work
states, manufacturers and their suppliers can act
collusively in competitive labor markets, thus
lowering wages in the affected industries.
(30)   Such a finding has important implications
regarding the demographics of employment and
wages in right-to-work states. Specifically, if
right-to-work laws lower wages by weakening
union power, minority workers can be expected to
(35)   suffer a relatively greater economic disadvantage in
right-to-work states than in union shop states. This
is so because, contrary to what was once thought,
unions tend to have a significant positive impact
on the economic position of minority workers,
(40)   especially Black workers, relative to White workers.
Most studies concerned with the impact of unionism
on the Black worker's economic position relative to
the White worker's have concentrated on the changes
in Black wages due to union membership. That is,
(45)   they have concentrated on union versus nonunion
wage differentials within certain occupational
groups. In a pioneering study, however, Ashenfelter
finds that these studies overlook an important
fact: although craft unionism increases the
(50)   differential between the wages of White workers
and Black workers due to the traditional exclusion
of minority workers from unions in the craft sectors
of the labor market, strong positive wage gains are
made by Black workers within industrial unions.
(55)   In fact, Ashenfelter estimates that industrial
unionism decreases the differential between the
wages of Black workers and White workers by

about 3 percent. If state right-to-work laws weaken
the economic power of unions to raise wages, Black
(60)   workers will experience a disproportionate decline
in their relative wage positions. Black workers in
right-to-work states would therefore experience a
decline in their relative economic positions unless
there is strong economic growth in right-to-work
(65)   states, creating labor shortages and thereby driving
up wages.

1. The reasoning behind the "literature" (line 9), as
    that reasoning is presented in the passage, is most
    analogous to the reasoning behind which one of the
    following situations?

    (A) A law is proposed that benefits many but
         disadvantages a few; those advocating
         passage of the law argue that the
         disadvantages to a few are not so serious
         that the benefits should be denied to many.
    (B) A new tax on certain categories of consumer
         items is proposed; those in favor of the tax
         argue that those affected by the tax are well
         able to pay it, since the items taxed are
         luxury items.
    (C) A college sets strict course requirements
         that every student must complete before
         graduating; students already enrolled argue
         that it is unfair for the new requirements to
         apply to those enrolled before the change.
    (D) The personnel office of a company designs
         a promotion policy requiring that all
         promotions become effective on January
         l; the managers protest that such a policy
         means that they cannot respond fast enough
         to changes in staffing needs.
    (E) A fare increase in a public transportation
         system does not significantly reduce the
         number of fares sold; the management of
         the public transportation system asserts,
         therefore, that the fare hike has had no
         negative effects.

2. According to the passage, which one of the following is true of Carroll's study?

(A) It implies that right-to-work laws have had a negligible effect on workers in right-to-work states.

(B) It demonstrates that right-to-work laws have significantly decreased union membership from what it once was in right-to-work states.

(C) It argues that right-to-work laws have affected wages in right-to-work states.

(D) It supports the findings of most earlier researchers.

(E) It explains the mechanisms by which collusion between manufacturers and suppliers is accomplished.

3. It can be inferred from the passage that the author believes which one of the following about craft unions?

(A) Craft unions have been successful in ensuring that the wages of their members remain higher than the wages of nonunion workers in the same occupational groups.

(B) The number of minority workers joining craft unions has increased sharply in states that have not adopted right-to-work legislation.

(C) Wages for workers belonging to craft unions have generally risen faster and more steadily than wages for workers belonging to industrial unions.

(D) The wages of workers belonging to craft unions have not been significantly affected by right-to-work legislation, although the wages of workers belonging to industrial unions have been negatively affected.

(E) The wages of workers belonging to craft unions are more likely to be driven up in the event of labor shortages than are the wages of workers belonging to industrial unions.

4. Which one of the following best describes the effect industrial unionism has had on the wages of Black workers relative to those of White workers, as that effect is presented in the passage?

(A) Prior to 1947, industrial unionism had little effect on the wages of Black workers relative to those of White workers; since 1947, it has had a slight positive effect.

(B) Prior to 1947, industrial unionism had a strong positive effect on the wages of Black workers relative to those of White workers; since 1947, it has had little effect.

(C) Prior to 1947, industrial unionism had a negative effect on the wages of Black workers relative to those of White workers; since 1947, it has had a significant positive effect.

(D) Industrial unionism has contributed moderately to an increase in the wage differential between Black workers and White workers.

(E) Industrial unionism has contributed strongly to a 3 percent decrease in the wage differential between Black workers and White workers.

5. According to the passage, which one of the following could counteract the effects of a decrease in unions' economic power to raise wages in right-to-work states?

(A) a decrease in the number of union shop agreements

(B) strong economic growth that creates labor shortages

(C) a decrease in membership in craft unions

(D) the merging of large industrial unions

(E) a decline in the craft sectors of the labor market

6. Which one of the following best describes the passage as a whole?

(A) an overview of a problem in research methodology and a recommended solution to that problem

(B) a comparison of two competing theories and a suggestion for reconciling them

(C) a critique of certain legislation and a proposal for modification of that legislation

(D) a review of research that challenges the conclusions of earlier researchers

(E) a presentation of a specific case that confirms the findings of an earlier study

Gray marketing, the selling of trademarked products through channels of distribution not authorized by the trademark holder, can involve distribution of goods either within a market region
(5) or across market boundaries. Gray marketing within a market region ("channel flow diversion") occurs when manufacturer-authorized distributors sell trademarked goods to unauthorized distributors who then sell the goods to consumers within the
(10) same region. For example, quantity discounts from manufacturers may motivate authorized dealers to enter the gray market because they can purchase larger quantities of a product than they themselves intend to stock if they can sell the extra units
(15) through gray market channels.

When gray marketing occurs across market boundaries, it is typically in an international setting and may be called "parallel importing." Manufacturers often produce and sell products in
(20) more than one country and establish a network of authorized dealers in each country. Parallel importing occurs when trademarked goods intended for one country are diverted from proper channels (channel flow diversion) and then exported to unauthorized
(25) distributors in another country.

Trademark owners justifiably argue against gray marketing practices since such practices clearly jeopardize the goodwill established by trademark owners: consumers who purchase trademarked
(30) goods in the gray market do not get the same "extended product," which typically includes pre- and postsale service. Equally important, authorized distributors may cease to promote the product if it becomes available for much lower prices through
(35) unauthorized channels.

Current debate over regulation of gray marketing focuses on three disparate theories in trademark law that have been variously and confusingly applied to parallel importation cases:
(40) universality, exhaustion, and territoriality. The theory of universality holds that a trademark is only an indication of the source or origin of the product. This theory does not recognize the goodwill functions of a trademark. When the courts apply
(45) this theory, gray marketing practices are allowed to continue because the origin of the product remains the same regardless of the specific route of the product through the channel of distribution. The exhaustion theory holds that a trademark owner
(50) relinquishes all rights once a product has been sold. When this theory is applied, gray marketing practices are allowed to continue because the trademark owners' rights cease as soon as their products are sold to a distributor. The theory of territoriality
(55) holds that a trademark is effective in the country in which it is registered. Under the theory of territoriality, trademark owners can stop gray

marketing practices in the registering countries on products bearing their trademarks. Since only the
(60) territoriality theory affords trademark owners any real legal protection against gray marketing practices, I believe it is inevitable as well as desirable that it will come to be consistently applied in gray marketing cases.

7. Which one of the following best expresses the main point of the passage?

(A) Gray marketing is unfair to trademark owners and should be legally controlled.
(B) Gray marketing is practiced in many different forms and places, and legislators should recognize the futility of trying to regulate it.
(C) The mechanisms used to control gray marketing across markets are different from those most effective in controlling gray marketing within markets.
(D) The three trademark law theories that have been applied in gray marketing cases lead to different case outcomes.
(E) Current theories used to interpret trademark laws have resulted in increased gray marketing activity.

8. The function of the passage as a whole is to

(A) criticize the motives and methods of those who practice gray marketing
(B) evaluate the effects of both channel flow diversion and parallel importation
(C) discuss the methods that have been used to regulate gray marketing and evaluate such methods' degrees of success
(D) describe a controversial marketing practice and evaluate several legal views regarding it
(E) discuss situations in which certain marketing practices are common and analyze the economic factors responsible for their development

9. Which one of the following does the author offer as an argument against gray marketing?

(A) Manufacturers find it difficult to monitor the effectiveness of promotional efforts made on behalf of products that are gray marketed.

(B) Gray marketing can discourage product promotion by authorized distributors.

(C) Gray marketing forces manufacturers to accept the low profit margins that result from quantity discounting.

(D) Gray marketing discourages competition among unauthorized dealers.

(E) Quality standards in the manufacture of products likely to be gray marketed may decline.

10. The information in the passage suggests that proponents of the theory of territoriality would probably differ from proponents of the theory of exhaustion on which one of the following issues?

(A) the right of trademark owners to enforce, in countries in which the trademarks are registered, distribution agreements intended to restrict distribution to authorized channels

(B) the right of trademark owners to sell trademarked goods only to those distributors who agree to abide by distribution agreements

(C) the legality of channel flow diversion that occurs in a country other than the one in which a trademark is registered

(D) the significance consumers attach to a trademark

(E) the usefulness of trademarks as marketing tools

11. The author discusses the impact of gray marketing on goodwill in order to

(A) fault trademark owners for their unwillingness to offer a solution to a major consumer complaint against gray marketing

(B) indicate a way in which manufacturers sustain damage against which they ought to be protected

(C) highlight one way in which gray marketing across markets is more problematic than gray marketing within a market

(D) demonstrate that gray marketing does not always benefit the interests of unauthorized distributors

(E) argue that consumers are unwilling to accept a reduction in price in exchange for elimination of service

12. The author's attitude toward the possibility that the courts will come to exercise consistent control over gray marketing practices can best be characterized as one of

(A) resigned tolerance
(B) utter dismay
(C) reasoned optimism
(D) unbridled fervor
(E) cynical indifference

13. It can be inferred from the passage that some channel flow diversion might be eliminated if

(A) profit margins on authorized distribution of goods were less than those on goods marketed through parallel importing

(B) manufacturers relieved authorized channels of all responsibility for product promotion

(C) manufacturers charged all authorized distributors the same unit price for products regardless of quantity purchased

(D) the postsale service policies of authorized channels were controlled by manufacturers

(E) manufacturers refused to provide the "extended product" to consumers who purchase goods in the gray market

Passage #4: February 1995 Questions 14-20

(The following passage was written in 1986.)

The legislature of a country recently considered a bill designed to reduce the uncertainty inherent in the ownership of art by specifying certain conditions that must be met before an allegedly stolen work of
(5) art can be reclaimed by a plaintiff. The bill places the burden of proof in reclamation litigation entirely on the plaintiff, who must demonstrate that the holder of an item knew at the time of purchase that it had been stolen. Additionally, the bill creates a
(10) uniform national statute of limitations for reclamation of stolen cultural property.

Testifying in support of the bill, James D. Burke, a citizen of the country and one of its leading art museum directors, specifically praised the inclusion
(15) of a statute of limitations; otherwise, he said, other countries could seek to reclaim valuable art objects, no matter how long they have been held by the current owner or how legitimately they were acquired. Any country could enact a patrimony
(20) law stating that anything ever made within the boundaries of that country is its cultural property. Burke expressed the fear that widespread reclamation litigation would lead to ruinous legal defense costs for museums.
(25) However, because such reclamation suits have not yet been a problem, there is little basis for Burke's concern. In fact, the proposed legislation would establish too many unjustifiable barriers to the location and recovery of stolen objects. The
(30) main barrier is that the bill considers the announcement of an art transaction in a museum publication to be adequate evidence of an attempt to notify a possible owner. There are far too many such publications for the victim of a theft to survey,
(35) and with only this form of disclosure, a stolen object could easily remain unlocated even if assiduously searched for. Another stipulation requires that a purchaser show the object to a scholar for verification that it is not stolen, but it is
(40) a rare academic who is aware of any but the most publicized art thefts. Moreover, the time limit specified by the statute of limitations is very short, and the requirement that the plaintiff demonstrate that the holder had knowledge of the theft is
(45) unrealistic. Typically, stolen art changes hands several times before rising to the level in the marketplace where a curator or collector would see it. At that point, the object bears no trace of the initial transaction between the thief and the first
(50) purchaser, perhaps the only one in the chain who knowingly acquired a stolen work of art.

Thus, the need for new legislation to protect holders of art is not obvious. Rather, what is necessary is legislation remedying the difficulties
(55) that legitimate owners of works of art, and countries from which such works have been stolen, have in locating and reclaiming these stolen works.

14. Which one of the following most accurately summarizes the main point of the passage?

(A) Various legal disputes have recently arisen that demonstrate the need for legislation clarifying the legal position of museums in suits involving the repossession of cultural property.

(B) A bill intended to prevent other governments from recovering cultural property was recently introduced into the legislature of a country at the behest of its museum directors.

(C) A bill intended to protect good-faith purchasers of works of art from reclamation litigation is unnecessary and fails to address the needs of legitimate owners attempting to recover stolen art works.

(D) Clashes between museum professionals and members of the academic community regarding governmental legislation of the arts can best be resolved by negotiation and arbitration, not by litigation.

(E) The desire of some governments to use legislation and litigation to recover cultural property stolen from their countries has led to abuses in international patrimony legislation.

15. The uncertainty mentioned in line 2 of the passage refers to the

(A) doubt that owners of works of art often harbor over whether individuals have a moral right to possess great art

(B) concern that owners of works of art often have that their possession of such objects may be legally challenged at any time

(C) questions that owners of works of art often have concerning the correct identification of the age and origin of their objects

(D) disputes that often arise between cultural institutions vying for the opportunity to purchase a work of art

(E) apprehension that owners of works of art often feel concerning the possibility that their objects may be damaged or stolen from them

16. Which one of the following is an example of the kind of action that Burke feared would pose a serious threat to museums in his country?

    (A) the passage of a law by another country forbidding the future export of any archaeological objects uncovered at sites within its territory
    (B) an international accord establishing strict criteria for determining whether a work of art can be considered stolen and specifying the circumstances under which it must be returned to its country of origin
    (C) the passage of a law by another country declaring that all objects created by its aboriginal people are the sole property of that country
    (D) an increase in the acquisition of culturally significant works of art by private collectors, who are more capable than museums of bearing the cost of litigation but who rarely display their collections to the public
    (E) the recommendation of a United Nations committee studying the problem of art theft that all international sales of cultural property be coordinated by a central regulatory body

17. According to the passage, Burke envisaged the most formidable potential adversaries of his country's museums in reclamation litigation to be

    (A) commercial dealers in art
    (B) law enforcement officials in his own country
    (C) governments of other countries
    (D) private collectors of art
    (E) museums in other countries

18. The author suggests that in the country mentioned in line 1, litigation involving the reclamation of stolen works of art has been

    (A) less common than Burke fears it will become without passage of a national statute of limitations for reclamation of stolen cultural property
    (B) increasing as a result of the passage of legislation that aids legitimate owners of art in their attempts to recover stolen works
    (C) a serious threat to museums and cultural institutions that have unwittingly added stolen artifacts to their collections
    (D) a signal of the legitimate frustrations of victims of art theft
    (E) increasing as a result of an increase in the amount of art theft

19. Which one of the following best describes the author's attitude toward the proposed bill?

    (A) impassioned support
    (B) measured advocacy
    (C) fearful apprehension
    (D) reasoned opposition
    (E) reluctant approval

20. Which one of the following best exemplifies the sort of legislation considered necessary by the author of the passage?

    (A) a law requiring museums to notify foreign governments and cultural institutions of all the catalogs and scholarly journals that they publish
    (B) a law providing for the creation of a national warehouse for storage of works of art that are the subject of litigation
    (C) a law instituting a national fund for assisting museums to bear the expenses of defending themselves against reclamation suits
    (D) a law declaring invalid all sales of cultural property during the last ten years by museums of one country to museums of another
    (E) a law requiring that a central archive be established for collecting and distributing information concerning all reported thefts of cultural property

One way governments can decrease air pollution is to impose a tax on industrial carbon dioxide emissions. But why should governments consider a carbon tax when they could control emissions by
(5) establishing energy efficiency and conservation standards, by legislating against coal use, or by increasing investment in nuclear power? The great virtue of such a tax is that it would provide incentives for industry to achieve emission
(10) reductions. Because oil emits more carbon dioxide per unit of energy generated than does natural gas, and coal more than oil, a carbon tax would vary with the type of fuel. Such a tax would induce industry to substitute less-polluting fuels for those carrying a
(15) higher tax, and also to reduce the total use of energy.

However, it is not clear how high such a tax should be or what its economic and environmental implications would be. At first glance, it is not
(20) difficult to estimate roughly the size of the tax needed to effect a given level of emission reduction. One writer estimates, for example, that a tax of 41 percent on the price of coal, 33 percent on oil, and 25 percent on gas would reduce the United
(25) Kingdom's emissions by 20 percent (using 1988 as the base year) by the year 2005, the target recommended by the 1988 Toronto Conference. It should be noted, however, that these numbers ignore the effect of the tax on economic growth, and
(30) hence on emissions, and assume that past responses to a price rise will be replicated in the future. These numbers are also based on the assumption that all countries will behave cooperatively in imposing a carbon tax.
(35) There are very strong reasons to believe that cooperation would be difficult to win. If most countries cooperated, then any country that chose not to cooperate would be advantaged: it would have no abatement costs, and the effect on the
(40) environment of its defection would be relatively small. Because of this "free rider" effect, cooperation on a scale needed to reduce carbon dioxide emissions might prove elusive.

Should countries act unilaterally to curb
(45) emissions? If a country were to act unilaterally, the benefits would be spread across the globe, whereas the costs would fall solely on the country taking the action. The action would reduce emissions globally, and the effect of this would be to reduce the benefit
(50) other countries would receive if they reduced emissions. As a consequence, other countries would have less incentive to reduce emissions and would probably emit more carbon dioxide than they would have if the unilateral action had not been taken.
(55) The entire effect of the emission reduction may not be lost, but it would surely be diminished by this free-riding behavior.

16. According to the passage, the size of the carbon tax levied on a given fuel would vary with the

(A) amount of that fuel used by a particular industry
(B) amount of pollution caused by the fuel being taxed
(C) size of the industries using the fuel being taxed
(D) effect that the tax would have on a country's economy
(E) number of users of a particular fuel at a particular time

17. The author mentions the estimates of "One writer" (line 22) primarily in order to

(A) indicate in a general way the size that a carbon tax must be for it to be effective
(B) provide the most accurate information available about the most practical size for a carbon tax
(C) suggest that the target recommended by the 1988 Toronto Conference is an unrealistic one
(D) undermine the argument that a carbon tax would provide incentives for users to achieve emissions reductions
(E) show how the size of an effective carbon tax can be calculated

18. Which one of the following circumstances would most seriously undermine the conclusion "Such a tax would induce industry to substitute less-polluting fuels for those carrying a higher tax" (lines 13-15)?

(A) The fuel taxed at the highest rate costs considerably less to buy than fuels taxed at lower rates.
(B) The goal set by the Toronto Conference cannot be reached unless each fuel is taxed at a much higher rate.
(C) The tax on coal represents a much greater cost increase than does the tax on oil or gas.
(D) It is discovered that gas produces even less carbon dioxide per unit of energy generated than was previously thought.
(E) It is discovered that coal produces even more carbon dioxide per unit of energy generated than was previously thought.

19. The passage is primarily intended to answer which one of the following questions?

    (A)   How high a tax should a country's government impose on carbon dioxide emissions?

    (B)   What issues should a country's government consider before deciding whether to impose a tax on carbon dioxide emissions?

    (C)   What assumptions underlie a country's decision to impose a tax on carbon dioxide emissions?

    (D)   How can the effects of industrial pollution on the Earth's atmosphere be decreased?

    (E)   What can be done to increase the effectiveness of any tax that a country imposes on carbon dioxide emissions?

20. In response to the question, "Should countries act unilaterally to curb emissions?" (lines 44-45), the author would be most likely to contend that a country should

    (A)   not act unilaterally because, although that country would receive some benefits from such action, other countries would most likely be harmed by it

    (B)   not act unilaterally because unilateral action would have no benefits for other countries

    (C)   not act unilaterally because the cost o that country would not be justified by the limited effect that such action would have on industrial pollution worldwide

    (D)   act unilaterally because that country's economy would benefit from the resulting reduction in industrial emissions worldwide

    (E)   act unilaterally because other countries might well be inspired to follow that country's example

21. Which one of the following is most parallel to the "free rider" effect mentioned in line 41?

    (A)   An industry agrees to base itself in a city where there has been little industrial development only if the city will rezone the specific property the industry desires.

    (B)   Because fares for public transportation are rising, a commuter decides to bicycle to work rather than to use public transportation in a city where auto emissions are a problem.

    (C)   An apartment dweller begins to recycle newspapers even though no one else in the building does so and recycling is not required by law.

    (D)   In an area where groundwater has become polluted, a homeowner continues to buy bottled water rather than contribute to a neighborhood fund to combat pollution.

    (E)   In an area where overgrazing is a severe problem, a shepherd allows his sheep to continue grazing common fields even though his neighbors have agreed to buy feed for their animals until regrowth occurs.

Chapter Seven:
Social Science

Social Science Passages

One scientific discipline, during its early stages of development, is often related to another as an antithesis to its thesis. The thesis discipline tends to concern itself with discovery and classification of
(5) phenomena, to offer holistic explanations emphasizing pattern and form, and to use existing theory to explain the widest possible range of phenomena. The paired or antidiscipline, on the other hand, can be characterized by a more focused
(10) approach, concentrating on the units of construction, and by a belief that the discipline can be reformulated in terms of the issues and explanations of the antidiscipline.

The relationship of cytology (cell biology) to
(15) biochemistry in the late nineteenth century, when both disciplines were growing at a rapid pace, exemplifies such a pattern. Researchers in cell biology found mounting evidence of an intricate cell architecture. They also deduced the mysterious
(20) choreography of the chromosomes during cell division. Many biochemists, on the other hand, remained skeptical of the idea that so much structure existed, arguing that the chemical reactions that occur in cytological preparations might create
(25) the appearance of such structures. Also, they stood apart from the debate then raging over whether protoplasm, the complex of living material within a cell, is homogeneous, networklike, granular, or foamlike. Their interest lay in the more
(30) "fundamental" issues of the chemical nature of protoplasm, especially the newly formulated enzyme theory of life.

In general, biochemists judged cytologists to be too ignorant of chemistry to grasp the basic
(35) processes, whereas cytologists considered the methods of biochemists inadequate to characterize the structures of the living cell. The renewal of Mendelian genetics and, later, progress in chromosome mapping did little at first to effect a
(40) synthesis.

Both sides were essentially correct. Biochemistry has more than justified its extravagant early claims by explaining so much of the cellular machinery. But in achieving this feat (mostly since 1950) it has
(45) been partially transformed into the new discipline of molecular biology—biochemistry that deals with spatial arrangements and movements of large molecules. At the same time cytology has metamorphosed into modern cellular biology. Aided
(50) by electron microscopy, it has become more similar in language and outlook to molecular biology. The interaction of a discipline and its antidiscipline has moved both sciences toward a synthesis, namely molecular genetics.

(55) This interaction between paired disciplines can have important results. In the case of late nineteenth century cell research, progress was fueled by competition among the various attitudes and issues derived from cell biology and biochemistry. Joseph
(60) Fruton, a biochemist, has suggested that such competition and the resulting tensions among researchers are a principal source of vitality and "are likely to lead to unexpected and exciting novelties in the future, as they have in the past."

9. Which one of the following best states the central idea of the passage?

(A) Antithetical scientific disciplines can both stimulate and hinder one another's research in complex ways.

(B) Antithetical scientific disciplines often interact with one another in ways that can be highly useful.

(C) As disciplines such as cytology and biochemistry advance, their interaction necessarily leads to a synthesis of their approaches.

(D) Cell research in the late nineteenth century was plagued by disagreements between cytologists and biochemists.

(E) In the late nineteenth century, cytologists and biochemists made many valuable discoveries that advanced scientific understanding of the cell.

10. The passage states that in the late nineteenth century cytologists deduced the

(A) maps of chromosomes
(B) chemical nature of protoplasm
(C) spatial relationship of molecules within the cell
(D) role of enzymes in biological processes
(E) sequence of the movement of chromosomes during cell division

11. It can be inferred from the passage that in the late nineteenth century the debate over the structural nature of protoplasm (lines 25-29) was most likely carried on

(A) among cytologists
(B) among biochemists
(C) between cytologists and biochemists
(D) between cytologists and geneticists
(E) between biochemists and geneticists

12. According to the passage, cytologists in the late nineteenth century were critical of the cell research of biochemists because cytologists believed that

    (A) the methods of biochemistry were inadequate to account for all of the chemical reactions that occurred in cytological preparations
    (B) the methods of biochemistry could not adequately discover and explain the structures of living cells
    (C) biochemists were not interested in the nature of protoplasm
    (D) biochemists were not interested in cell division
    (E) biochemists were too ignorant of cytology to understand the basic processes of the cell

13. The author quotes Fruton (lines 63-64) primarily in order to

    (A) restate the author's own conclusions
    (B) provide new evidence about the relationship of cytology to biochemistry
    (C) summarize the position of the biochemists described in the passage
    (D) illustrate the difficulties encountered in the synthesis of disciplines
    (E) emphasize the ascendancy of the theories of biochemists over those of cytologists

14. Which one of the following inferences about when the enzyme theory of life was formulated can be drawn from the passage?

    (A) The theory was formulated before the appearance of molecular biology.
    (B) The theory was formulated before the initial discovery of cell architecture.
    (C) The theory was formulated after the completion of chromosome mapping.
    (D) The theory was formulated after a synthesis of the ideas of cytologists and biochemists had occurred.
    (E) The theory was formulated at the same time as the beginning of the debate over the nature of protoplasm.

15. Which one of the following statements about cells is most compatible with the views of late nineteenth-century biochemists as those views are described in the passage?

    (A) The secret of cell function resides in the structure of the cell.
    (B) Only by discovering the chemical composition of protoplasm can the processes of the cell be understood.
    (C) Scientific knowledge about the chemical composition of the cell can help to explain behavioral patterns in organisms.
    (D) The most important issue to be resolved with regard to the cell is determining the physical characteristics of protoplasm.
    (E) The methods of chemistry must be supplemented before a full account of the cell's structure can be made.

16. Which one of the following best describes the organization of the material presented in the passage?

    (A) An account of a process is given, and then the reason for its occurrence is stated.
    (B) A set of examples is provided, and then a conclusion is drawn from them.
    (C) A general proposition is stated, and then an example is given.
    (D) A statement of principles is made, and then a rationale for them is debated.
    (E) A problem is analyzed, and then a possible solution is discussed.

Historians attempting to explain how scientific work was done in the laboratory of the seventeenth-century chemist and natural philosopher Robert Boyle must address a fundamental discrepancy
(5) between how such experimentation was actually performed and the seventeenth-century rhetoric describing it. Leaders of the new Royal Society of London in the 1660's insisted that authentic science depended upon actual experiments performed,
(10) observed, and recorded by the scientists themselves. Rejecting the traditional contempt for manual operations, these scientists, all members of the English upper class, were not to think themselves demeaned by the mucking about with chemicals,
(15) furnaces, and pumps; rather, the willingness of each of them to become, as Boyle himself said, a mere "drudge" and "under-builder" in the search for God's truth in nature was taken as a sign of their nobility and Christian piety.
(20) This rhetoric has been so effective that one modern historian assures us that Boyle himself actually performed all of the thousand or more experiments he reported. In fact, due to poor eyesight, fragile health, and frequent absences from
(25) his laboratory, Boyle turned over much of the labor of obtaining and recording experimental results to paid technicians, although published accounts of the experiments rarely, if ever, acknowledged the technicians' contributions. Nor was Boyle unique in
(30) relying on technicians without publicly crediting their work.
Why were the contributions of these technicians not recognized by their employers? One reason is the historical tendency, which has persisted into
(35) the twentieth century, to view scientific discovery as resulting from momentary flashes of individual insight rather than from extended periods of cooperative work by individuals with varying levels of knowledge and skill. Moreover, despite the clamor of
(40) seventeenth-century scientific rhetoric commending a hands-on approach, science was still overwhelmingly an activity of the English upper class, and the traditional contempt that genteel society maintained for manual labor was pervasive and deeply rooted.
(45) Finally, all of Boyle's technicians were "servants," which in seventeenth- century usage meant anyone who worked for pay. To seventeenth-century sensibilities, the wage relationship was charged with political significance. Servants, meaning wage
(50) earners, were excluded from the franchise because they were perceived as ultimately dependent on their wages and thus controlled by the will of their employers. Technicians remained invisible in the political economy of science for the same reasons
(55) that underlay servants' general political exclusion. The technicians' contributions, their observations and judgment, if acknowledged, would not have been perceived in the larger scientific community as objective because the technicians were dependent on
(60) the wages paid to them by their employers. Servants might have made the apparatus work, but their contributions to the making of scientific knowledge were largely—and conveniently—ignored by their employers.

8. Which one of the following best summarizes the main idea of the passage?

(A) Seventeenth-century scientific experimentation would have been impossible without the work of paid laboratory technicians.

(B) Seventeenth-century social conventions prohibited upper-class laboratory workers from taking public credit for their work.

(C) Seventeenth-century views of scientific discovery combined with social class distinctions to ensure that laboratory technicians' scientific work was never publicly acknowledged.

(D) Seventeenth-century scientists were far more dependent on their laboratory technicians than are scientists today, yet far less willing to acknowledge technicians' scientific contributions.

(E) Seventeenth-century scientists liberated themselves from the stigma attached to manual labor by relying heavily on the work of laboratory technicians.

9. It can be inferred from the passage that the "seventeenth-century rhetoric" mentioned in line 6 would have more accurately described the experimentation performed in Boyle's laboratory if which one of the following were true?

(A) Unlike many seventeenth-century scientists, Boyle recognized that most scientific discoveries resulted from the cooperative efforts of many individuals.

(B) Unlike many seventeenth-century scientists, Boyle maintained a deeply rooted and pervasive contempt for manual labor.

(C) Unlike many seventeenth-century scientists, Boyle was a member of the Royal Society of London.

(D) Boyle generously acknowledged the contribution of the technicians who worked in his laboratory.

(E) Boyle himself performed the actual labor of obtaining and recording experimental results.

10. According to the author, servants in seventeenth-century England were excluded from the franchise because of the belief that

(A) their interests were adequately represented by their employers

(B) their education was inadequate to make informed political decisions

(C) the independence of their political judgment would be compromised by their economic dependence on their employers

(D) their participation in the elections would be a polarizing influence on the political process

(E) the manual labor that they performed did not constitute a contribution to the society that was sufficient to justify their participation in elections

11. According to the author, the Royal Society of London insisted that scientists abandon the

(A) belief that the primary purpose of scientific discovery was to reveal the divine truth that could be found in nature
(B) view that scientific knowledge results largely from the insights of a few brilliant individuals rather than from the cooperative efforts of many workers
(C) seventeenth-century belief that servants should be denied the right to vote because they were dependent on wages paid to them by their employers
(D) traditional disdain for manual labor that was maintained by most members of the English upper class during the seventeenth century
(E) idea that the search for scientific truth was a sign of piety

12. The author implies that which one of the following beliefs was held in both the seventeenth and the twentieth centuries?

(A) Individual insights rather than cooperative endeavors produce most scientific discoveries.
(B) How science is practiced is significantly influenced by the political beliefs and assumptions of scientists.
(C) Scientific research undertaken for pay cannot be considered objective.
(D) Scientific discovery can reveal divine truth in nature.
(E) Scientific discovery often relies on the unacknowledged contributions of laboratory technicians.

13. Which one of the following best describes the organization of the last paragraph?

(A) Several alternative answers are presented to a question posed in the previous paragraph, and the last is adopted as the most plausible.
(B) A question regarding the cause of the phenomenon described in the previous paragraph is posed, two possible explanations are rejected, and evidence is provided in support of a third.
(C) A question regarding the phenomenon described in the previous paragraph is posed, and several incompatible views are presented.
(D) A question regarding the cause of the phenomenon described in the previous paragraph is posed, and several contributing factors are then discussed.
(E) Several possible answers to a question are evaluated in light of recent discoveries cited earlier in the passage.

14. The author's discussion of the political significance of the "wage relationship" (line 48) serves to

(A) place the failure of seventeenth-century scientists to acknowledge the contributions of their technicians in the larger context of relations between workers and their employers in seventeenth-century England
(B) provide evidence in support of the author's more general thesis regarding the relationship of scientific discovery to the economic conditions of societies in which it takes place
(C) provide evidence in support of the author's explanation of why scientists in seventeenth-century England were reluctant to rely on their technicians for the performance of anything but the most menial tasks
(D) illustrate political and economic changes in the society of seventeenth-century England that had a profound impact on how scientific research was conducted
(E) undermine the view that scientific discovery results from individual enterprise rather than from the collective endeavor of many workers

15. It can be inferred from the passage that "the clamor of seventeenth-century scientific rhetoric" (lines 39-40) refers to

(A) the claim that scientific discovery results largely from the insights of brilliant individuals working alone
(B) ridicule of scientists who were members of the English upper class and who were thought to demean themselves by engaging in the manual labor required by their experiments
(C) criticism of scientists who publicly acknowledged the contributions of their technicians
(D) assertions by members of the Royal Society of London that scientists themselves should be responsible for obtaining and recording experimental results
(E) the claim by Boyle and his colleagues that the primary reason for scientific research is to discover evidence of divine truth in the natural world

Passage #3: December 1991 Questions 16-20

One type of violation of the antitrust laws is the abuse of monopoly power. Monopoly power is the ability of a firm to raise its prices above the competitive level—that is, above the level that
(5) would exist naturally if several firms had to compete—without driving away so many customers as to make the price increase unprofitable. In order to show that a firm has abused monopoly power, and thereby violated the antitrust laws, two essential
(10) facts must be established. First, a firm must be shown to possess monopoly power, and second, that power must have been used to exclude competition in the monopolized market or related markets.

The price a firm may charge for its product is
(15) constrained by the availability of close substitutes for the product. If a firm attempts to charge a higher price—a supracompetitive price—customers will turn to other firms able to supply substitute products at competitive prices. If a firm provides a
(20) large percentage of the products actually or potentially available, however, customers may find it difficult to buy from alternative suppliers. Consequently, a firm with a large share of the relevant market of substitutable products may be
(25) able to raise its price without losing many customers. For this reason courts often use market share as a rough indicator of monopoly power.

Supracompetitive prices are associated with a loss of consumers' welfare because such prices
(30) force some consumers to buy a less attractive mix of products than they would ordinarily buy. Supracompetitive prices, however, do not themselves constitute an abuse of monopoly power. Antitrust laws do not attempt to counter the mere
(35) existence of monopoly power, or even the use of monopoly power to extract extraordinarily high profits. For example, a firm enjoying economies of scale—that is, low unit production costs due to high volume—does not violate the antitrust laws when it
(40) obtains a large market share by charging prices that are profitable but so low that its smaller rivals cannot survive. If the antitrust laws posed disincentives to the existence and growth of such firms, the laws could impair consumers' welfare.
(45) Even if the firm, upon acquiring monopoly power, chose to raise prices in order to increase profits, it would not be in violation of the antitrust laws.

The antitrust prohibitions focus instead on abuses of monopoly power that exclude competition
(50) in the monopolized market or involve leverage—the use of power in one market to reduce competition in another. One such forbidden practice is a tying arrangement, in which a monopolist conditions the sale of a product in one market on the buyer's

(55) purchase of another product in a different market. For example, a firm enjoying a monopoly in the communications systems market might not sell its products to a customer unless that customer also buys its computer systems, which are competing
(60) with other firms' computer systems.

The focus on the abuse of monopoly power, rather than on monopoly itself, follows from the primary purpose of the antitrust laws: to promote consumers' welfare through assurance of the quality
(65) and quantity of products available to consumers.

16. Which one of the following distinctions between monopoly power and the abuse of monopoly power would the author say underlies the antitrust laws discussed in the passage?

(A) Monopoly power is assessed in terms of market share, whereas abuse of monopoly power is assessed in terms of market control.
(B) Monopoly power is easy to demonstrate, whereas abuse of monopoly power is difficult to demonstrate.
(C) Monopoly power involves only one market, whereas abuse of monopoly power involves at least two or more related markets.
(D) Monopoly power is the ability to charge supracompetitive prices, whereas abuse of monopoly power is the use of that ability.
(E) Monopoly power does not necessarily hurt consumer welfare, whereas abuse of monopoly power does.

17. Would the use of leverage meet the criteria for abuse of monopoly power outlined in the first paragraph?

(A) No, because leverage involves a nonmonopolized market.
(B) No, unless the leverage involves a tying arrangement.
(C) Yes, because leverage is a characteristic of monopoly power.
(D) Yes, unless the firm using leverage is charging competitive prices.
(E) Yes, because leverage is used to eliminate competition in a related market.

18. What is the main purpose of the third paragraph (lines 28-47)?

  (A) to distinguish between supracompetitive prices and supracompetitive profits
  (B) to describe the positive uses of monopoly power
  (C) to introduce the concept of economies of scale
  (D) to distinguish what is not covered by the antitrust laws under discussion from what is covered
  (E) to remind the reader of the issue of consumers' welfare

19. Given only the information in the passage, with which one of the following statements about competition would those responsible for the antitrust laws most likely agree?

  (A) Competition is essential to consumers' welfare.
  (B) There are acceptable and unacceptable ways for firms to reduce their competition.
  (C) The preservation of competition is the principal aim of the antitrust laws.
  (D) Supracompetitive prices lead to reductions in competition.
  (E) Competition is necessary to ensure high-quality products at low prices.

20. Which one of the following sentences would best complete the last paragraph of the passage?

  (A) By limiting consumers' choices, abuse of monopoly power reduces consumers' welfare, but monopoly alone can sometimes actually operate in the consumers' best interests.
  (B) What is needed now is a set of related laws to deal with the negative impacts that monopoly itself has on consumers' ability to purchase products at reasonable cost.
  (C) Over time, the antitrust laws have been very effective in ensuring competition and, consequently, consumers' welfare in the volatile communications and computer systems industries.
  (D) By controlling supracompetitive prices and corresponding supracompetitive profits, the antitrust laws have, indeed, gone a long way toward meeting that objective.
  (E) As noted above, the necessary restraints on monopoly itself have been left to the market, where competitive prices and economies of scale are rewarded through increased market share.

Nico Frijda writes that emotions are governed by a psychological principle called the "law of apparent reality": emotions are elicited only by events appraised as real, and the intensity of these
(5) emotions corresponds to the degree to which these events are appraised as real. This observation seems psychologically plausible, but emotional responses elicited by works of art raise counterexamples.

Frijda's law accounts for my panic if I am afraid
(10) of snakes and see an object I correctly appraise as a rattlesnake, and also for my identical response if I see a coiled garden hose I mistakenly perceive to be a snake. However, suppose I am watching a movie and see a snake gliding toward its victim. Surely I
(15) might experience the same emotions of panic and distress, though I know the snake is not real. These responses extend even to phenomena not conventionally accepted as real. A movie about ghosts, for example, may be terrifying to all viewers,
(20) even those who firmly reject the possibility of ghosts, but this is not because viewers are confusing cinematic depiction with reality. Moreover, I can feel strong emotions in response to objects of art that are interpretations, rather than
(25) representations, of reality: I am moved by Mozart's *Requiem*, but I know that I am not at a real funeral. However, if Frijda's law is to explain all emotional reactions, there should be no emotional response at all to aesthetic objects or events, because we know
(30) they are not real in the way a living rattlesnake is real.

Most psychologists, perplexed by the feelings they acknowledge are aroused by aesthetic experience, have claimed that these emotions are
(35) genuine, but different in kind from nonaesthetic emotions. This, however, is a descriptive distinction rather than an empirical observation and consequently lacks explanatory value. On the other hand, Gombrich argues that emotional responses to
(40) art are ersatz: art triggers remembrances of previously experienced emotions. These debates have prompted the psychologist Radford to argue that people do experience real melancholy or joy in responding to art, but that these are irrational
(45) responses precisely because people know they are reacting to illusory stimuli. Frijda's law does not help us to untangle these positions, since it simply implies that events we recognize as being represented rather than real cannot elicit emotion
(50) in the first place.

Frijda does suggest that a vivid imagination has "properties of reality"—implying, without explanation, that we make aesthetic objects or events "real" in the act of experiencing them.
(55) However, as Scruton argues, a necessary characteristic of the imaginative construction that can occur in an emotional response to art is that

the person knows he or she is pretending. This is what distinguishes imagination from psychotic fantasy.

9. Which one of the following best states the central idea of the passage?

    (A) The law of apparent reality fails to account satisfactorily for the emotional nature of belief.
    (B) Theories of aesthetic response fail to account for how we distinguish unreasonable from reasonable responses to art.
    (C) The law of apparent reality fails to account satisfactorily for emotional responses to art.
    (D) Psychologists have been unable to determine what accounts for the changeable nature of emotional responses to art.
    (E) Psychologists have been unable to determine what differentiates aesthetic from nonaesthetic emotional responses.

10. According to the passage, Frijda's law asserts that emotional responses to events are

    (A) unpredictable because emotional responses depend on how aware the person is of the reality of an event
    (B) weaker if the person cannot distinguish illusion from reality
    (C) more or less intense depending on the degree to which the person perceives the event to be real
    (D) more intense if the person perceives an event to be frightening
    (E) weaker if the person judges an event to be real but unthreatening

11. The author suggests that Frijda's notion of the role of imagination in aesthetic response is problematic because it

    (A) ignores the unselfconsciousness that is characteristic of emotional responses to art
    (B) ignores the distinction between genuine emotion and ersatz emotion
    (C) ignores the fact that a person who is imagining knows that he or she is imagining
    (D) makes irrelevant distinctions between vivid and weak imaginative capacities
    (E) suggests, in reference to the observation of art, that there is no distinction between real and illusory stimuli

12. The passage supports all of the following statements about the differences between Gombrich and Radford EXCEPT:

    (A)   Radford's argument relies on a notion of irrationality in a way that Gombrich's argument does not.
    (B)   Gombrich's position is closer to the position of the majority of psychologists than is Radford's.
    (C)   Gombrich, unlike Radford, argues that we do not have true emotions in response to art.
    (D)   Gombrich's argument rests on a notion of memory in a way that Radford's argument does not.
    (E)   Radford's argument, unlike Gombrich's, is not focused on the artificial quality of emotional responses to art.

13. Which one of the following best captures the progression of the author's argument in lines 9-31?

    (A)   The emotional responses to events ranging from the real to the depicted illustrate the irrationality of emotional response.
    (B)   A series of events that range from the real to the depicted conveys the contrast between real events and cinematic depiction.
    (C)   An intensification in emotional response to a series of events that range from the real to the depicted illustrates Frijda's law.
    (D)   A progression of events that range from the real to the depicted examines the precise nature of panic in relation to a feared object.
    (E)   The consistency of emotional responses to events that range from the real to the depicted challenges Frijda's law.

14. The author's assertions concerning movies about ghosts imply that all of the following statements are false EXCEPT:

    (A)   Movies about ghosts are terrifying in proportion to viewers' beliefs in the phenomenon of ghosts.
    (B)   Movies about imaginary phenomena like ghosts may be just as terrifying as movies about phenomena like snakes.
    (C)   Movies about ghosts and snakes are not terrifying because people know that what they are viewing is not real.
    (D)   Movies about ghosts are terrifying to viewers who previously rejected the possibility of ghosts because movies permanently alter the viewers' sense of reality.
    (E)   Movies about ghosts elicit a very different emotional response from viewers who do not believe in ghosts than movies about snakes elicit from viewers who are frightened by snakes.

15. Which one of the following statements best exemplifies the position of Radford concerning the nature of emotional response to art?

    (A)   A person watching a movie about guerrilla warfare irrationally believes that he or she is present at the battle.
    (B)   A person watching a play about a kidnapping feels nothing because he or she rationally realizes it is not a real event.
    (C)   A person gets particular enjoyment out of writing fictional narratives in which he or she figures as a main character.
    (D)   A person irrationally bursts into tears while reading a novel about a destructive fire, even while realizing that he or she is reading about a fictional event.
    (E)   A person who is afraid of snakes trips over a branch and irrationally panics.

Passage #5: October 1992 Questions 21-27

Although the United States steel industry faces
widely publicized economic problems that have
eroded its steel production capacity, not all branches
of the industry have been equally affected. The steel
(5) industry is not monolithic: it includes integrated
producers, minimills, and specialty-steel mills. The
integrated producers start with iron ore and coal
and produce a wide assortment of shaped steels.
The minimills reprocess scrap steel into a limited
(10) range of low-quality products, such as reinforcing
rods for concrete. The specialty-steel mills are
similar to minimills in that they tend to be smaller
than the integrated producers and are based on
scrap, but they manufacture much more expensive
(15) products than minimills do and commonly have an
active in-house research-and-development effort.
    Both minimills and specialty-steel mills have
succeeded in avoiding the worst of the economic
difficulties that are afflicting integrated steel
(20) producers, and some of the mills are quite
profitable. Both take advantage of new technology
for refining and casting steel, such as continuous
casting, as soon as it becomes available. The
minimills concentrate on producing a narrow range
(25) of products for sale in their immediate geographic
area, whereas specialty-steel mills preserve
flexibility in their operations in order to fulfill a
customer's particular specifications.
    Among the factors that constrain the
(30) competitiveness of integrated producers are
excessive labor, energy, and capital costs, as well as
manufacturing inflexibility. Their equipment is old
and less automated, and does not incorporate many
of the latest refinements in steelmaking technology.
(35) (For example, only about half of the United States
integrated producers have continuous casters,
which combine pouring and rolling into one
operation and thus save the cost of separate rolling
equipment.) One might conclude that the older,
(40) labor-intensive machinery still operating in United
States integrated plants is at fault for the poor
performance of the United States industry, but this
cannot explain why Japanese integrated producers,
who produce a higher-quality product using less
(45) energy and labor, are also experiencing economic
trouble. The fact is that the common technological
denominator of integrated producers is an inherently
inefficient process that is still rooted in the
nineteenth century.
(50)   Integrated producers have been unable to
compete successfully with minimills because the
minimills, like specialty-steel mills, have dispensed
almost entirely with the archaic energy-and
capital-intensive front end of integrated steelmaking:
(55) the iron-smelting process, including the mining and
preparation of the raw materials and the
blast-furnace operation. In addition, minimills have

found a profitable way to market steel products:
as indicated above, they sell their finished products
(60) locally, thereby reducing transportation costs, and
concentrate on a limited range of shapes and sizes
within a narrow group of products that can be
manufactured economically. For these reasons,
minimills have been able to avoid the economic
(65) decline affecting integrated steel producers.

21. Which one of the following best expresses the main
idea of the passage?

(A) United States steel producers face economic
problems that are shared by producers in
other nations.
(B) Minimills are the most successful steel
producers because they best meet market
demands for cheap steel.
(C) Minimills and specialty-steel mills are more
economically competitive than integrated
producers because they use new technology
and avoid the costs of the iron-smelting
process.
(D) United States steel producers are
experiencing an economic decline that can
be traced back to the nineteenth century.
(E) New steelmaking technologies such
as continuous casting will replace
blast-furnace operations to reverse the
decline in United States steel production.

22. The author mentions all of the following as features
of minimills EXCEPT

(A) flexibility in their operations
(B) local sale of their products
(C) avoidance of mining operations
(D) use of new steel-refining technology
(E) a limited range of low-quality products

23. The author of the passage refers to "Japanese
integrated producers" (line 43) primarily in order to
support the view that

(A) different economic difficulties face the steel
industries of different nations
(B) not all integrated producers share a common
technological denominator
(C) labor-intensive machinery cannot be blamed
for the economic condition of United States
integrated steel producers
(D) modern steelmaking technology is generally
labor- and energy-efficient
(E) labor-intensive machinery is an economic
burden on United States integrated steel
producers

24. Which one of the following best describes the organization of the third paragraph?

    (A) A hypothesis is proposed and supported; then an opposing view is presented and criticized.
    (B) A debate is described and illustrated; then a contrast is made and the debate is resolved.
    (C) A dilemma is described and cited as evidence for a broader criticism.
    (D) A proposition is stated and argued, then rejected in favor of a more general statement, which is supported with additional evidence.
    (E) General statements are made and details given; then an explanation is proposed and rejected, and an alternative is offered.

25. It can be inferred from the passage that United States specialty-steel mills generally differ from integrated steel producers in that the specialty-steel mills

    (A) sell products in a restricted geographical area
    (B) share the economic troubles of the minimills
    (C) resemble specialty-steel mills found in Japan
    (D) concentrate on producing a narrow range of products
    (E) do not operate blast furnaces

26. Each of the following describes an industry facing a problem also experienced by United States integrated steel producers EXCEPT

    (A) a paper-manufacturing company that experiences difficulty in obtaining enough timber and other raw materials to meet its orders
    (B) a food-canning plant whose canning machines must constantly be tended by human operators
    (C) a textile firm that spends heavily on capital equipment and energy to process raw cotton before it is turned into fabric
    (D) a window-glass manufacturer that is unable to produce quickly different varieties of glass with special features required by certain customers
    (E) a leather-goods company whose hand-operated cutting and stitching machines were manufactured in Italy in the 1920s

27. Which one of the following, if true, would best serve as supporting evidence for the author's explanation of the economic condition of integrated steel producers?

    (A) Those nations that derive a larger percentage of their annual steel production from minimills than the United States does also have a smaller per capita trade deficit.
    (B) Many integrated steel producers are as adept as the specialty-steel mills at producing high-quality products to meet customer specifications.
    (C) Integrated steel producers in the United States are rapidly adopting the production methods of Japanese integrated producers.
    (D) Integrated steel producers in the United States are now attempting to develop a worldwide market by advertising heavily.
    (E) Those nations in which iron-smelting operations are carried out independently of steel production must heavily subsidize those operations in order to make them profitable.

After thirty years of investigation into cell genetics, researchers made startling discoveries in the 1960s and early 1970s which culminated in the development of processes, collectively known as
(5) recombinant deoxyribonucleic acid (rDNA) technology, for the active manipulation of a cell's genetic code. The technology has created excitement and controversy because it involves altering DNA—which contains the building blocks
(10) of the genetic code.

Using rDNA technology, scientists can transfer a portion of the DNA from one organism to a single living cell of another. The scientist chemically "snips" the DNA chain of the host cell at a
(15) predetermined point and attaches another piece of DNA from a donor cell at that place, creating a completely new organism.

Proponents of rDNA research and development claim that it will allow scientists to find cures for
(20) disease and to better understand how genetic information controls an organism's development. They also see many other potentially practical benefits, especially in the pharmaceutical industry. Some corporations employing the new technology
(25) even claim that by the end of the century all major diseases will be treated with drugs derived from microorganisms created through rDNA technology. Pharmaceutical products already developed, but not yet marketed, indicate that these predictions may be
(30) realized.

Proponents also cite nonmedical applications for this technology. Energy production and waste disposal may benefit: genetically altered organisms could convert sewage and other organic material
(35) into methane fuel. Agriculture might also take advantage of rDNA technology to produce new varieties of crops that resist foul weather, pests, and the effects of poor soil.

A major concern of the critics of rDNA research
(40) is that genetically altered microorganisms might escape from the laboratory. Because these micro-organisms are laboratory creations that, in all probability, do not occur in nature, their interaction with the natural world cannot be predicted with
(45) certainty. It is possible that they could cause previously unknown, perhaps incurable diseases. The effect of genetically altered microorganisms on the world's microbiological predator-prey relation-ships is another potentially serious problem pointed
(50) out by the opponents of rDNA research. Introducing a new species may disrupt or even destroy the existing ecosystem. The collapse of interdependent relationships among species, extrapolated to its extreme, could eventually result in the destruction
(55) of humanity.

Opponents of rDNA technology also cite ethical problems with it. For example, it gives scientists the power to instantly cross evolutionary and species boundaries that nature took millennia to establish.
(60) The implications of such power would become particularly profound if genetic engineers were to tinker with human genes, a practice that would bring us one step closer to Aldous Huxley's grim vision in *Brave New World* of a totalitarian society
(65) that engineers human beings to fulfill specific roles.

1. In the passage, the author is primarily concerned with doing which one of the following?

   (A) explaining the process and applications of rDNA technology
   (B) advocating continued rDNA research and development
   (C) providing evidence indicating the need for regulation of rDNA research and development
   (D) summarizing the controversy surrounding rDNA research and development
   (E) arguing that the environmental risks of rDNA technology may outweigh its medical benefits

2. According to the passage, which one of the following is an accurate statement about research into the genetic code of cells?

   (A) It led to the development of processes for the manipulation of DNA.
   (B) It was initiated by the discovery of rDNA technology.
   (C) It led to the use of new treatments for major diseases.
   (D) It was universally heralded as a great benefit to humanity.
   (E) It was motivated by a desire to create new organisms.

3. The potential benefits of rDNA technology referred to in the passage include all of the following EXCEPT

   (A) new methods of waste treatment
   (B) new biological knowledge
   (C) enhanced food production
   (D) development of less expensive drugs
   (E) increased energy production

4. Which one of the following, if true, would most weaken an argument of opponents of rDNA technology?

   (A) New safety procedures developed by rDNA researchers make it impossible for genetically altered microorganisms to escape from laboratories.
   (B) A genetically altered microorganism accidentally released from a laboratory is successfully contained.
   (C) A particular rDNA-engineered microorganism introduced into an ecosystem attracts predators that keep its population down.
   (D) Genetically altered organisms designed to process sewage into methane cannot survive outside the waste treatment plant.
   (E) A specific hereditary disease that has plagued humankind for generations is successfully eradicated.

5. The author's reference in the last sentence of the passage to a society that engineers human beings to fulfill specific roles serves to

   (A) emphasize the potential medical dangers of rDNA technology
   (B) advocate research on the use of rDNA technology in human genetics
   (C) warn of the possible disasters that could result from upsetting the balance of nature
   (D) present *Brave New World* as an example of a work of fiction that accurately predicted technological developments
   (E) illustrate the sociopolitical ramifications of applying genetic engineering to humans

6. Which one of the following, if true, would most strengthen an argument of the opponents of rDNA technology?

   (A) Agricultural products developed through rDNA technology are no more attractive to consumers than are traditional crops.
   (B) Genetically altered microorganisms have no natural predators but can prey on a wide variety of other microorganisms.
   (C) Drugs produced using rDNA technology cost more to manufacture than drugs produced with traditional technologies.
   (D) Ecosystems are impermanent systems that are often liable to collapse, and occasionally do so.
   (E) Genetically altered microorganisms generally cannot survive for more than a few hours in the natural environment.

A conventional view of nineteenth-century Britain holds that iron manufacturers and textile manufacturers from the north of England became the wealthiest and most powerful people in society (5) after about 1832. According to Marxist historians, these industrialists were the target of the working class in its struggle for power. A new study by Rubinstein, however, suggests that the real wealth lay with the bankers and merchants of London. (10) Rubinstein does not deny that a northern industrial elite existed but argues that it was consistently outnumbered and outdone by a London-based commercial elite. His claims are provocative and deserve consideration.

(15) Rubinstein's claim about the location of wealth comes from his investigation of probate records. These indicate the value of personal property, excluding real property (buildings and land), left by individuals at death. It does seem as if large (20) fortunes were more frequently made in commerce than in industry and, within industry, more frequently from alcohol or tobacco than from textiles or metal. However, such records do not unequivocally make Rubinstein's case. Uncertainties (25) abound about how the probate rules for valuing assets were actually applied. Mills and factories, being real property, were clearly excluded; machinery may also have been, for the same reason. What the valuation conventions were for stock-in- (30) trade (goods for sale) is also uncertain. It is possible that their probate values were much lower than their actual market values; cash or near-cash, such as bank balances or stocks, were, on the other hand, invariably considered at full face value. A further (35) complication is that probate valuations probably took no notice of a business's goodwill (favor with the public) which, since it represents expectations about future profit-making, would today very often be a large fraction of market value. Whether factors (40) like these introduced systematic biases into the probate valuations of individuals with different types of businesses would be worth investigating.

The orthodox view that the wealthiest individuals were the most powerful is also questioned by (45) Rubinstein's study. The problem for this orthodox view is that Rubinstein finds many millionaires who are totally unknown to nineteenth-century historians; the reason for their obscurity could be that they were not powerful. Indeed, Rubinstein (50) dismisses any notion that great wealth had anything to do with entry into the governing elite, as represented by bishops, higher civil servants, and chairmen of manufacturing companies. The only requirements were university attendance and a father (55) with a middle-class income.

Rubinstein, in another study, has begun to buttress his findings about the location of wealth by analyzing income tax returns, which reveal a geographical distribution of middle-class incomes (60) similar to that of wealthy incomes revealed by probate records. But until further confirmatory investigation is done, his claims can only be considered partially convincing.

21. The main idea of the passage is that

(A) the Marxist interpretation of the relationship between class and power in nineteenth-century Britain is no longer viable

(B) a simple equation between wealth and power is unlikely to be supported by new data from nineteenth-century British archives

(C) a recent historical investigation has challenged but not disproved the orthodox view of the distribution of wealth and the relationship of wealth to power in nineteenth-century Britain

(D) probate records provide the historian with a revealing but incomplete glimpse of the extent and location of wealth in nineteenth-century Britain

(E) an attempt has been made to confirm the findings of a new historical study of nineteenth-century Britain, but complete confirmation is likely to remain elusive

22. The author of the passage implies that probate records as a source of information about wealth in nineteenth-century Britain are

(A) self-contradictory and misleading
(B) ambiguous and outdated
(C) controversial but readily available
(D) revealing but difficult to interpret
(E) widely used by historians but fully understandable only by specialists

23. The author suggests that the total probate valuations of the personal property of individuals holding goods for sale in nineteenth-century Britain may have been

   (A)   affected by the valuation conventions for such goods
   (B)   less accurate than the valuations for such goods provided by income tax returns
   (C)   less, on average, if such goods were tobacco-related than if they were alcohol-related
   (D)   greater, on average, than the total probate valuations of those individuals who held bank balances
   (E)   dependent on whether such goods were held by industrialists or by merchants or bankers

24. According to the passage, Rubinstein has provided evidence that challenges which one of the following claims about nineteenth-century Britain?

   (A)   The distribution of great wealth between commerce and industry was not equal.
   (B)   Large incomes were typically made in alcohol and tobacco rather than in textiles and metal.
   (C)   A London-based commercial elite can be identified.
   (D)   An official governing elite can be identified.
   (E)   There was a necessary relationship between great wealth and power.

25. The author mentions that goodwill was probably excluded from the probate valuation of a business in nineteenth-century Britain most likely in order to

   (A)   give an example of a business asset about which little was known in the nineteenth century
   (B)   suggest that the probate valuations of certain businesses may have been significant underestimations of their true market value
   (C)   make the point that this exclusion probably had an equal impact on the probate valuations of all nineteenth-century British businesses
   (D)   indicate that expectations about future profit-making is the single most important factor in determining the market value of certain businesses
   (E)   argue that the twentieth-century method of determining probate valuations of a business may be consistently superior to the nineteenth-century method

26. Which one of the following studies would provide support for Rubinstein's claims?

   (A)   a study that indicated that many members of the commercial elite in nineteenth-century London had insignificant holdings of real property
   (B)   a study that indicated that, in the nineteenth century, industrialists from the north of England were in fact a target for working-class people
   (C)   a study that indicated that, in nineteenth-century Britain, probate values of goods for sale were not as high as probate values of cash assets
   (D)   a study that indicated that the wealth of nineteenth-century British industrialists did not appear to be significantly greater when the full value of their real property holdings was actually considered
   (E)   a study that indicated that at least some members of the official governing elite in nineteenth-century Britain owned more real property than had previously been thought to be the case

27. Which one of the following, if true, would cast the most doubt on Rubinstein's argument concerning wealth and the official governing elite in nineteenth-century Britain?

   (A)   Entry into this elite was more dependent on university attendance than on religious background.
   (B)   Attendance at a prestigious university was probably more crucial than a certain minimum family income in gaining entry into this elite.
   (C)   Bishops as a group were somewhat wealthier at the point of entry into this elite, than were higher civil servants or chairmen of manufacturing companies.
   (D)   The families of many members of this elite owned few, if any, shares in iron industries and textile industries in the north of England.
   (E)   The composition of this elite included vice-chancellors, many of whom held office because of their wealth.

Passage #8: June 1994 Questions 1-7

Nearly every writer on the philosophy of civil rights activist Martin Luther King, Jr., makes a connection between King and Henry David Thoreau, usually via Thoreau's famous essay,
(5) "Civil Disobedience" (1849). In his book *Stride Toward Freedom* (1958), King himself stated that Thoreau's essay was his first intellectual contact with the theory of passive resistance to governmental laws that are perceived as morally
(10) unjust. However, this emphasis on Thoreau's influence on King is unfortunate: first, King would not have agreed with many other aspects of Thoreau's philosophy, including Thoreau's ultimate acceptance of violence as a form of protest; second,
(15) an overemphasis on the influence of one essay has kept historians from noting other correspondences between King's philosophy and transcendentalism. "Civil Disobedience" was the only example of transcendentalist writing with which King was
(20) familiar, and in many other transcendentalist writings, including works by Ralph Waldo Emerson and Margaret Fuller, King would have found ideas more nearly akin to his own.
    The kind of civil disobedience King had in mind
(25) was, in fact, quite different from Thoreau's view of civil disobedience. Thoreau, like most other transcendentalists, was primarily interested in reform of the individual, whereas King was primarily interested in reform of society. As a
(30) protest against the Mexican War, Thoreau refused to pay taxes, but he did not hope by his action to force a change in national policy. While he encouraged others to adopt similar protests, he did not attempt to mount any mass protest action
(35) against unjust laws. In contrast to Thoreau, King began to advocate the use of mass civil disobedience to effect revolutionary changes within the social system.
    However, King's writings suggest that, without
(40) realizing it, he was an incipient transcendentalist. Most transcendentalists subscribed to the concept of "higher law" and included civil disobedience to unjust laws as part of their strategy. They often invoked the concept of higher law to justify their
(45) opposition to slavery and to advocate disobedience to the strengthened Fugitive Slave Law of 1850. In his second major book, King's discussion of just and unjust laws and the responsibility of the individual is very similar to the transcendentalists'
(50) discussion of higher law. In reference to how one can advocate breaking some laws and obeying others, King notes that there are two types of laws, just and unjust; he describes a just law as a "code that squares with the moral law" and an unjust law

(55) as a "code that is out of harmony with the moral law." Thus, King's opposition to the injustice of legalized segregation in the twentieth century is philosophically akin to the transcendentalists' opposition to the Fugitive Slave Law in the
(60) nineteenth century.

1. Which one of the following best states the main idea of the passage?

    (A) King's philosophy was more influenced by Thoreau's essay on civil disobedience than by any other writing of the transcendentalists.
    (B) While historians may have overestimated Thoreau's influence on King, King was greatly influenced by a number of the transcendentalist philosophers.
    (C) Thoreau's and King's views on civil disobedience differed in that King was more concerned with the social reform than with the economic reform of society.
    (D) Although historians have overemphasized Thoreau's influence on King, there are parallels between King's philosophy and transcendentalism that have not been fully appreciated.
    (E) King's ideas about law and civil disobedience were influenced by transcendentalism in general and Thoreau's essays in particular.

2. Which one of the following statements about "Civil Disobedience" would the author consider most accurate?

    (A) It was not King's first contact with the concept of passive resistance to unjust laws.
    (B) It was one of many examples of transcendentalist writing with which King was familiar.
    (C) It provided King with a model for using passive resistance to effect social change.
    (D) It contains a number of ideas with which other transcendentalists strongly disagreed.
    (E) It influenced King's philosophy on passive resistance to unjust laws.

3. In the first paragraph, the author is primarily concerned with

   (A) chronicling the development of King's philosophy on passive resistance to unjust law
   (B) suggesting that a common emphasis on one influence on King's philosophy has been misleading
   (C) providing new information about the influence of twentieth century philosophers on King's work
   (D) summarizing the work of historians on the most important influences on King's philosophy
   (E) providing background information about nineteenth-century transcendentalist philosophers

4. According to the passage, which one of the following is true of Emerson and Fuller?

   (A) Some of their ideas were less typical of transcendentalism than were some of Thoreau's ideas.
   (B) They were more concerned with the reform of society than with the reform of the individual.
   (C) They would have been more likely than Thoreau to agree with King on the necessity of mass protest in civil disobedience.
   (D) Their ideas about civil disobedience and unjust laws are as well known as Thoreau's are.
   (E) Some of their ideas were more similar to King's than were some of Thoreau's.

5. According to the passage, King differed from most transcendentalists in that he

   (A) opposed violence as a form of civil protest
   (B) opposed war as an instrument of foreign policy under any circumstances
   (C) believed that just laws had an inherent moral value
   (D) was more interested in reforming society than in reforming the individual
   (E) protested social and legal injustice in United States society rather than United States foreign policy

6. The passage suggests which one of the following about Thoreau?

   (A) He was the first to develop fully the theory of civil disobedience.
   (B) His work has had a greater influence on contemporary thinkers than has the work of Emerson and Fuller.
   (C) His philosophy does not contain all of the same elements as the philosophies of the other transcendentalists.
   (D) He advocated using civil disobedience to force the federal government to change its policies on war.
   (E) He is better known for his ideas on social and legal reform than for his ideas on individual reform.

7. The passage provides support for which one of the following statements about the quotations in lines 53-56?

   (A) They are an example of a way in which King's ideas differed from Thoreau's but were similar to the ideas of other transcendentalists.
   (B) They provide evidence that proves that King's philosophy was affected by transcendentalist thought.
   (C) They suggest that King, like the transcendentalists, judged human laws by ethical standards.
   (D) They suggest a theoretical basis for King's philosophy of government.
   (E) They provide a paraphrase of Thoreau's position on just and unjust laws.

In *Democracy and its Critics*, Robert Dahl defends both democratic values and pluralist democracies, or polyarchies (a rough shorthand term for Western political systems). Dahl argues
(5) convincingly that the idea of democracy rests on political equality—the equal capacity of all citizens to determine or influence collective decisions. Of course, as Dahl recognizes, if hierarchical ordering is inevitable in any structure of government, and if
(10) no society can guarantee perfect equality in the resources that may give rise to political influence, the democratic principle of political equality is incapable of full realization. So actual systems can be deemed democratic only as approximations to
(15) the ideal. It is on these grounds that Dahl defends polyarchy.
    As a representative system in which elected officials both determine government policy and are accountable to a broad-based electorate, polyarchy
(20) reinforces a diffusion of power away from any single center and toward a variety of individuals, groups, and organizations. It is this centrifugal characteristic, Dahl argues, that makes polyarchy the nearest possible approximation to the democratic
(25) ideal. Polyarchy achieves this diffusion of power through party competition and the operation of pressure groups. Competing for votes, parties seek to offer different sections of the electorate what they most want; they do not ask what the majority
(30) thinks of an issue, but what policy commitments will sway the electoral decisions of particular groups. Equally, groups that have strong feelings about an issue can organize in pressure groups to influence public policy.
(35)   During the 1960s and 1970s, criticism of the theory of pluralist democracy was vigorous. Many critics pointed to a gap between the model and the reality of Western political systems. They argued that the distribution of power resources other than
(40) the vote was so uneven that the political order systematically gave added weight to those who were already richer or organizationally more powerful. So the power of some groups to exclude issues altogether from the political agenda effectively
(45) countered any diffusion of influence on decision-making.
    Although such criticism became subdued during the 1980s, Dahl himself seems to support some of the earlier criticism. Although he regrets that some
(50) Western intellectuals demand more democracy from polyarchies than is possible, and is cautious about the possibility of further democratization, he nevertheless ends his book by asking what changes in structures and consciousness might make political
(55) life more democratic in present polyarchies. One answer, he suggests, is to look at the economic order of polyarchies from the point of view of the citizen as well as from that of producers and consumers. This would require a critical examination

(60) of both the distribution of those economic resources that are at the same time political resources, and the relationship between political structures and economic enterprises.

8. The characterization of polyarchies as "centrifugal" (line 22) emphasizes the

    (A) way in which political power is decentralized in a polyarchy
    (B) central role of power resources in a polyarchy
    (C) kind of concentrated power that political parties generate in a polyarchy
    (D) dynamic balance that exists between economic enterprises and elected officials in a polyarchy
    (E) dynamic balance that exists between voters and elected officials in a polyarchy

9. In the third paragraph, the author of the passage refers to criticism of the theory of pluralist democracy primarily in order to

    (A) refute Dahl's statement that Western intellectuals expect more democracy from polyarchies than is possible
    (B) advocate the need for rethinking the basic principles on which the theory of democracy rests
    (C) suggest that the structure of government within pluralist democracies should be changed
    (D) point out a flaw in Dahl's argument that the principle of political equality cannot be fully realized
    (E) point out an objection to Dahl's defense of polyarchy

10. According to the passage, the aim of a political party in a polyarchy is to do which one of the following?

    (A) determine what the position of the majority of voters is on a particular issue
    (B) determine what position on an issue will earn the support of particular groups of voters
    (C) organize voters into pressure groups in order to influence public policy on a particular issue
    (D) ensure that elected officials accurately represent the position of the party on specific issues
    (E) ensure that elected officials accurately represent the position of the electorate on specific issues

11. It can be inferred from the passage that Dahl assumes which one of the following in his defense of polyarchies?

(A) Polyarchies are limited in the extent to which they can embody the idea of democracy.
(B) The structure of polyarchical governments is free of hierarchical ordering.
(C) The citizens of a polyarchy have equal access to the resources that provide political influence.
(D) Polyarchy is the best political system to foster the growth of political parties.
(E) Polyarchy is a form of government that is not influenced by the interests of economic enterprises.

12. Which one of the following is most closely analogous to pluralist democracies as they are described in relation to the democratic principle of political equality?

(A) an exact copy of an ancient artifact that is on display in a museum
(B) a performance of a musical score whose range of tonality cannot be completely captured by any actual instruments
(C) a lecture by a former astronaut to a class of young students who would like to be astronauts
(D) the commemoration of a historical event each year by a historian presenting a lecture on a topic related to the event
(E) the mold from which a number of identical castings of a sculpture are made

13. Which one of the following, if true, would most strengthen Dahl's defense of polyarchy?

(A) The political agenda in a polyarchy is strongly influenced by how power resources other than the vote are distributed.
(B) The outcome of elections is more often determined by the financial resources candidates are able to spend during campaigns than by their stands on political issues.
(C) Public policy in a polyarchy is primarily determined by decision-makers who are not accountable to elected officials.
(D) Political parties in a polyarchy help concentrate political power in the central government.
(E) Small and diverse pressure groups are able to exert as much influence on public policy in a polyarchy as are large and powerful groups.

14. The passage can best be described as

(A) an inquiry into how present-day polyarchies can be made more democratic
(B) a commentary on the means pressure groups employ to exert influence within polyarchies
(C) a description of the relationship between polyarchies and economic enterprises
(D) a discussion of the strengths and weaknesses of polyarchy as a form of democracy
(E) an overview of the similarities between political parties and pressure groups in a polyarchy

When catastrophe strikes, analysts typically blame some combination of powerful mechanisms. An earthquake is traced to an immense instability along a fault line; a stock market crash is blamed on
(5) the destabilizing effect of computer trading. These explanations may well be correct. But systems as large and complicated as the Earth's crust or the stock market can break down not only under the force of a mighty blow but also at the drop of a pin.
(10) In a large interactive system, a minor event can start a chain reaction that leads to a catastrophe.

   Traditionally, investigators have analyzed large interactive systems in the same way they analyze small orderly systems, mainly because the methods
(15) developed for small systems have proved so successful. They believed they could predict the behavior of a large interactive system by studying its elements separately and by analyzing its component mechanisms individually. For lack of better
(20) theory, they assumed that in large interactive systems the response to a disturbance is proportional to that disturbance.

   During the past few decades, however, it has become increasingly apparent that many large
(25) complicated systems do not yield to traditional analysis. Consequently, theorists have proposed a "theory of self-organized criticality": many large interactive systems evolve naturally to a critical state in which a minor event starts a chain reaction
(30) that can affect any number of elements in the system. Although such systems produce more minor events than catastrophes, the mechanism that leads to minor events is the same one that leads to major events.

(35)   A deceptively simple system serves as a paradigm for self-organized criticality: a pile of sand. As sand is poured one grain at a time onto a flat disk, the grains at first stay close to the position where they land. Soon they rest on top of one
(40) another, creating a pile that has a gentle slope. Now and then, when the slope becomes too steep, the grains slide down, causing a small avalanche. The system reaches its critical state when the amount of sand added is balanced, on average, by the amount
(45) falling off the edge of the disk.

   Now when a grain of sand is added, it can start an avalanche of any size, including a "catastrophic" event. Most of the time the grain will fall so that no avalanche occurs. By studying a specific area of the
(50) pile, one can even predict whether avalanches will occur there in the near future. To such a local observer, however, large avalanches would remain unpredictable because they are a consequence of the total history of the entire pile. No matter what
(55) the local dynamics are, catastrophic avalanches would persist at a relative frequency that cannot be altered. Criticality is a global property of the sandpile.

16. The passage provides support for all of the following generalizations about large interactive systems EXCEPT:

(A) They can evolve to a critical state.
(B) They do not always yield to traditional analysis.
(C) They make it impossible for observers to make any predictions about them.
(D) They are subject to the effects of chain reactions.
(E) They are subject to more minor events than major events.

17. According to the passage, the criticality of a sandpile is determined by the

(A) size of the grains of sand added to the sandpile
(B) number of grains of sand the sandpile contains
(C) rate at which sand is added to the sandpile
(D) shape of the surface on which the sandpile rests
(E) balance between the amount of sand added to and the amount lost from the sandpile

SOCIAL SCIENCE

18. It can be inferred from the passage that the theory employed by the investigators mentioned in the second paragraph would lead one to predict that which one of the following would result from the addition of a grain of sand to a sandpile?

   (A)   The grain of sand would never cause anything more than a minor disturbance.
   (B)   The grain of sand would usually cause a minor disturbance, but would occasionally cause a small avalanche.
   (C)   The grain of sand would usually cause either a minor disturbance or a small avalanche, but would occasionally cause a catastrophic event.
   (D)   The grain of sand would usually cause a catastrophic event, but would occasionally cause only a small avalanche or an even more minor disturbance.
   (E)   The grain of sand would invariably cause a catastrophic event.

19. Which one of the following best describes the organization of the passage?

   (A)   A traditional procedure is described and its application to common situations is endorsed; its shortcomings in certain rare but critical circumstances are then revealed.
   (B)   A common misconception is elaborated and its consequences are described; a detailed example of one of these consequences is then given.
   (C)   A general principle is stated and supported by several examples; an exception to the rule is then considered and its importance evaluated.
   (D)   A number of seemingly unrelated events are categorized; the underlying processes that connect them are then detailed.
   (E)   A traditional method of analysis is discussed and the reasons for its adoption are explained; an alternative is then described and clarified by means of an example.

20. Which one of the following is most analogous to the method of analysis employed by the investigators mentioned in the second paragraph?

   (A)   A pollster gathers a sample of voter preferences and on the basis of this information makes a prediction about the outcome of an election.
   (B)   A historian examines the surviving documents detailing the history of a movement and from these documents reconstructs a chronology of the events that initiated the movement.
   (C)   A meteorologist measures the rainfall over a certain period of the year and from this data calculates the total annual rainfall for the region.
   (D)   A biologist observes the behavior of one species of insect and from these observations generalizes about the behavior of insects as a class.
   (E)   An engineer analyzes the stability of each structural element of a bridge and from these analyses draws a conclusion about the structural soundness of the bridge.

21. In the passage, the author is primarily concerned with

   (A)   arguing against the abandonment of a traditional approach
   (B)   describing the evolution of a radical theory
   (C)   reconciling conflicting points of view
   (D)   illustrating the superiority of a new theoretical approach
   (E)   advocating the reconsideration of an unfashionable explanation

A recent generation of historians of science, far from portraying accepted scientific views as objectively accurate reflections of a natural world, explain the acceptance of such views in terms of the
(5) ideological biases of certain influential scientists or the institutional and rhetorical power such scientists wield. As an example of ideological bias, it has been argued that Pasteur rejected the theory of spontaneous generation not because of
(10) experimental evidence but because he rejected the materialist ideology implicit in that doctrine. These historians seem to find allies in certain philosophers of science who argue that scientific views are not imposed by reality but are free inventions of
(15) creative minds, and that scientific claims are never more than brave conjectures, always subject to inevitable future falsification. While these philosophers of science themselves would not be likely to have much truck with the recent historians,
(20) it is an easy step from their views to the extremism of the historians.

While this rejection of the traditional belief that scientific views are objective reflections of the world may be fashionable, it is deeply implausible.
(25) We now know, for example, that water is made of hydrogen and oxygen and that parents each contribute one-half of their children's complement of genes. I do not believe any serious-minded and informed person can claim that these statements are
(30) not factual descriptions of the world or that they will inevitably be falsified.

However, science's accumulation of lasting truths about the world is not by any means a straightforward matter. We certainly need to
(35) get beyond the naive view that the truth will automatically reveal itself to any scientist who looks in the right direction; most often, in fact, a whole series of prior discoveries is needed to tease reality's truths from experiment and observation.
(40) And the philosophers of science mentioned above are quite right to argue that new scientific ideas often correct old ones by indicating errors and imprecisions (as, say, Newton's ideas did to Kepler's). Nor would I deny that there are
(45) interesting questions to be answered about the social processes in which scientific activity is embedded. The persuasive processes by which particular scientific groups establish their experimental results as authoritative are themselves social activities and
(50) can be rewardingly studied as such. Indeed, much of the new work in the history of science has been extremely revealing about the institutional interactions and rhetorical devices that help determine whose results achieve prominence.
(55) But one can accept all this without accepting the

thesis that natural reality never plays any part at all in determining what scientists believe. What the new historians ought to be showing us is how those doctrines that do in fact fit reality work their way
(60) through the complex social processes of scientific activity to eventually receive general scientific acceptance.

8. It can be inferred from the passage that the author would be most likely to agree with which one of the following characterizations of scientific truth?

(A) It is often implausible.
(B) It is subject to inevitable falsification.
(C) It is rarely obvious and transparent.
(D) It is rarely discovered by creative processes.
(E) It is less often established by experimentation than by the rhetorical power of scientists.

9. According to the passage, Kepler's ideas provide an example of scientific ideas that were

(A) corrected by subsequent inquiries
(B) dependent on a series of prior observations
(C) originally thought to be imprecise and then later confirmed
(D) established primarily by the force of an individual's rhetorical power
(E) specifically taken up for the purpose of falsification by later scientists

10. In the third paragraph of the passage, the author is primarily concerned with

(A) presenting conflicting explanations for a phenomenon
(B) suggesting a field for possible future research
(C) qualifying a previously expressed point of view
(D) providing an answer to a theoretical question
(E) attacking the assumptions that underlie a set of beliefs

11. The use of the words "any serious-minded and informed person" (lines 28-29) serves which one of the following functions in the context of the passage?

    (A)   to satirize chronologically earlier notions about the composition of water

    (B)   to reinforce a previously stated opinion about certain philosophers of science

    (C)   to suggest the author's reservations about the "traditional belief" mentioned in line 22

    (D)   to anticipate objections from someone who would argue for an objectively accurate description of the world

    (E)   to discredit someone who would argue that certain scientific assertions do not factually describe reality

12. It can be inferred from the passage that the author would most likely agree with which one of the following statements about the relationship between the views of "certain philosophers of science" (lines 12-13) and those of the recent historians?

    (A)   These two views are difficult to differentiate.

    (B)   These two views share some similarities.

    (C)   The views of the philosophers ought to be seen as the source of the historians' views.

    (D)   Both views emphasize the rhetorical power of scientists.

    (E)   The historians explicitly acknowledge that their views are indebted to those of the philosophers.

13. Which one of the following best characterizes the author's assessment of the opinions of the new historians of science, as these opinions are presented in the passage?

    (A)   They lack any credibility.

    (B)   They themselves can be rewardingly studied as social phenomena.

    (C)   They are least convincing when they concern the actions of scientific groups.

    (D)   Although they are gross overstatements, they lead to some valuable insights.

    (E)   Although they are now popular, they are likely to be refuted soon.

14. In concluding the passage, the author does which one of the following?

    (A)   offers a prescription

    (B)   presents a paradox

    (C)   makes a prediction

    (D)   concedes an argument

    (E)   anticipates objections

15. The author's attitude toward the "thesis" mentioned in line 56 is revealed in which one of the following pairs of words?

    (A)   "biases" (line 5) and "rhetorical" (line 6)

    (B)   "wield" (line 7) and "falsification" (line 17)

    (C)   "conjectures" (line 16) and "truck with" (line 19)

    (D)   "extremism" (line 20) and "implausible" (line 24)

    (E)   "naive" (line 35) and "errors" (line 42)

Chapter Eight:
Hard Science

Hard Science Passages

Three basic adaptive responses—regulatory, acclimatory, and developmental—may occur in organisms as they react to changing environmental conditions. In all three, adjustment of biological
(5) features (morphological adjustment) or of their use (functional adjustment) may occur. Regulatory responses involve rapid changes in the organism's use of its physiological apparatus—increasing or decreasing the rates of various processes, for
(10) example. Acclimation involves morphological change—thickening of fur or red blood cell proliferation—which alters physiology itself. Such structural changes require more time than regulatory response changes. Regulatory and acclimatory
(15) responses are both reversible.

Developmental responses, however, are usually permanent and irreversible; they become fixed in the course of the individual's development in response to environmental conditions at the time the response
(20) occurs. One such response occurs in many kinds of water bugs. Most water-bug species inhabiting small lakes and ponds have two generations per year. The first hatches during the spring, reproduces during the summer, then dies. The eggs laid in the summer
(25) hatch and develop into adults in late summer. They live over the winter before breeding in early spring. Individuals in the second (overwintering) generation have fully developed wings and leave the water in autumn to overwinter in forests, returning in spring
(30) to small bodies of water to lay eggs. Their wings are absolutely necessary for this seasonal dispersal. The summer (early) generation, in contrast, is usually dimorphic—some individuals have normal functional (macropterous) wings; others have much reduced
(35) (micropterous) wings of no use for flight. The summer generation's dimorphism is a compromise strategy, for these individuals usually do not leave the ponds and thus generally have no use for fully developed wings. But small ponds occasionally dry up
(40) during the summer, forcing the water bugs to search for new habitats, an eventuality that macropterous individuals are well adapted to meet.

The dimorphism of micropterous and macropterous individuals in the summer generation
(45) expresses developmental flexibility; it is not genetically determined. The individual's wing form is environmentally determined by the temperature to which developing eggs are exposed prior to their being laid. Eggs maintained in a warm environment
(50) always produce bugs with normal wings, but exposure to cold produces micropterous individuals. Eggs producing the overwintering brood are all formed during the late summer's warm temperatures. Hence, all individuals in the
(55) overwintering brood have normal wings. Eggs laid by the overwintering adults in the spring, which develop into the summer generation of adults, are formed in

early autumn and early spring. Those eggs formed in autumn are exposed to cold winter temperatures, and
(60) thus produce micropterous adults in the summer generation. Those formed during the spring are never exposed to cold temperatures, and thus yield individuals with normal wings. Adult water bugs of the overwintering generation, brought into the
(65) laboratory during the cold months and kept warm, produce only macropterous offspring.

14. The primary purpose of the passage is to

(A) illustrate an organism's functional adaptive response to changing environmental conditions

(B) prove that organisms can exhibit three basic adaptive responses to changing environmental conditions

(C) explain the differences in form and function between micropterous and macropterous water bugs and analyze the effect of environmental changes on each

(D) discuss three different types of adaptive responses and provide an example that explains how one of those types of responses works

(E) contrast acclimatory responses with developmental responses and suggest an explanation for the evolutionary purposes of these two responses to changing environmental conditions

15. The passage supplies information to suggest that which one of the following would happen if a pond inhabited by water bugs were to dry up in June?

(A) The number of developmental responses among the water-bug population would decrease.

(B) Both micropterous and macropterous water bugs would show an acclimatory response.

(C) The generation of water bugs to be hatched during the subsequent spring would contain an unusually large number of macropterous individuals.

(D) The dimorphism of the summer generation would enable some individuals to survive.

(E) The dimorphism of the summer generation would be genetically transferred to the next spring generation.

16. It can be inferred from the passage that if the winter months of a particular year were unusually warm, the

(A) eggs formed by water bugs in the autumn would probably produce a higher than usual proportion of macropterous individuals

(B) eggs formed by water bugs in the autumn would probably produce an entire summer generation of water bugs with smaller than normal wings

(C) eggs of the overwintering generation formed in the autumn would not be affected by this temperature change

(D) overwintering generation would not leave the ponds for the forest during the winter

(E) overwintering generation of water bugs would most likely form fewer eggs in the autumn and more in the spring

17. According to the passage, the dimorphic wing structure of the summer generation of water bugs occurs because

(A) the overwintering generation forms two sets of eggs, one exposed to the colder temperatures of winter and one exposed only to the warmer temperatures of spring

(B) the eggs that produce micropterous and macropterous adults are morphologically different

(C) water bugs respond to seasonal changes by making an acclimatory functional adjustment in the wings

(D) water bugs hatching in the spring live out their life spans in ponds and never need to fly

(E) the overwintering generation, which produces eggs developing into the dimorphic generation, spends the winter in the forest and the spring in small ponds

18. It can be inferred from the passage that which one of the following is an example of a regulatory response?

(A) thickening of the plumage of some birds in the autumn

(B) increase in pulse rate during vigorous exercise

(C) gradual darkening of the skin after exposure to sunlight

(D) gradual enlargement of muscles as a result of weight lifting

(E) development of a heavy fat layer in bears before hibernation

19. According to the passage, the generation of water bugs hatching during the summer is likely to

(A) be made up of equal numbers of macropterous and micropterous individuals

(B) lay its eggs during the winter in order to expose them to cold

(C) show a marked inability to fly from one pond to another

(D) exhibit genetically determined differences in wing form from the early spring-hatched generation

(E) contain a much greater proportion of macropterous water bugs than the early spring-hatched generation

20. The author mentions laboratory experiments with adult water bugs (lines 63-66) in order to illustrate which one of the following?

(A) the function of the summer generation's dimorphism

(B) the irreversibility of most developmental adaptive responses in water bugs

(C) the effect of temperature on developing water-bug eggs

(D) the morphological difference between the summer generation and the overwintering generation of water bugs

(E) the functional adjustment of water bugs in response to seasonal temperature variation

21. Which one of the following best describes the organization of the passage?

(A) Biological phenomena are presented, examples of their occurrence are compared and contrasted, and one particular example is illustrated in detail.

(B) A description of related biological phenomena is stated, and two of those phenomena are explained in detail with illustrated examples.

(C) Three related biological phenomena are described, a hypothesis explaining their relationship is presented, and supporting evidence is produced.

(D) Three complementary biological phenomena are explained, their causes are examined, and one of them is described by contrasting its causes with the other two.

(E) A new way of describing biological phenomena is suggested, its applications are presented, and one specific example is examined in detail.

Until recently many astronomers believed that asteroids travel about the solar system unaccompanied by satellites. These astronomers assumed this because they considered asteroid-
(5) satellite systems inherently unstable. Theoreticians could have told them otherwise: even minuscule bodies in the solar system can theoretically have satellites, as long as everything is in proper scale. If a bowling ball were orbiting about the Sun in the
(10) asteroid belt, it could have a pebble orbiting it as far away as a few hundred radii (or about 50 meters) without losing the pebble to the Sun's gravitational pull.

Observations now suggest that asteroid satellites
(15) may exist not only in theory but also in reality. Several astronomers have noticed, while watching asteroids pass briefly in front of stars, that something besides the known asteroid sometimes blocks out the star as well. Is that something a
(20) satellite?

The most convincing such report concerns the asteroid Herculina, which was due to pass in front of a star in 1978. Astronomers waiting for the predicted event found not just one occultation, or
(25) eclipse, of the star, but two distinct drops in brightness. One was the predicted occultation, exactly on time. The other, lasting about five seconds, preceded the predicted event by about two minutes. The presence of a secondary body near
(30) Herculina thus seemed strongly indicated. To cause the secondary occultation, an unseen satellite would have to be about 45 kilometers in diameter, a quarter of the size of Herculina, and at a distance of 990 kilometers from the asteroid at the time. These
(35) values are within theoretical bounds, and such an asteroid-satellite pair could be stable.

With the Herculina event, apparent secondary occultations became "respectable"—and more commonly reported. In fact, so common did reports
(40) of secondary events become that they are now simply too numerous for all of them to be accurate. Even if every asteroid has as many satellites as can be fitted around it without an undue number of collisions, only one in every hundred primary
(45) occultations would be accompanied by a secondary event (one in every thousand if asteroidal satellite systems resembled those of the planets).

Yet even astronomers who find the case for asteroid satellites unconvincing at present say they
(50) would change their minds if a photoelectric record were made of a well-behaved secondary event. By "well-behaved" they mean that during occultation the observed brightness must drop sharply as the star winks out and must rise sharply as it reappears
(55) from behind the obstructing object, but the

brightness during the secondary occultation must drop to that of the asteroid, no higher and no lower. This would make it extremely unlikely that an airplane or a glitch in the instruments was
(60) masquerading as an occulting body.

1. Which one of the following best expresses the main idea of the passage?

   (A) The observation of Herculina represented the crucial event that astronomical observers and theoreticians had been waiting for to establish a convincing case for the stability of asteroid-satellite systems.

   (B) Although astronomers long believed that observation supports the existence of stable asteroid-satellite systems, numerous recent reports have increased skepticism on this issue in astronomy.

   (C) Theoreticians' views on the stability of asteroid satellite systems may be revised in the light of reports like those about Herculina.

   (D) Astronomers continue to consider it respectable to doubt the stability of asteroid-satellite systems, but new theoretical developments may change their views.

   (E) The Herculina event suggests that theoreticians' views about asteroid-satellite systems may be correct, and astronomers agree about the kind of evidence needed to clearly resolve the issue.

2. Which one of the following is mentioned in the passage as providing evidence that Herculina has a satellite?

   (A) the diameter of a body directly observed near Herculina

   (B) the distance between Herculina and the planet nearest to it

   (C) the shortest possible time in which satellites of Herculina, if any, could complete a single orbit

   (D) the occultation that occurred shortly before the predicted occultation by Herculina

   (E) the precise extent to which observed brightness dropped during the occultation by Herculina

3. According to the passage, the attitude of astronomers toward asteroid satellites since the Herculina event can best be described as

(A) open-mindedness combined with a concern for rigorous standards of proof
(B) contempt for and impatience with the position held by theoreticians
(C) bemusement at a chaotic mix of theory, inadequate or spurious data, and calls for scientific rigor
(D) hardheaded skepticism, implying rejection of all data not recorded automatically by state-of-the-art instruments
(E) admiration for the methodical process by which science progresses from initial hypothesis to incontrovertible proof

4. The author implies that which one of the following was true prior to reports of the Herculina event?

(A) Since no good theoretical model existed, all claims that reports of secondary occultations were common were disputed.
(B) Some of the reported observations of secondary occultations were actually observations of collisions of satellites with one another.
(C) If there were observations of phenomena exactly like the phenomena now labeled secondary occultations, astronomers were less likely then to have reported such observations.
(D) The prevailing standards concerning what to classify as a well-behaved secondary event were less stringent than they are now.
(E) Astronomers were eager to publish their observations of occultations of stars by satellites of asteroids.

5. The passage suggests that which one of the following would most help to resolve the question of whether asteroids have satellites?

(A) a review of pre-1978 reports of secondary occultations
(B) an improved theoretical model of stable satellite systems
(C) a photoelectric record of a well-behaved secondary occultation
(D) a more stringent definition of what constitutes a well-behaved secondary occultation
(E) a powerful telescope that would permit a comparison of ground-based observations with those made from airplanes

6. The information presented in the passage implies which one of the following about the frequency of reports of secondary occultations after the Herculina event?

(A) The percentage of reports of primary occultations that also included reports of secondary occultations increased tenfold compared to the time before the Herculina event.
(B) Primary occultations by asteroids were reported to have been accompanied by secondary occultations in about one out of every thousand cases.
(C) The absolute number of reports of secondary occultations increased tenfold compared to the time before the Herculina event.
(D) Primary occultations by asteroids were reported to have been accompanied by secondary occultations in more than one out of every hundred cases.
(E) In more than one out of every hundred cases, primary occultations were reported to have been accompanied by more than one secondary occultation.

7. The primary purpose of the passage is to

(A) cast doubt on existing reports of secondary occultations of stars
(B) describe experimental efforts by astronomers to separate theoretically believable observations of satellites of asteroids from spurious ones
(C) review the development of ideas among astronomers about whether or not satellites of asteroids exist
(D) bring a theoretician's perspective to bear on an incomplete discussion of satellites of asteroids
(E) illustrate the limits of reasonable speculation concerning the occultation of stars

The human species came into being at the time of the greatest biological diversity in the history of the Earth. Today, as human populations expand and alter the natural environment, they are reducing

(5) biological diversity to its lowest level since the end of the Mesozoic era, 65 million years ago. The ultimate consequences of this biological collision are beyond calculation, but they are certain to be harmful. That, in essence, is the biodiversity crisis.

(10) The history of global diversity can be summarized as follows: after the initial flowering of multicellular animals, there was a swift rise in the number of species in early Paleozoic times (between 600 and 430 million years ago), then plateau-like stagnation

(15) for the remaining 200 million years of the Paleozoic era, and finally a slow but steady climb through the Mesozoic and Cenozoic eras to diversity's all-time high. This history suggests that biological diversity was hard won and a long time in coming.

(20) Furthermore, this pattern of increase was set back by five massive extinction episodes. The most recent of these, during the Cretaceous period, is by far the most famous, because it ended the age of the dinosaurs, conferred hegemony on the mammals, and

(25) ultimately made possible the ascendancy of the human species. But the Cretaceous crisis was minor compared with the Permian extinctions 240 million years ago, during which between 77 and 96 percent of marine animal species perished. It took 5 million

(30) years, well into Mesozoic times, for species diversity to begin a significant recovery.

Within the past 10,000 years biological diversity has entered a wholly new era. Human activity has had a devastating effect on species diversity, and the

(35) rate of human-induced extinctions is accelerating. Half of the bird species of Polynesia have been eliminated through hunting and the destruction of native forests. Hundreds of fish species endemic to Lake Victoria are now threatened with extinction

(40) following the careless introduction of one species of fish, the Nile perch. The list of such biogeographic disasters is extensive.

Because every species is unique and irreplaceable, the loss of biodiversity is the most profound process

(45) of environmental change. Its consequences are also the least predictable because the value of the Earth's biota (the fauna and flora collectively) remains largely unstudied and unappreciated; unlike material and cultural wealth, which we understand because

(50) they are the substance of our everyday lives, biological wealth is usually taken for granted. This is a serious strategic error, one that will be increasingly regretted as time passes. The biota is not only part of a country's heritage, the product of millions of years

(55) of evolution centered on that place; it is also a potential source for immense untapped material wealth in the form of food, medicine, and other commercially important substances.

7. Which one of the following best expresses the main idea of the passage?

(A) The reduction in biodiversity is an irreversible process that represents a setback both for science and for society as a whole.

(B) The material and cultural wealth of a nation are insignificant when compared with the country's biological wealth.

(C) The enormous diversity of life on Earth could not have come about without periodic extinctions that have conferred preeminence on one species at the expense of another.

(D) The human species is in the process of initiating a massive extinction episode that may make past episodes look minor by comparison.

(E) The current decline in species diversity is a human induced tragedy of incalculable proportions that has potentially grave consequences for the human species.

8. Which one of the following situations is most analogous to the history of global diversity summarized in lines 10-18 of the passage?

(A) The number of fish in a lake declines abruptly as a result of water pollution, then makes a slow comeback after cleanup efforts and the passage of ordinances against dumping.

(B) The concentration of chlorine in the water supply of a large city fluctuates widely before stabilizing at a constant and safe level.

(C) An old-fashioned article of clothing goes in and out of style periodically as a result of features in fashion magazines and the popularity of certain period films.

(D) After valuable mineral deposits are discovered, the population of a geographic region booms, then levels off and begins to decrease at a slow and steady rate.

(E) The variety of styles stocked by a shoe store increases rapidly after the store opens, holds constant for many months, and then gradually creeps upward.

9. The author suggests which one of the following about the Cretaceous crisis?

(A) It was the second most devastating extinction episode in history.
(B) It was the most devastating extinction episode up until that time.
(C) It was less devastating to species diversity than is the current biodiversity crisis.
(D) The rate of extinction among marine animal species as a result of the crisis did not approach 77 percent.
(E) The dinosaurs comprised the great majority of species that perished during the crisis.

10. The author mentions the Nile perch in order to provide an example of

(A) a species that has become extinct through human activity
(B) the typical lack of foresight that has led to biogeographic disaster
(C) a marine animal species that survived the Permian extinctions
(D) a species that is a potential source of material wealth
(E) the kind of action that is necessary to reverse the decline in species diversity

11. All of the following are explicitly mentioned in the passage as contributing to the extinction of species EXCEPT

(A) hunting
(B) pollution
(C) deforestation
(D) the growth of human populations
(E) human-engineered changes in the environment

12. The passage suggests which one of the following about material and cultural wealth?

(A) Because we can readily assess the value of material and cultural wealth, we tend not to take them for granted.
(B) Just as the biota is a source of potential material wealth, it is an untapped source of cultural wealth as well.
(C) Some degree of material and cultural wealth may have to be sacrificed if we are to protect our biological heritage.
(D) Material and cultural wealth are of less value than biological wealth because they have evolved over a shorter period of time.
(E) Material wealth and biological wealth are interdependent in a way that material wealth and cultural wealth are not.

13. The author would be most likely to agree with which one of the following statements about the consequences of the biodiversity crisis?

(A) The loss of species diversity will have as immediate an impact on the material wealth of nations as on their biological wealth.
(B) The crisis will likely end the hegemony of the human race and bring about the ascendancy of another species.
(C) The effects of the loss of species diversity will be dire, but we cannot yet tell how dire.
(D) It is more fruitful to discuss the consequences of the crisis in terms of the potential loss to humanity than in strictly biological terms.
(E) The consequences of the crisis can be minimized, but the pace of extinctions cannot be reversed.

Although bacteria are unicellular and among the simplest autonomous forms of life, they show a remarkable ability to sense their environment. They are attracted to materials they need and are repelled
(5) by harmful substances. Most types of bacteria swim very erratically; short smooth runs in relatively straight lines are followed by brief tumbles, after which the bacteria shoot off in random directions. This leaves researchers with the question of how
(10) such bacteria find their way to an attractant such as food or, in the case of photosynthetic bacteria, light, if their swimming pattern consists only of smooth runs and tumbles, the latter resulting in random changes in direction.
(15) One clue comes from the observation that when a chemical attractant is added to a suspension of such bacteria, the bacteria swim along a gradient of the attractant, from an area where the concentration of the attractant is weaker to an area where it is
(20) stronger. As they do so, their swimming is charac-terized by a decrease in tumbling and an increase in straight runs over relatively longer distances. As the bacteria encounter increasing concentrations of the attractant, their tendency to tumble is suppressed,
(25) whereas tumbling increases whenever they move away from the attractant. The net effect is that runs in the direction of higher concentrations of the attractant become longer and straighter as a result of the suppression of tumbling, whereas runs away
(30) from it are shortened by an increased tendency of the bacteria to tumble and change direction.

Biologists have proposed two mechanisms that bacteria might use in detecting changes in the concentration of a chemical attractant. First, a
(35) bacterium might compare the concentration of a chemical at the front and back of its cell body simultaneously. If the concentration is higher at the front of the cell, then it knows it is moving up the concentration gradient, from an area where the
(40) concentration is lower to an area where it is higher. Alternatively, it might measure the concentration at one instant and again after a brief interval, in which case the bacterium must retain a memory of the initial concentration. Researchers reasoned that if
(45) bacteria do compare concentrations at different times, then when suddenly exposed to a uniformly high concentration of an attractant, the cells would behave as if they were swimming up a concen-tration gradient, with long, smooth runs and
(50) relatively few tumbles. If, on the other hand, bacteria detect a chemical gradient by measuring it simultaneously at two distinct points, front and back, on the cell body, they would not respond to the jump in concentration because the concentration

(55) of the attractant in front and back of the cells, though high, would be uniform. Experimental evidence suggests that bacteria compare concentrations at different times.

16. It can be inferred from the passage that which one of the following experimental results would suggest that bacteria detect changes in the concentration of an attractant by measuring its concentration in front and back of the cell body simultaneously?

(A) When suddenly transferred from a medium in which the concentration of an attractant was uniformly low to one in which the concentration was uniformly high, the tendency of the bacteria to tumble and undergo random changes in direction increased.

(B) When suddenly transferred from a medium in which the concentration of an attractant was uniformly low to one in which the concentration was uniformly high, the bacteria exhibited no change in the pattern of their motion.

(C) When suddenly transferred from a medium in which the concentration of an attractant was uniformly low to one in which the concentration was uniformly high, the bacteria's movement was characterized by a complete absence of tumbling.

(D) When placed in a medium in which the concentration of an attractant was in some areas low and in others high, the bacteria exhibited an increased tendency to tumble in those areas where the concentration of the attractant was high.

(E) When suddenly transferred from a medium in which the concentration of an attractant was uniformly low to one that was completely free of attractants, the bacteria exhibited a tendency to suppress tumbling and move in longer, straighter lines.

17. It can be inferred from the passage that a bacterium would increase the likelihood of its moving away from an area where the concentration of a harmful substance is high if it did which one of the following?

   (A) increased the speed at which it swam immediately after undergoing the random changes in direction that result from tumbling

   (B) detected the concentration gradient of an attractant toward which it could begin to swim

   (C) relied on the simultaneous measurement of the concentration of the substance in front and back of its body, rather than on the comparison of the concentration at different points in time

   (D) exhibited a complete cessation of tumbling when it detected increases in the concentration of the substance

   (E) exhibited an increased tendency to tumble as it encountered increasing concentrations of the substance, and suppressed tumbling as it detected decreases in the concentration of the substance

18. It can be inferred from the passage that when describing bacteria as "swimming up a concentration gradient" (lines 48-49), the author means that they were behaving as if they were swimming

   (A) against a resistant medium that makes their swimming less efficient

   (B) away from a substance to which they are normally attracted

   (C) away from a substance that is normally harmful to them

   (D) from an area where the concentration of a repellent is weaker to an area where it is completely absent

   (E) from an area where the concentration of a substance is weaker to an area where it is stronger

19. The passage indicates that the pattern that characterizes a bacterium's motion changes in response to

   (A) the kinds of chemical attractants present in different concentration gradients

   (B) the mechanism that the bacterium adopts in determining the presence of an attractant

   (C) the bacterium's detection of changes in the concentration of an attractant

   (D) the extent to which neighboring bacteria are engaged in tumbling

   (E) changes in the intervals of time that occur between the bacterium's measurement of the concentration of an attractant

20. Which one of the following best describes the organization of the third paragraph of the passage?

   (A) Two approaches to a problem are discussed, a test that would determine which is more efficient is described, and a conclusion is made, based on experimental evidence.

   (B) Two hypotheses are described, a way of determining which of them is more likely to be true is discussed, and one is said to be more accurate on the basis of experimental evidence.

   (C) Two hypotheses are described, the flaws inherent in one of them are elaborated, and experimental evidence confirming the other is cited.

   (D) An assertion that a species has adopted two different mechanisms to solve a particular problem is made, and evidence is then provided in support of that assertion.

   (E) An assertion that one mechanism for solving a particular problem is more efficient than another is made, and evidence is then provided in support of that assertion.

21. The passage provides information in support of which one of the following assertions?

   (A) The seemingly erratic motion exhibited by a microorganism can in fact reflect a mechanism by which it is able to control its movement.

   (B) Biologists often overstate the complexity of simple organisms such as bacteria.

   (C) A bacterium cannot normally retain a memory of a measurement of the concentration of an attractant.

   (D) Bacteria now appear to have less control over their movement than biologists had previously hypothesized.

   (E) Photosynthetic bacteria appear to have more control over their movement than do bacteria that are not photosynthetic.

Cultivation of a single crop on a given tract of land leads eventually to decreased yields. One reason for this is that harmful bacterial phytopathogens, organisms parasitic on plant
(5) hosts, increase in the soil surrounding plant roots. The problem can be cured by crop rotation, denying the pathogens a suitable host for a period of time. However, even if crops are not rotated, the severity of diseases brought on by such
(10) phytopathogens often decreases after a number of years as the microbial population of the soil changes and the soil becomes "suppressive" to those diseases. While there may be many reasons for this phenomenon, it is clear that levels of certain
(15) bacteria, such as *Pseudomonas fluorescens,* a bacterium antagonistic to a number of harmful phytopathogens, are greater in suppressive than in nonsuppressive soil. This suggests that the presence of such bacteria suppresses phytopathogens. There
(20) is now considerable experimental support for this view. Wheat yield increases of 27 percent have been obtained in field trials by treatment of wheat seeds with fluorescent pseudomonads. Similar treatment of sugar beets, cotton, and potatoes has
(25) had similar results.

These improvements in crop yields through the application of *Pseudomonas fluorescens* suggest that agriculture could benefit from the use of bacteria genetically altered for specific purposes. For
(30) example, a form of phytopathogen altered to remove its harmful properties could be released into the environment in quantities favorable to its competing with and eventually excluding the harmful normal strain. Some experiments suggest
(35) that deliberately releasing altered nonpathogenic *Pseudomonas syringae* could crowd out the nonaltered variety that causes frost damage. Opponents of such research have objected that the deliberate and large-scale release of genetically
(40) altered bacteria might have deleterious results. Proponents, on the other hand, argue that this particular strain is altered only by the removal of the gene responsible for the strain's propensity to cause frost damage, thereby rendering it safer than
(45) the phytopathogen from which it was derived.

Some proponents have gone further and suggest that genetic alteration techniques could create organisms with totally new combinations of desirable traits not found in nature. For example,
(50) genes responsible for production of insecticidal compounds have been transposed from other bacteria into pseudomonads that colonize corn roots. Experiments of this kind are difficult and require great care: such bacteria are developed in highly

(55) artificial environments and may not compete well with natural soil bacteria. Nevertheless, proponents contend that the prospects for improved agriculture through such methods seem excellent. These prospects lead many to hope that current efforts to
(60) assess the risks of deliberate release of altered microorganisms will successfully answer the concerns of opponents and create a climate in which such research can go forward without undue impediment.

15. Which one of the following best summarizes the main idea of the passage?

(A) Recent field experiments with genetically altered *Pseudomonas* bacteria have shown that releasing genetically altered bacteria into the environment would not involve any significant danger.

(B) Encouraged by current research, advocates of agricultural use of genetically altered bacteria are optimistic that such use will eventually result in improved agriculture, though opponents remain wary.

(C) Current research indicates that adding genetically altered *Pseudomonas syringae* bacteria to the soil surrounding crop plant roots will have many beneficial effects, such as the prevention of frost damage in certain crops.

(D) Genetic alteration of a number of harmful phytopathogens has been advocated by many researchers who contend that these techniques will eventually replace such outdated methods as crop rotation.

(E) Genetic alteration of bacteria has been successful in highly artificial laboratory conditions, but opponents of such research have argued that these techniques are unlikely to produce organisms that are able to survive in natural environments.

16. It can be inferred from the passage that crop rotation can increase yields in part because

(A) moving crop plants around makes them hardier and more resistant to disease

(B) the number of *Pseudomonas fluorescens* bacteria in the soil usually increases when crops are rotated

(C) the roots of many crop plants produce compounds that are antagonistic to phytopathogens harmful to other crop plants

(D) the presence of phytopathogenic bacteria is responsible for the majority of plant diseases

(E) phytopathogens typically attack some plant species but find other species to be unsuitable hosts

17. The author discusses naturally occurring *Pseudomonas fluorescens* bacteria in the first paragraph primarily in order to do which one of the following?

(A) prove that increases in the level of such bacteria in the soil are the sole cause of soil suppressivity

(B) explain why yields increased after wheat fields were sprayed with altered *Pseudomonas fluorescens* bacteria

(C) detail the chemical processes that such bacteria use to suppress organisms parasitic to crop plants, such as wheat, sugar beets, and potatoes

(D) provide background information to support the argument that research into the agricultural use of genetically altered bacteria would be fruitful

(E) argue that crop rotation is unnecessary, since diseases brought on by phytopathogens diminish in severity and eventually disappear on their own

18. It can be inferred from the author's discussion of *Pseudomonas fluorescens* bacteria that which one of the following would be true of crops impervious to parasitical organisms?

(A) *Pseudomonas fluorescens* bacteria would be absent from the soil surrounding their roots.

(B) They would crowd out and eventually exclude other crop plants if their growth were not carefully regulated.

(C) Their yield would not be likely to be improved by adding *Pseudomonas fluorescens* bacteria to the soil.

(D) They would mature more quickly than crop plants that were susceptible to parasitical organisms.

(E) Levels of phytopathogenic bacteria in the soil surrounding their roots would be higher compared with other crop plants.

19. According to the passage, proponents of the use of genetically altered bacteria in agriculture argue that which one of the following is true of the altered bacteria used in the frost-damage experiments?

(A) The altered bacteria had a genetic constitution differing from that of the normal strain only in that the altered variety had one less gene.

(B) Although the altered bacteria competed effectively with the nonaltered strain in the laboratory, they were not as viable in natural environments.

(C) The altered bacteria were much safer and more effective than the naturally occurring *Pseudomonas fluorescens* bacteria used in earlier experiments.

(D) The altered bacteria were antagonistic to several types of naturally occurring phytopathogens in the soil surrounding the roots of frost-damaged crops.

(E) The altered bacteria were released into the environment in numbers sufficient to guarantee the validity of experimental results.

20. Which one of the following, if true, would most seriously weaken the proponents' argument regarding the safety of using altered *Pseudomonas syringae* bacteria to control frost damage?

(A) *Pseudomonas syringae* bacteria are primitive and have a simple genetic constitution.

(B) The altered bacteria are derived from a strain that is parasitic to plants and can cause damage to crops.

(C) Current genetic-engineering techniques permit the large-scale commercial production of such bacteria.

(D) Often genes whose presence is responsible for one harmful characteristic must be present in order to prevent other harmful characteristics.

(E) The frost-damage experiments with *Pseudomonas syringae* bacteria indicate that the altered variety would only replace the normal strain if released in sufficient numbers.

Oil companies need offshore platforms primarily because the oil or natural gas the companies extract from the ocean floor has to be processed before pumps can be used to move the substances ashore.
(5) But because processing crude (unprocessed oil or gas) on a platform rather than at facilities onshore exposes workers to the risks of explosion and to an unpredictable environment, researchers are attempting to diminish the need for human labor
(10) on platforms and even to eliminate platforms altogether by redesigning two kinds of pumps to handle crude. These pumps could then be used to boost the natural pressure driving the flow of crude, which, by itself, is sufficient only to bring
(15) the crude to the platform, located just above the wellhead. Currently, pumps that could boost this natural pressure sufficiently to drive the crude through a pipeline to the shore do not work consistently because of the crude's content. Crude
(20) may consist of oil or natural gas in multiphase states—combinations of liquids, gases, and solids under pressure—that do not reach the wellhead in constant proportions. The flow of crude oil, for example, can change quickly from 60 percent liquid
(25) to 70 percent gas. This surge in gas content causes loss of "head," or pressure inside a pump, with the result that a pump can no longer impart enough energy to transport the crude mixture through the pipeline and to the shore.
(30)   Of the two pumps being redesigned, the positive-displacement pump is promising because it is immune to sudden shifts in the proportion of liquid to gas in the crude mixture. But the pump's design, which consists of a single or twin screw
(35) pushing the fluid from one end of the pump to the other, brings crude into close contact with most parts of the pump, and thus requires that it be made of expensive, corrosion-resistant material. The alternative is the centrifugal pump, which has a
(40) rotating impeller that sucks fluid in at one end and forces fluid out at the other. Although this pump has a proven design and has worked for years with little maintenance in waste-disposal plants, researchers have discovered that because the swirl
(45) of its impeller separates gas out from the oil that normally accompanies it, significant reductions in head can occur as it operates.
   Research in the development of these pumps is focused mainly on trying to reduce the cost of the
(50) positive-displacement pump and attempting to make the centrifugal pump more tolerant of gas. Other researchers are looking at ways of adapting either kind of pump for use underwater, so that crude could be moved directly from the sea bottom
(55) to processing facilities onshore, eliminating platforms.

1. Which one of the following best expresses the main idea of the passage?

    (A)   Oil companies are experimenting with technologies that may help diminish the danger to workers from offshore crude processing.
    (B)   Oil companies are seeking methods of installing processing facilities underwater.
    (C)   Researchers are developing several new pumps designed to enhance human labor efficiency in processing facilities.
    (D)   Researchers are seeking to develop equipment that would preempt the need for processing facilities onshore.
    (E)   Researchers are seeking ways to separate liquids from gases in crude in order to enable safer processing.

2. The passage supports which one of the following statements about the natural pressure driving the flow of crude?

    (A)   It is higher than that created by the centrifugal pump.
    (B)   It is constant, regardless of relative proportions of gas and liquid.
    (C)   It is able to carry the crude only as far as the wellhead.
    (D)   It is able to carry the crude to the platform.
    (E)   It is able to carry the crude to the shore.

3. Which one of the following best describes the relationship of the second paragraph to the passage as a whole?

(A) It offers concrete detail designed to show that the argument made in the first paragraph is flawed.
(B) It provides detail that expands upon the information presented in the first paragraph.
(C) It enhances the author's discussion by objectively presenting in detail the pros and cons of a claim made in the first paragraph.
(D) It detracts from the author's discussion by presenting various problems that qualify the goals presented.
(E) It modifies an observation made in the first paragraph by detailing viewpoints against it.

4. Which one of the following phrases, if substituted for the word "head" in line 47, would LEAST change the meaning of the sentence?

(A) the flow of the crude inside the pump
(B) the volume of oil inside the pump
(C) the volume of gas inside the pump
(D) the speed of the impeller moving the crude
(E) the pressure inside of the pump

5. With which one of the following statements regarding offshore platforms would the author most likely agree?

(A) If a reduction of human labor on offshore platforms is achieved, there is no real need to eliminate platforms altogether.
(B) Reducing human labor on offshore platforms is desirable because researchers' knowledge about the transportation of crude is dangerously incomplete.
(C) The dangers involved in working on offshore platforms make their elimination a desirable goal.
(D) The positive-displacement pump is the better alternative for researchers, because it would allow them to eliminate platforms altogether.
(E) Though researchers have succeeded in reducing human labor on offshore platforms, they think that it would be inadvisable to eliminate platforms altogether, because these platforms have other uses.

6. Which one of the following can be inferred from the passage about pumps that are currently available to boost the natural pressure of crude?

(A) The efficiency of these pumps depends on there being no gas in the flow of crude.
(B) These pumps are more efficient when the crude is less subject to sudden increases in the proportion of gas to liquid.
(C) A sudden change from solid to liquid in the flow of crude increases the efficiency of these pumps.
(D) The proportion of liquid to gas in the flow of crude does not affect the efficiency of these pumps.
(E) A sudden change from liquid to gas in the flow of crude increases the risk of explosion due to rising pressure inside these pumps.

7. The passage implies that the positive-displacement pump differs from the centrifugal pump in that the positive-displacement pump

(A) is more promising, but it also is more expensive and demands more maintenance
(B) is especially well researched, since it has been used in other settings
(C) involves the use of a single or twin screw that sucks fluid in at one end of the pump
(D) is problematic because it causes rapid shifts from liquid to gas content in crude
(E) involves exposure of many parts of the pump to crude

8. The passage implies that the current state of technology necessitates that crude be moved to shore

(A) in a multiphase state
(B) in equal proportions of gas to liquid
(C) with small proportions of corrosive material
(D) after having been processed
(E) largely in the form of a liquid

The old belief that climatic stability accounts for the high level of species diversity in the Amazon River basin of South America emerged, strangely enough, from observations of the deep sea. Sanders
(5) discovered high diversity among the mud-dwelling animals of the deep ocean. He argued that such diversity could be attributed to the absence of significant fluctuations in climate and physical conditions, without which the extinction of species
(10) should be rare. In the course of time new species would continue to evolve, and so the rate of speciation would be greater than the rate of extinction, resulting in the accumulation of great diversity. Sanders argued that the Amazon tropical
(15) rain forest is analogous to the deep sea: because the rain forest has a stable climate, extinction should be rare. Evidence that some species of rain-forest trees have persisted for some 30 million years in the Amazon basin, added to the absence of
(20) winter and glaciation, supports this view.

Recently, however, several observations have cast doubt on the validity of the stability hypothesis and suggest that the climate of the Amazon basin has fluctuated significantly in the past. Haffer
(25) noted that different species of birds inhabit different corners of the basin in spite of the fact that essentially unbroken green forest spreads from the western edge to the eastern edge of the region. This pattern presented a puzzle to biologists
(30) studying the distributions of plants and animals: why would different species inhabit different parts of the forest if the habitat in which they lived had a stable climate?

Haffer proposed a compelling explanation for
(35) the distribution of species. Observing that species found on high ground are different from those on low ground, and knowing that in the Amazon lowlands are drier than uplands, he proposed that during the ice ages the Amazon lowlands became a
(40) near-desert arid plain; meanwhile, the more elevated regions became islands of moisture and hence served as refuges for the fauna and flora of the rain forest. Populations that were once continuous diverged and became permanently
(45) separated. Haffer's hypothesis appears to explain the distribution of species as well as the unusual species diversity. The ice-age refuges would have protected existing species from extinction. But the periodic geographic isolation of related populations
(50) (there have been an estimated 13 ice ages to date) would have facilitated the development of new species as existing species on the lowlands adapted to changing climates.

Although no conclusive proof has yet been
(55) found to support Haffer's hypothesis, it has led

other researchers to gauge the effects of climatic changes, such as storms and flooding, on species diversity in the Amazon basin. Their research suggests that climatic disturbances help account for
(60) the splendid diversity of the Amazon rain forest today.

15. As discussed in the first paragraph of the passage, Sanders' analogy between the deep sea and the Amazon basin involves which one of the following assumptions?

(A) Both the Amazon basin and the deep sea support an unusually high rate of speciation.

(B) Both the rain-forest trees in the Amazon basin and the mud-dwelling animals in the deep sea have survived for 30 million years.

(C) Both the deep sea and the Amazon basin have not experienced dramatic changes in climate or physical conditions.

(D) A dependable supply of water to the Amazon basin and the deep sea has moderated the rate of extinction in both habitats.

(E) The rate of speciation in the Amazon basin is equivalent to the rate of speciation in the deep sea.

16. The author of the passage would most likely agree with which one of the following statements about Haffer's hypothesis?

(A) It provides an intriguing and complete explanation for the high rate of species diversity in the Amazon basin.

(B) It is partially correct in that a number of climatic disturbances account for species diversity in the Amazon basin.

(C) It has not yet been verified, but it has had an influential effect on current research on species diversity in the Amazon basin.

(D) It is better than Sanders' theory in accounting for the low rate of species extinction in the Amazon basin.

(E) It provides a compelling explanation for the distribution of species in the Amazon basin but does not account for the high species diversity.

17. According to the passage, lowlands in the Amazon basin currently differ from uplands in which one of the following respects?

    (A)   Lowlands are desertlike, whereas uplands are lush.

    (B)   Lowlands are less vulnerable to glaciation during the ice ages than are uplands.

    (C)   Uplands support a greater diversity of species than do lowlands.

    (D)   Uplands are wetter than are lowlands.

    (E)   Uplands are more densely populated than are lowlands.

18. Which one of the following best describes the organization of the passage?

    (A)   A hypothesis is discussed, evidence that undercuts that hypothesis is presented, and a new hypothesis that may account for the evidence is described.

    (B)   A recently observed phenomenon is described, an explanation for that phenomenon is discussed, and the explanation is evaluated in light of previous research findings.

    (C)   Several hypotheses that may account for a puzzling phenomenon are described and discounted, and a more promising hypothesis is presented.

    (D)   A hypothesis and the assumptions on which it is based are described, and evidence is provided to suggest that the hypothesis is only partially correct.

    (E)   Two alternative explanations for a phenomenon are presented and compared, and experiments designed to test each theory are described.

19. The author of the passage mentions the number of ice ages in the third paragraph most probably in order to

    (A)   provide proof that cooler and drier temperatures are primarily responsible for the distribution of species in the Amazon

    (B)   explain how populations of species were protected from extinction in the Amazon basin

    (C)   explain how most existing species were able to survive periodic climatic disturbances in the Amazon basin

    (D)   suggest that certain kinds of climatic disturbances cause more species diversity than do other kinds of climatic disturbances

    (E)   suggest that geographic isolation may have occurred often enough to cause high species diversity in the Amazon basin

20. The passage suggests that which one of the following is true of Sanders' hypothesis?

    (A)   He underestimated the effects of winter and glaciation in the Amazon basin on the tropical rain forest.

    (B)   He failed to recognize the similarity in physical conditions of the Amazon lowlands and the Amazon uplands.

    (C)   He failed to take into account the relatively high rate of extinction during the ice ages in the Amazon basin.

    (D)   He overestimated the length of time that species have survived in the Amazon basin.

    (E)   He failed to account for the distribution of species in the Amazon basin.

21. Which one of the following is evidence that would contribute to the "proof" mentioned in line 54?

    (A)   Accurately dated sediment cores from a freshwater lake in the Amazon indicate that the lake's water level rose significantly during the last ice age.

    (B)   Data based on radiocarbon dating of fossils suggest that the Amazon uplands were too cold to support rain forests during the last ice age.

    (C)   Computer models of climate during global ice ages predict only insignificant reductions of monsoon rains in tropical areas such as the Amazon.

    (D)   Fossils preserved in the Amazon uplands during the last ice age are found together with minerals that are the products of an arid landscape.

    (E)   Fossilized pollen from the Amazon lowlands indicates that during the last ice age the Amazon lowlands supported vegetation that needs little water rather than the rain forests they support today.

How does the brain know when carbohydrates have been or should be consumed? The answer to this question is not known, but one element in the explanation seems to be the neurotransmitter
(5) serotonin, one of a class of chemical mediators that may be released from a presynaptic neuron and that cause the transmission of a nerve impulse across a synapse to an adjacent postsynaptic neuron. In general, it has been found that drugs that selectively
(10) facilitate serotonin-mediated neurotransmission tend to cause weight loss, whereas drugs that block serotonin-mediated transmission often have the opposite effect: they often induce carbohydrate craving and consequent weight gain.
(15)   Serotonin is a derivative of tryptophan, an amino acid that is normally present at low levels in the bloodstream. The rate of conversion is affected by the proportion of carbohydrates in an individual's diet: carbohydrates stimulate the secretion of
(20) insulin, which facilitates the uptake of most amino acids into peripheral tissues, such as muscles. Blood tryptophan levels, however, are unaffected by insulin, so the proportion of tryptophan in the blood relative to the other amino acids increases when
(25) carbohydrates are consumed. Since tryptophan competes with other amino acids for transport across the blood-brain barrier into the brain, insulin secretion indirectly speeds tryptophan's entry into the central nervous system where, in a special
(30) cluster of neurons, it is converted into serotonin.
    The level of serotonin in the brain in turn affects the amount of carbohydrate an individual chooses to eat. Rats that are allowed to choose among synthetic foods containing different proportions of
(35) carbohydrate and protein will normally alternate between foods containing mostly protein and those containing mostly carbohydrate. However, if rats are given drugs that enhance the effect of serotonin, the rats' carbohydrate intake is reduced. On the
(40) other hand, when rats are given drugs that interrupt serotonin-mediated neurotransmission, their brains fail to respond when carbohydrates are eaten, so the desire for them persists.
    In human beings a serotoninlike drug,
(45) d-fenfluramine (which releases serotonin into brain synapses and then prolongs its action by blocking its reabsorption into the presynaptic neuron), selectively suppresses carbohydrate snacking (and its associated weight gain) in people who crave
(50) carbohydrates. In contrast, drugs that block serotonin-mediated transmission or that interact with neurotransmitters other than serotonin have the opposite effect: they often induce carbohydrate craving and subsequent weight gain. People who

(55) crave carbohydrates report feeling refreshed and invigorated after eating a carbohydrate-rich meal (which would be expected to increase brain serotonin levels). In contrast, those who do not crave carbohydrates become sleepy following a
(60) high-carbohydrate meal. These findings suggest that serotonin has other effects that may be useful indicators of serotonin levels in human beings.

21. Which one of the following best states the main idea of the passage?

    (A)   The body's need for carbohydrates varies with the level of serotonin in the blood.
    (B)   The body's use of carbohydrates can be regulated by the administration of serotoninlike drugs.
    (C)   The role of serotonin in regulating the consumption of carbohydrates is similar in rats and in humans.
    (D)   The body's desire for carbohydrates can be influenced by serotonin or serotoninlike drugs.
    (E)   Tryptophan initiates a chain of events that regulates the body's use of carbohydrates.

22. The term "rate" (line 17) refers to the rate at which

    (A)   serotonin is produced from tryptophan
    (B)   carbohydrates are taken into the body
    (C)   carbohydrates stimulate the secretion of insulin
    (D)   insulin facilitates the uptake of amino acids into peripheral tissues
    (E)   tryptophan enters the bloodstream

23. It can be inferred that a person is likely to crave carbohydrates when

    (A)   the amount of insulin produced is too high
    (B)   the amount of serotonin in the brain is too low
    (C)   more tryptophan than usual crosses the blood-brain barrier
    (D)   neurotransmission by neurotransmitters other than serotonin is interrupted
    (E)   amino acids other than tryptophan are taken up by peripheral tissues

24. The information in the passage indicates that if human beings were given a drug that inhibits the action of serotonin, which one of the following might be expected to occur?

    (A) Subjects would probably show a preference for carbohydrate-rich snacks rather than protein-rich snacks.

    (B) Subjects would probably become sleepy after eating a carbohydrate-rich meal.

    (C) Subjects would be more likely to lose weight than before they took the drug.

    (D) Subjects' blood tryptophan levels would probably increase.

    (E) Subjects' desire for both carbohydrates and proteins would increase.

25. The primary purpose of the second paragraph in the passage is to

    (A) provide an overview of current research concerning the effect of serotonin on carbohydrate consumption

    (B) contrast the role of tryptophan in the body with that of serotonin

    (C) discuss the role of serotonin in the transmission of neural impulses

    (D) explain how the brain knows that carbohydrates should be consumed

    (E) establish a connection between carbohydrate intake and the production of serotonin

26. It can be inferred that after a person has taken *d*-fenfluramine, he or she will probably be

    (A) inclined to gain weight
    (B) sleepy much of the time
    (C) unlikely to crave carbohydrates
    (D) unable to sleep as much as usual
    (E) likely to secrete more insulin than usual

27. The author's primary purpose is to

    (A) defend a point of view
    (B) correct a misconception
    (C) assess conflicting evidence
    (D) suggest new directions for investigation
    (E) provide information that helps explain a phenomenon

A major tenet of the neurosciences has been that all neurons (nerve cells) in the brains of vertebrate animals are formed early in development. An adult vertebrate, it was believed, must make do with a
(5) fixed number of neurons: those lost through disease or injury are not replaced, and adult learning takes place not through generation of new cells but through modification of connections among existing ones.

(10) However, new evidence for neurogenesis (the birth of new neurons) has come from the study of canary song. Young canaries and other songbirds learn to sing much as humans learn to speak, by imitating models provided by their elders. Several
(15) weeks after birth, a young bird produces its first rudimentary attempts at singing; over the next few months the song becomes more structured and stable, reaching a fully developed state by the time the bird approaches its first breeding season. But
(20) this repertoire of song is not permanently learned. After each breeding season, during late summer and fall, the bird loses mastery of its developed "vocabulary," and its song becomes as unstable as that of a juvenile bird. During the following winter
(25) and spring, however, the canary acquires new songs, and by the next breeding season it has developed an entirely new repertoire.

Recent neurological research into this learning and relearning process has shown that the two most
(30) important regions of the canary's brain related to the learning of songs actually vary in size at different times of the year. In the spring, when the bird's song is highly developed and uniform, the regions are roughly twice as large as they are in the
(35) fall. Further experiments tracing individual nerve cells within these regions have shown that the number of neurons drops by about 38 percent after the breeding season, but by the following breeding season, new ones have been generated to replace
(40) them. A possible explanation for this continual replacement of nerve cells may have to do with the canary's relatively long life span and the requirements of flight. Its brain would have to be substantially larger and heavier than might be
(45) feasible for flying if it had to carry all the brain cells needed to process and retain all the information gathered over a lifetime.

Although the idea of neurogenesis in the adult mammalian brain is still not generally accepted,
(50) these findings might help uncover a mechanism that would enable the human brain to repair itself through neurogenesis. Whether such replacement of neurons would disrupt complex learning processes or long-term memory is not known, but

(55) songbird research challenges scientists to identify the genes or hormones that orchestrate neurogenesis in the young human brain and to learn how to activate them in the adult brain.

1. Which one of the following best expresses the main idea of the passage?

    (A) New evidence of neurogenesis in canaries challenges an established neurological theory concerning brain cells in vertebrates and suggests the possibility that human brains may repair themselves.
    (B) The brains of canaries differ from the brains of other vertebrate animals in that the brains of adult canaries are able to generate neurons.
    (C) Recent studies of neurogenesis in canaries, building on established theories of vertebrate neurology, provide important clues as to why researchers are not likely to discover neurogenesis in adult humans.
    (D) Recent research into neurogenesis in canaries refutes a long-held belief about the limited supply of brain cells and provides new information about neurogenesis in the adult human brain.
    (E) New information about neurogenesis in canaries challenges older hypotheses and clarifies the importance of the yearly cycle in learning processes and neurological replacement among vertebrates.

2. According to the passage, which one of the following is true of the typical adult canary during the late summer and fall?

    (A) The canary's song repertoire takes on a fully structured and stable quality.
    (B) A process of neurogenesis replaces the song-learning neurons that were lost during the preceding months.
    (C) The canary begins to learn an entirely new repertoire of songs based on the models of other canaries.
    (D) The regions in the canary's brain that are central to the learning of song decrease in size.
    (E) The canary performs slightly modified versions of the songs it learned during the preceding breeding season.

3. Information in the passage suggests that the author would most likely regard which one of the following as LEAST important in future research on neurogenesis in humans?

    (A) research on possible similarities between the neurological structures of humans and canaries
    (B) studies that compare the ratio of brain weight to body weight in canaries to that in humans
    (C) neurological research on the genes or hormones that activate neurogenesis in the brain of human infants
    (D) studies about the ways in which long-term memory functions in the human brain
    (E) research concerning the processes by which humans learn complicated tasks

4. Which one of the following, if true, would most seriously undermine the explanation proposed by the author in the third paragraph?

    (A) A number of songbird species related to the canary have a shorter life span than the canary and do not experience neurogenesis.
    (B) The brain size of several types of airborne birds with life spans similar to those of canaries has been shown to vary according to a two-year cycle of neurogenesis.
    (C) Several species of airborne birds similar to canaries in size are known to have brains that are substantially heavier than the canary's brain.
    (D) Individual canaries that have larger-than-average repertoires of songs tend to have better developed muscles for flying.
    (E) Individual canaries with smaller and lighter brains than the average tend to retain a smaller-than-average repertoire of songs.

5. The use of the word "vocabulary" (line 23) serves primarily to

    (A) demonstrate the presence of a rudimentary grammatical structure in canary song
    (B) point out a similarity between the patterned groupings of sounds in a canary's song and the syllabic structures of words
    (C) stress the stability and uniformity of the canary's song throughout its lifetime
    (D) suggest a similarity between the possession of a repertoire of words among humans and a repertoire of songs among canaries
    (E) imply that the complexity of the canary's song repertoire is equal to that of human language

6. According to the passage, which one of the following factors may help account for the occurrence of neurogenesis in canaries?

    (A) the life span of the average canary
    (B) the process by which canaries learn songs
    (C) the frequency of canary breeding seasons
    (D) the number of regions in the canary brain related to song learning
    (E) the amount of time an average canary needs to learn a repertoire of songs

7. Which one of the following best describes the organization of the third paragraph?

    (A) A theory is presented, analyzed, and modified, and a justification for the modification is offered.
    (B) Research results are advanced and reconciled with results from other studies, and a shared principle is described.
    (C) Research results are presented, further details are provided, and a hypothesis is offered to explain the results.
    (D) Research findings are described, their implications are explained, and an application to a related field is proposed.
    (E) Research results are reported, their significance is clarified, and they are reconciled with previously established neurological tenets.

8. It can be inferred from the passage that the author would most likely describe the current understanding of neurogenesis as

    (A) exhaustive
    (B) progressive
    (C) incomplete
    (D) antiquated
    (E) incorrect

It is a fundamental tenet of geophysics that the Earth's magnetic field can exist in either of two polarity states: a "normal" state, in which north-seeking compass needles point to the
(5) geographic north, and a "reverse" state, in which they point to the geographic south. Geological evidence shows that periodically the field's polarity reverses, and that these reversals have been taking place at an increasing rate. Evidence also indicates
(10) that the field does not reverse instantaneously from one polarity state to another; rather, the process involves a transition period that typically spans a few thousand years.

Though this much is known, the underlying
(15) causes of the reversal phenomenon are not well understood. It is generally accepted that the magnetic field itself is generated by the motion of free electrons in the outer core, a slowly churning mass of molten metal sandwiched between the
(20) Earth's mantle (the region of the Earth's interior lying below the crust) and its solid inner core. In some way that is not completely understood, gravity and the Earth's rotation, acting on temperature and density differences within the outer core fluid,
(25) provide the driving forces behind the generation of the field. The reversal phenomenon may be triggered when something disturbs the heat circulation pattern of the outer core fluid, and with it the magnetic field.

(30) Several explanations for this phenomenon have been proposed. One proposal, the "heat-transfer hypothesis," is that the triggering process is intimately related to the way the outer core vents its heat into the mantle. For example, such heat
(35) transfer could create hotter (rising) or cooler (descending) blobs of material from the inner and outer boundaries of the fluid core, thereby perturbing the main heat-circulation pattern. A more controversial alternative proposal is the
(40) "asteroid-impact hypothesis." In this scenario an extended period of cold and darkness results from the impact of an asteroid large enough to send a great cloud of dust into the atmosphere. Following this climatic change, ocean temperatures drop and
(45) the polar ice caps grow, redistributing the Earth's seawater. This redistribution increases the rotational acceleration of the mantle, causing friction and turbulence near the outer core-mantle boundary and initiating a reversal of the magnetic field.

(50) How well do these hypotheses account for such observations as the long-term increase in the frequency of reversal? In support of the asteroid-impact model, it has been argued that the gradual cooling of the average ocean temperature

(55) would enable progressively smaller asteroid impacts (which are known to occur more frequently than larger impacts) to cool the Earth's climate sufficiently to induce ice-cap growth and reversals. But theories that depend on extraterrestrial
(60) intervention seem less convincing than theories like the first, which account for the phenomenon solely by means of the thermodynamic state of the outer core and its effect on the mantle.

1. Which one of the following statements regarding the Earth's outer core is best supported by information presented in the passage?

(A) Heat circulation in the outer core controls the growth and diminution of the polar ice caps.

(B) Impact of asteroids on the Earth's surface alters the way in which the outer core vents its heat into the mantle.

(C) Motion of electrons within the metallic fluid in the outer core produces the Earth's magnetic field.

(D) Friction and turbulence near the boundary between the outer core and the mantle are typically caused by asteroid impacts.

(E) Cessation of heat circulation within the outer core brings on multiple reversals in the Earth's magnetic field.

HARD SCIENCE

2. The author's objection to the second hypothesis discussed in the passage is most applicable to which one of the following explanations concerning the extinction of the dinosaurs?

(A) The extinction of the dinosaurs was the result of gradual changes in the composition of the Earth's atmosphere that occurred over millions of years.
(B) The dinosaurs became extinct when their food supply was disrupted following the emergence of mammals.
(C) The dinosaurs succumbed to the new, colder environment brought about by a buildup of volcanic ash in the atmosphere.
(D) After massively overpopulating the planet, dinosaurs disappeared due to widespread starvation and the rapid spread of disease.
(E) After radical climatic changes resulted from the impact of a comet, dinosaurs disappeared from the Earth.

3. The author mentions the creation of blobs of different temperatures in the Earth's outer core (lines 34-38) primarily in order to

(A) present a way in which the venting of heat from the outer core might disturb the heat-circulation pattern within the outer core
(B) provide proof for the proposal that ventilation of heat from the outer core into the mantle triggers polarity reversal
(C) give an example of the way in which heat circulates between the Earth's outer core and the Earth's exterior
(D) describe how the outer core maintains its temperature by venting its excess heat into the Earth's mantle
(E) argue in favor of the theory that heat circulation in the Earth's interior produces the magnetic field

4. Which one of the following statements regarding the polarity of the Earth's magnetic field is best supported by information in the passage?

(A) Most, but not all, geophysicists agree that the Earth's magnetic field may exist in two distinct polarity states.
(B) Changes in the polarity of the Earth's magnetic field have occurred more often in the recent past than in the distant past.
(C) Heat transfer would cause reversals of the polarity of the Earth's magnetic field to occur more quickly than would asteroid impact.
(D) Geophysicists' understanding of the reversal of the Earth's magnetic field has increased significantly since the introduction of the heat-transfer hypothesis.
(E) Friction near the boundary of the inner and outer cores brings on reversal of the polarity of the geomagnetic field.

5. Which one of the following can be inferred regarding the two proposals discussed in the passage?

(A) Since their introduction they have sharply divided the scientific community.
(B) Both were formulated in order to explain changes in the frequency of polarity reversal.
(C) Although no firm conclusions regarding them have yet been reached, both have been extensively investigated.
(D) They are not the only proposals scientists have put forward to explain the phenomenon of polarity reversal.
(E) Both were introduced some time ago and have since fallen into disfavor among geophysicists.

6. The author mentions each of the following as possible contributing causes to reversals of the Earth's magnetic field EXCEPT

(A) changes in the way heat circulates within the outer core fluid
(B) extended periods of colder temperatures on the Earth's surface
(C) the creation of circulating blobs of outer core material of different temperatures
(D) changes in circulation patterns in the Earth's oceans
(E) clouding of the Earth's atmosphere by a large amount of dust

Until the 1980s, most scientists believed that noncatastrophic geological processes caused the extinction of dinosaurs that occurred approximately 66 million years ago, at the end of the Cretaceous
(5) period. Geologists argued that a dramatic drop in sea level coincided with the extinction of the dinosaurs and could have caused the climatic changes that resulted in this extinction as well as the extinction of many ocean species.
(10) This view was seriously challenged in the 1980s by the discovery of large amounts of iridium in a layer of clay deposited at the end of the Cretaceous period. Because iridium is extremely rare in rocks on the Earth's surface but common in meteorites,
(15) researchers theorized that it was the impact of a large meteorite that dramatically changed the Earth's climate and thus triggered the extinction of the dinosaurs.

Currently available evidence, however, offers
(20) more support for a new theory, the volcanic-eruption theory. A vast eruption of lava in India coincided with the extinctions that occurred at the end of the Cretaceous period, and the release of carbon dioxide from this episode of volcanism could
(25) have caused the climatic change responsible for the demise of the dinosaurs. Such outpourings of lava are caused by instability in the lowest layer of the Earth's mantle, located just above the Earth's core. As the rock that constitutes this layer is heated by
(30) the Earth's core, it becomes less dense and portions of it eventually escape upward as blobs of molten rock, called "diapirs," that can, under certain circumstances, erupt violently through the Earth's crust.
(35) Moreover, the volcanic-eruption theory, like the impact theory, accounts for the presence of iridium in sedimentary deposits; it also explains matters that the meteorite-impact theory does not. Although iridium is extremely rare on the Earth's
(40) surface, the lower regions of the Earth's mantle have roughly the same composition as meteorites and contain large amounts of iridium, which in the case of a diapir eruption would probably be emitted as iridium hexafluoride, a gas that would disperse
(45) more uniformly in the atmosphere than the iridium-containing matter thrown out from a meteorite impact. In addition, the volcanic-eruption theory may explain why the end of the Cretaceous period was marked by a gradual change in sea level.
(50) Fossil records indicate that for several hundred thousand years prior to the relatively sudden disappearance of the dinosaurs, the level of the sea gradually fell, causing many marine organisms to die out. This change in sea level might well have

(55) been the result of a distortion in the Earth's surface that resulted from the movement of diapirs upward toward the Earth's crust, and the more cataclysmic extinction of the dinosaurs could have resulted from the explosive volcanism that occurred as material
(60) from the diapirs erupted onto the Earth's surface.

1. The passage suggests that during the 1980s researchers found meteorite impact a convincing explanation for the extinction of dinosaurs, in part because

(A) earlier theories had failed to account for the gradual extinction of many ocean species at the end of the Cretaceous period

(B) geologists had, up until that time, underestimated the amount of carbon dioxide that would be released during an episode of explosive volcanism

(C) a meteorite could have served as a source of the iridium found in a layer of clay deposited at the end of the Cretaceous period

(D) no theory relying on purely geological processes had, up until that time, explained the cause of the precipitous drop in sea level that occurred at the end of the Cretaceous period

(E) the impact of a large meteorite could have resulted in the release of enough carbon dioxide to cause global climatic change

2. According to the passage, the lower regions of the Earth's mantle are characterized by

(A) a composition similar to that of meteorites

(B) the absence of elements found in rocks on the Earth's crust

(C) a greater stability than that of the upper regions

(D) the presence of large amounts of carbon dioxide

(E) a uniformly lower density than that of the upper regions

3. It can be inferred from the passage that which one of the following was true of the lava that erupted in India at the end of the Cretaceous period?

(A) It contained less carbon dioxide than did the meteorites that were striking the Earth's surface during that period.

(B) It was more dense than the molten rock located just above the Earth's core.

(C) It released enough iridium hexafluoride into the atmosphere to change the Earth's climate dramatically.

(D) It was richer in iridium than rocks usually found on the Earth's surface.

(E) It was richer in iridium than were the meteorites that were striking the Earth's surface during that period.

4. In the passage, the author is primarily concerned with doing which one of the following?

(A) describing three theories and explaining why the latest of these appears to be the best of the three

(B) attacking the assumptions inherent in theories that until the 1980s had been largely accepted by geologists

(C) outlining the inadequacies of three different explanations of the same phenomenon

(D) providing concrete examples in support of the more general assertion that theories must often be revised in light of new evidence

(E) citing evidence that appears to confirm the skepticism of geologists regarding a view held prior to the 1980s

5. The passage supports which one of the following claims about the volcanic-eruption theory?

(A) It does not rely on assumptions concerning the temperature of molten rock at the lowest part of the Earth's mantle.

(B) It may explain what caused the gradual fall in sea level that occurred for hundreds of thousands of years prior to the more sudden disappearance of the dinosaurs.

(C) It bases its explanation on the occurrence of periods of increased volcanic activity similar to those shown to have caused earlier mass extinctions.

(D) It may explain the relative scarcity of iridium in rocks on the Earth's surface, compared to its abundance in meteorites.

(E) It accounts for the relatively uneven distribution of iridium in the layer of clay deposited at the end of the Cretaceous period.

6. The author implies that if the theory described in the third paragraph is true, which one of the following would have been true of iridium in the atmosphere at the end of the Cretaceous period?

(A) Its level of concentration in the Earth's atmosphere would have been high due to a slow but steady increase in the atmospheric iridium that began in the early Cretaceous period.

(B) Its concentration in the Earth's atmosphere would have increased due to the dramatic decrease in sea level that occurred during the Cretaceous period.

(C) It would have been directly responsible for the extinction of many ocean species.

(D) It would have been more uniformly dispersed than iridium whose source had been the impact of a meteorite on the Earth's surface.

(E) It would have been more uniformly dispersed than iridium released into the atmosphere as a result of normal geological processes that occur on Earth.

7. Which one of the following, if true, would cast the most doubt on the theory described in the last paragraph of the passage?

(A) Fragments of meteorites that have struck the Earth are examined and found to have only minuscule amounts of iridium hexafluoride trapped inside of them.

(B) Most diapir eruptions in the geological history of the Earth have been similar in size to the one that occurred in India at the end of the Cretaceous period and have not been succeeded by periods of climatic change.

(C) There have been several periods in the geological history of the Earth, before and after the Cretaceous period, during which large numbers of marine species have perished.

(D) The frequency with which meteorites struck the Earth was higher at the end of the Cretaceous period than at the beginning of the period.

(E) Marine species tend to be much more vulnerable to extinction when exposed to a dramatic and relatively sudden change in sea level than when they are exposed to a gradual change in sea level similar to the one that preceded the extinction of the dinosaurs.

HARD SCIENCE

Some meteorologists have insisted that the severity of the drought in sub-Saharan West Africa and its long duration (nearly 40 years to date) must be a sign of a long-term alteration in climate.
(5) Among the theories proposed to explain this change, one hypothesis that has gained widespread attention attributes the drought to a cooling of the Northern Hemisphere. This hypothesis is based on the fact that, between 1945 and the early 1970s, the
(10) average annual air temperatures over the landmasses of the Northern Hemisphere decreased by about half a degree Fahrenheit (approximately one quarter of a degree Celsius—a small but significant amount). Several meteorologists have
(15) suggested that this cooling was caused by an increase in atmospheric dust emanating from volcanic eruptions and from urban and industrial pollution; the dust reflected incoming sunlight, causing the ground to receive less solar radiation
(20) and to transfer less heat to the atmosphere. The cooling seemed to be more pronounced in the middle and high latitudes than in the tropics, an observation that is consistent with the fact that the Sun's rays enter the atmosphere at a greater angle
(25) farther north, and so have to pass through more dust-laden atmosphere on the way to the Earth.
Since winds are set in motion by differences in air pressure caused by unequal heating of the atmosphere, supporters of the cooling hypothesis
(30) have argued that a growing temperature differential between the unusually cool middle and high latitudes and the warm tropical latitudes is causing a southward expansion of the circumpolar vortex—the high-altitude westerly winds that circle
(35) the Northern Hemisphere at middle latitudes. According to this hypothesis, as the circumpolar vortex expands, it forces south other components of large-scale atmospheric circulation and, in effect, displaces the northward-moving monsoon that
(40) ordinarily brings sub-Saharan rain. Proponents have further argued that this change in atmospheric circulation might be long-term since cooling in the Northern Hemisphere could be perpetuated by increases in ice and snow coverage there, which
(45) would lead to reflection of more sunlight away from the Earth, to further cooling, and, indirectly, to further drought in sub-Saharan West Africa.
Despite these dire predictions, and even though the current African drought has lasted longer than
(50) any other in this century, the notion that the drought is caused by cooling of the Northern Hemisphere is, in fact, not well supported. Contrary to the predictions of the cooling hypothesis, during one period of rapid Northern Hemisphere cooling
(55) in the early 1950s, the sub-Sahara was unusually rainy. Moreover, in the early 1980s, when the drought was particularly severe, Northern Hemisphere lands actually warmed slightly. And

further doubt has been cast on the hypothesis by
(60) recent analyses suggesting that, when surface temperatures of water as well as land are taken into account, the Northern Hemisphere may not have cooled at all.

22. Which one of the following best expresses the main idea of the passage?

(A) There is strong evidence to support the theory that an increase in atmospheric dust has contributed to the severity of the drought in sub-Saharan West Africa.
(B) The suggestion that Northern Hemisphere cooling is contributing to a decline of rainfall in sub-Saharan West Africa is open to question.
(C) The expansion of the circumpolar vortex has caused a dramatic shift in the atmospheric circulation patterns above sub-Saharan West Africa.
(D) The drought in sub-Saharan West Africa represents a long-term, permanent alteration in global climate patterns.
(E) Meteorologists cannot determine when the drought in sub-Saharan West Africa is likely to end.

23. The author's attitude toward the cooling hypothesis is best described as one of

(A) vehement opposition
(B) cautious skepticism
(C) growing ambivalence
(D) guarded enthusiasm
(E) strong support

24. According to the passage, proponents of the cooling hypothesis suggested that the circumpolar vortex is likely to expand when which one of the following occurs?

(A) The average annual atmospheric temperature of the tropics is significantly higher than normal for an extended period of time.
(B) The average annual snowfall in the Northern Hemisphere is lower than normal for an extended period of time.
(C) The average annual surface temperature of Northern Hemisphere waters is higher than the average annual surface temperature of Northern Hemisphere landmasses.
(D) There is a significant increase in the difference between the average annual atmospheric temperature of the tropics and that of the more northern latitudes.
(E) There is a significant increase in the difference between the average annual atmospheric temperatures of the middle and the high latitudes in the Northern Hemisphere.

25. Which one of the following can be inferred from the passage about the average annual temperature of the air over Northern Hemisphere landmasses before 1945?

(A) It was higher than it was between 1945 and the early 1970s.

(B) It was lower than it was during the early 1980s.

(C) It was the same as it was between 1945 and the early 1970s.

(D) It was the same as the annual average surface temperature of Northern Hemisphere landmasses and bodies of water between 1945 and the early 1970s.

(E) It was higher than the annual average surface temperature of Northern Hemisphere landmasses and bodies of water between 1945 and the early 1970s.

26. Which one of the following best describes the organization of the passage?

(A) Opposing points of view are presented, evidence supporting each point of view is discussed, and then one point of view is developed into a formal hypothesis.

(B) A theory is discussed, and different points of view about the theory are discussed, supported, and then reconciled.

(C) A hypothesis is proposed, contradictory evidence is discussed, and then the hypothesis is amended.

(D) A theory explaining a phenomenon is proposed, supporting evidence is considered, and then the theory is disputed.

(E) A point of view is presented, a theory supporting the view is proposed, contradictory evidence is presented, and then a different theory is proposed.

27. A proponent of the cooling hypothesis would most likely argue that the return of the monsoon rains to sub-Saharan West Africa would indicate that which one of the following has also occurred?

(A) The amount of ice and snow coverage over the landmasses of the Northern Hemisphere has increased.

(B) The average annual temperature of the atmosphere over the middle and high latitudes of the Northern Hemisphere has decreased.

(C) The average annual temperature of the atmosphere over the tropics in the Northern Hemisphere has increased.

(D) Other components of large-scale atmospheric circulation, besides the circumpolar vortex, have expanded and moved southward.

(E) The atmospheric circulation pattern of the high-altitude westerly winds has resumed its normal pattern.

Passage #13: June 1996 Questions 15-20

When the same habitat types (forests, oceans, grasslands, etc.) in regions of different latitudes are compared, it becomes apparent that the overall number of species increases from pole to equator.
(5) This latitudinal gradient is probably even more pronounced than current records indicate, since researchers believe that most undiscovered species live in the tropics.
     One hypothesis to explain this phenomenon, the
(10) "time theory," holds that diverse species adapted to today's climatic conditions have had more time to emerge in the tropical regions, which, unlike the temperate and arctic zones, have been unaffected by a succession of ice ages. However, ice ages have
(15) caused less disruption in some temperate regions than in others and have not interrupted arctic conditions.
     Alternatively, the species-energy hypothesis proposes the following positive correlations:
(20) incoming energy from the Sun correlated with rates of growth and reproduction; rates of growth and reproduction with the amount of living matter (biomass) at a given moment; and the amount of biomass with number of species. However, since
(25) organisms may die rapidly, high production rates can exist with low biomass. And high biomass can exist with few species. Moreover, the mechanism proposed—greater energy influx leading to bigger populations, thereby lowering the probability of
(30) local extinction—remains untested.
     A third hypothesis centers on the tropics' climatic stability, which provides a more reliable supply of resources. Species can thus survive even with few types of food, and competing species can
(35) tolerate greater overlap between their respective niches. Both capabilities enable more species to exist on the same resources. However, the ecology of local communities cannot account for the origin of the latitudinal gradient. Localized ecological
(40) processes such as competition do not generate regional pools of species, and it is the total number of species available regionally for colonizing any particular area that makes the difference between, for example, a forest at the equator and one at a
(45) higher latitude.
     A fourth and most plausible hypothesis focuses on regional speciation, and in particular on rates of speciation and extinction. According to this hypothesis, if speciation rates become higher toward
(50) the tropics, and are not negated by extinction rates, then the latitudinal gradient would result—and become increasingly steep.
     The mechanism for this rate-of-speciation hypothesis is that most new animal species, and

(55) perhaps plant species, arise because a population subgroup becomes isolated. This subgroup evolves differently and eventually cannot interbreed with members of the original population. The uneven spread of a species over a large geographic area
(60) promotes this mechanism: at the edges, small populations spread out and form isolated groups. Since subgroups in an arctic environment are more likely to face extinction than those in the tropics, the latter are more likely to survive long enough to
(65) adapt to local conditions and ultimately become new species.

15. Which one of the following most accurately expresses the main idea of the passage?

(A) At present, no single hypothesis explaining the latitudinal gradient in numbers of species is more widely accepted than any other.
(B) The tropical climate is more conducive to promoting species diversity than are arctic or temperate climates.
(C) Several explanations have been suggested for global patterns in species distribution, but a hypothesis involving rates of speciation seems most promising.
(D) Despite their differences, the various hypotheses regarding a latitudinal gradient in species diversity concur in predicting that the gradient can be expected to increase.
(E) In distinguishing among the current hypotheses for distribution of species, the most important criterion is whether a hypothesis proposes a mechanism that can be tested and validated.

16. Which one of the following situations is most consistent with the species-energy hypothesis as described in the passage?

(A) The many plants in a large agricultural tract represent a limited range of species.
(B) An animal species experiences a death rate almost as rapid as its rate of growth and reproduction.
(C) Within the small number of living organisms in a desert habitat, many different species are represented.
(D) In a tropical rain forest, a species with a large population is found to exhibit instances of local extinction.
(E) In an arctic tundra, the plants and animals exhibit a slow rate of growth and reproduction.

17. As presented in the passage, the principles of the time theory most strongly support which one of the following predictions?

    (A)   In the absence of additional ice ages, the number of species at high latitudes could eventually increase significantly.

    (B)   No future ice ages are likely to change the climatic conditions that currently characterize temperate regions.

    (C)   If no further ice ages occur, climatic conditions at high latitudes might eventually resemble those at today's tropical latitudes.

    (D)   Researchers will continue to find many more new species in the tropics than in the arctic and temperate zones.

    (E)   Future ice ages are likely to interrupt the climatic conditions that now characterize high-latitude regions.

18. Which one of the following, if true, most clearly weakens the rate-of-speciation hypothesis as it is described in the passage?

    (A)   A remote subgroup of a tropical species is reunited with the original population and proves unable to interbreed with members of this original population.

    (B)   Investigation of a small area of a tropical rain forest reveals that many competing species are able to coexist on the same range of resources.

    (C)   A correlation between higher energy influx, larger populations, and lower probability of local extinction is definitively established.

    (D)   Researchers find more undiscovered species during an investigation of an arctic region than they had anticipated.

    (E)   Most of the isolated subgroups of mammalian life within a tropical zone are found to experience rapid extinction.

19. Which one of the following inferences about the biological characteristics of a temperate-zone grassland is most strongly supported by the passage?

    (A)   It has more different species than does a tropical-zone forest.

    (B)   Its climatic conditions have been severely interrupted in the past by a succession of ice ages.

    (C)   If it has a large amount of biomass, it also has a large number of different species.

    (D)   It has a larger regional pool of species than does an arctic grassland.

    (E)   If population groups become isolated at its edges, they are likely to adapt to local conditions and become new species.

20. With which one of the following statements concerning possible explanations for the latitudinal gradient in number of species would the author be most likely to agree?

    (A)   The time theory is the least plausible of proposed hypotheses, since it does not correctly assess the impact of ice ages upon tropical conditions.

    (B)   The rate-of-speciation hypothesis addresses a principal objection to the climatic-stability hypothesis.

    (C)   The major objection to the time theory is that it does not accurately reflect the degree to which the latitudinal gradient exists, especially when undiscovered species are taken into account.

    (D)   Despite the claims of the species-energy hypothesis, a high rate of biological growth and reproduction is more likely to exist with low biomass than with high biomass.

    (E)   An important advantage of the rate-of-speciation theory is that it considers species competition in a regional rather than local context.

Many birds that form flocks compete through aggressive interaction for priority of access to resources such as food and shelter. The result of repeated interactions between flock members is that
(5) each bird gains a particular social status related to its fighting ability, with priority of access to resources increasing with higher status. As the number and intensity of interactions between birds increase, however, so increase the costs to each bird in terms of
(10) energy expenditure, time, and risk of injury. Thus, birds possessing attributes that reduce the number of costly interactions in which they must be involved, without leading to a reduction in status, are at an advantage. An external signal, such as a plumage type,
(15) announcing fighting ability and thereby obviating the actual need to fight, could be one such attribute.

The zoologist Rohwer asserted that plumage variations in "Harris sparrows" support the status signaling hypothesis (SSH). He reported that almost
(20) without exception birds with darker throats win conflicts with individuals having lighter plumage. He claimed that even among birds of the same age and sex the amount of dark plumage predicts relative dominance status.

(25) However, Rohwer's data do not support his assertions: in one of his studies darker birds won only 57 out of 75 conflicts; within another, focusing on conflicts between birds of the same age group or sex, darker birds won 63 and lost 62. There are indications
(30) that plumage probably does signal broad age-related differences in status among Harris sparrows: adults, usually dark throated, have higher status than juveniles, who are usually light throated; moreover, juveniles dyed to resemble adults are dominant over undyed
(35) juveniles. However, the Harris sparrows' age-related plumage differences do not signal the status of *individual* birds within an age class, and thus cannot properly be included under the term "status signaling."

(40) The best evidence for status signaling is from the greater titmouse. Experiments show a strong correlation between the width of the black breast plumage stripe and status as measured by success in aggressive interactions. An analysis of factors likely to be associated with breast-stripe width (sex, age, wing
(45) length, body weight) has demonstrated social status to be the only variable that correlates with stripe width when the other variables are held constant.

An ingenious experiment provided further evidence for status signaling in the greater titmouse. One of
(50) three stuffed titmouse dummies was mounted on a feeding tray. When a live bird approached, the dummy was fumed by radio control to face the bird and present its breast stripe in "display." When presented with a dummy having a narrower breast stripe than their own,
(55) birds approached closely and behaved aggressively.

However, when presented with a dummy having a broader breast stripe than their own, live birds acted submissive and did not approach.

15. According to the passage, the status signaling hypothesis holds that the ability to display a recognizable external signal would have the effect on an individual bird of

(A) enabling it to attract a mate of high status
(B) allowing it to avoid costly aggressive interactions
(C) decreasing its access to limited resources
(D) making it less attractive to predatory species
(E) increasing its fighting ability

16. The author refers to the fact that adult Harris sparrows are usually dark throated (lines 31-32), in order to do which one of the following?

(A) support the conclusion that plumage variation among Harris sparrows probably does not signal individual status
(B) argue that plumage variation among Harris sparrows helps to confirm the status signaling hypothesis
(C) indicate that in light of plumage variation patterns among Harris sparrows, the status signaling hypothesis should probably be modified
(D) demonstrate that Harris sparrows are the most appropriate subjects for the study of status signaling among birds
(E) suggest that the signaling of age-related differences in status is widespread among birds that form flocks

17. Which one of the following, if true, would most seriously undermine the validity of the results of the experiment discussed in the last paragraph?

    (A) The live birds all came from different titmouse flocks.

    (B) The physical characteristics of the stuffed dummies varied in ways other than just breaststripe width.

    (C) No live juvenile birds were included in the experiment.

    (D) The food placed in the feeding tray was not the kind of food normally eaten by titmice in the wild.

    (E) Even the live birds that acted aggressively did not actually physically attack the stuffed dummies.

18. Which one of the following best describes the organization of the passage?

    (A) A hypothesis is introduced and studies relevant to the hypothesis are discussed and evaluated.

    (B) A natural phenomenon is presented and several explanations for the phenomenon are examined in detail.

    (C) Behavior is described, possible underlying causes for the behavior are reported, and the likelihood of each cause is assessed.

    (D) A scientific conundrum is explained and the history of the issue is recounted.

    (E) A scientific theory is outlined and opinions for and against its validity as well as experiments supporting each side are compared.

19. According to the passage, which one of the following is true of Rohwer's relationship to the status signaling hypothesis (SSH)?

    (A) Although his research was designed to test the SSH, his data proved to be more relevant to other issues.

    (B) He set out to confirm the SSH, but ended up revising it.

    (C) He set out to disprove the SSH, but ended up accepting it.

    (D) He altered the SSH by expanding it to encompass various types of signals.

    (E) He advocated the SSH, but his research data failed to confirm it.

20. The passage suggests that among birds that form flocks, a bird of high status is most likely to have which one of the following?

    (A) dark throat plumage
    (B) greater-than-average body weight
    (C) offspring of high status
    (D) strong fighting ability
    (E) frequent injuries

21. Which one of the following can be inferred about Harris sparrows from the passage?

    (A) Among Harris sparrows, plumage differences signal individual status only within age groups.

    (B) Among Harris sparrows, adults have priority of access to food over juveniles.

    (C) Among Harris sparrows, juveniles with relatively dark plumage have status equal to that of adults with relatively light plumage.

    (D) juvenile Harris sparrows engage in aggressive interaction more frequently than do adult Harris sparrows.

    (E) Harris sparrows engage in aggressive interaction less frequently than do greater titmice.

SCIENCE

Chapter Nine: Humanities

Humanities Passages

Outside the medical profession, there are various efforts to cut medicine down to size: not only widespread malpractice litigation and massive governmental regulation, but also attempts by
(5) consumer groups and others to redefine medicine as a trade rather than as a profession, and the physician as merely a technician for hire under contract. Why should physicians (or indeed all sensible people) resist such efforts to give the
(10) practice of medicine a new meaning? We can gain some illumination from etymology. "Trade," from Germanic and Anglo-Saxon roots meaning "a course or pathway," has come to mean derivatively a habitual occupation and has been related to certain
(15) skills and crafts. On the other hand, while "profession" today also entails a habit of work, the word "profession" itself traces to an act of self-conscious and public—even confessional—speech. "To profess" preserves the meaning of its Latin
(20) source, "to declare publicly; to announce, affirm, avow." A profession is an activity or occupation to which its practitioner publicly professes, that is, confesses, devotion. But public announcement seems insufficient; publicly declaring devotion
(25) to plumbing or auto repair would not turn these trades into professions.

Some believe that learning and knowledge are the diagnostic signs of a profession. For reasons probably linked to the medieval university, the term
(30) "profession" has been applied to the so-called learned professions—medicine, law, and theology— the practices of which are founded upon inquiry and knowledge rather than mere "know-how." Yet it is not only the pursuit and acquisition of knowledge
(35) that makes one a professional. The knowledge involved makes the profession one of the learned variety, but its professional quality is rooted in something else.

Some mistakenly seek to locate that something
(40) else in the prestige and honor accorded professionals by society, evidenced in their special titles and the special deference and privileges they receive. But externalities do not constitute medicine a profession. Physicians are not professionals
(45) because they are honored; rather, they are honored because of their profession. Their titles and the respect they are shown superficially signify and acknowledge something deeper, that physicians are persons of the professional sort, knowingly and
(50) freely devoting themselves to a way of life worthy of such devotion. Just as lawyers devote themselves to rectifying injustices, looking up to what is lawful and right; just as teachers devote themselves to the education of the young, looking up to truth and
(55) wisdom; so physicians heal the sick, looking up to

health and wholesomeness. Being a professional is thus rooted in our moral nature and in that which warrants and impels making a public confession to a way of life.
(60) Professing oneself a professional is an ethical act because it is not a silent and private act, but an articulated and public one; because it promises continuing devotion to a way of life, not merely announces a present preference or a way to a
(65) livelihood; because it is an activity in service to some high good that insists on devotion; because it is difficult and demanding. A profession engages one's character and heart, not merely one's mind and hands.

22. According to the author, which one of the following is required in order that one be a professional?

(A) significant prestige and a title
(B) "know-how" in a particular field
(C) a long and difficult educational endeavor
(D) a commitment to political justice
(E) a public confession of devotion to a way of life

23. Which one of the following best expresses the main point made by the author in the passage?

(A) Medicine is defined as a profession because of the etymology of the word "profession."
(B) It is a mistake to pay special honor to the knowledge and skills of physicians.
(C) The work of physicians is under attack only because it is widely misunderstood.
(D) The correct reason that physicians are professionals is that their work involves public commitment to a high good.
(E) Physicians have been encouraged to think of themselves as technicians and need to reorient themselves toward ethical concerns.

24. The question posed by the author in lines 8-10 of the passage introduces which one of the following?

(A) the author's belief that it is futile to resist the trend toward defining the physician's work as a trade
(B) the author's dislike of governmental regulation and consumer advocacy
(C) the author's inquiry into the nature of the practice of medicine
(D) the author's suggestions for rallying sensible people to a concentrated defense of physicians
(E) the author's fascination with the origins of words

25. In the passage, the author mentions or suggests all of the following EXCEPT

(A) how society generally treats physicians
(B) that the practice of medicine is analogous to teaching
(C) that being a professional is in part a public act
(D) the specific knowledge on which trades are based
(E) how a livelihood is different from a profession

26. The author's attitude toward professionals is best described as

(A) eager that the work of one group of professionals, physicians, be viewed from a new perspective
(B) sympathetic toward professionals who have become demoralized by public opinion
(C) surprised that professionals have been balked by governmental regulations and threats of litigation
(D) dismayed that most professionals have come to be considered technicians
(E) certain that professionals confess a commitment to ethical ideals

27. Based on the information in the passage, it can be inferred that which one of the following would most logically begin a paragraph immediately following the passage?

(A) A skilled handicraft is a manual art acquired by habituation that enables tradespeople to tread regularly and reliably along the same path.
(B) Critics might argue that being a doctor, for example, requires no ethical or public act; thus medicine, as such, is morally neutral, does not bind character, and can be used for good or ill.
(C) Sometimes the pursuit of personal health competes with the pursuit of other goods, and it has always been the task of the community to order and define competing ends.
(D) Not least among the myriad confusions and uncertainties of our time are those attending efforts to discern and articulate the essential characteristics of the medical profession.
(E) When, in contrast, we come to physicians of the whole body, we come tacitly acknowledging the meaning of illness and its potential threat to all that we hold dear.

28. Which one of the following best describes the author's purpose in lines 19-44 of the passage?

(A) The author locates the "something else" that truly constitutes a profession.
(B) The author dismisses efforts to redefine the meaning of the term "profession."
(C) The author considers, and largely criticizes, several definitions of what constitutes a profession.
(D) The author clarifies the meaning of the term "profession" by advocating a return to its linguistic and historical roots.
(E) The author distinguishes trades such as plumbing and auto repair from professions such as medicine, law, and theology.

In recent years the early music movement, which advocates performing a work as it was performed at the time of its composition, has taken on the character of a crusade, particularly as it has moved
(5) beyond the sphere of medieval and baroque music and into music from the late eighteenth and early nineteenth centuries by composers such as Mozart and Beethoven. Granted, knowledge about the experience of playing old music on now-obsolete
(10) instruments has been of inestimable value to scholars. Nevertheless, the early music approach to performance raises profound and troubling questions.

Early music advocates assume that composers
(15) write only for the instruments available to them, but evidence suggests that composers of Beethoven's stature imagined extraordinarily high and low notes as part of their compositions, even when they recognized that such notes could not be played on
(20) instruments available at the time. In the score of Beethoven's first piano concerto, there is a "wrong" note, a high F-natural where the melody obviously calls for a high F-sharp, but pianos did not have this high an F-sharp when Beethoven composed
(25) the concerto. Because Beethoven once expressed a desire to revise his early works to exploit the extended range of pianos that became available to him some years later, it seems likely that he would have played the F-sharp if given the opportunity.
(30) To use a piano exactly contemporary with the work's composition would require playing a note that was probably frustrating for Beethoven himself to have had to play.

In addition, early music advocates often
(35) inadvertently divorce music and its performance from the life of which they were, and are, a part. The discovery that Haydn's and Mozart's symphonies were conducted during their lifetimes by a pianist who played the chords to keep the
(40) orchestra together has given rise to early music recordings in which a piano can be heard obtrusively in the foreground, despite evidence indicating that the orchestral piano was virtually inaudible to audiences at eighteenth-century
(45) concerts and was dropped as musically unnecessary when a better way to beat time was found. And although in the early nineteenth century the first three movements (sections) of Mozart's and Beethoven's symphonies were often played faster,
(50) and the last movement slower, than today, this difference can readily be explained by the fact that at that time audiences applauded at the end of each movement, rather than withholding applause until the end of the entire work. As a result, musicians
(55) were not forced into extra brilliance in the finale in order to generate applause, as they are now. To restore the original tempo of these symphonies represents an irrational denial of the fact that our concepts of musical intensity and excitement have,
(60) quite simply, changed.

13. It can be inferred from the passage that by "a piano exactly contemporary" (line 30) with the composition of Beethoven's first piano concerto, the author means the kind of piano that was

(A) designed to be inaudible to the audience when used by conductors of orchestras
(B) incapable of playing the high F-natural that is in the score of Beethoven's original version of the concerto
(C) unavailable to Mozart and Haydn
(D) incapable of playing the high F-sharp that the melody of the concerto calls for
(E) influential in Beethoven's decision to revise his early compositions

14. Which one of the following best expresses the main idea of the passage?

(A) The early music movement has yet to resolve a number of troubling questions regarding its approach to the performance of music.
(B) The early music movement, while largely successful in its approach to the performance of medieval and baroque music, has yet to justify its use of obsolete instruments in the performance of music by Beethoven and Mozart.
(C) The early music approach to performance often assumes that composers write music that is perfectly tailored to the limitations of the instruments on which it will be performed during their lifetimes.
(D) Although advocates of early music know much about the instruments used to perform music at the time it was composed, they lack information regarding how the style of such performances has changed since such music was written.
(E) The early music movement has not yet fully exploited the knowledge that it has gained from playing music on instruments available at the time such music was composed.

15. In the second paragraph, the author discusses Beethoven's first piano concerto primarily in order to

(A) illustrate how piano music began to change in response to the extended range of pianos that became available during Beethoven's lifetime
(B) illustrate how Beethoven's work failed to anticipate the changes in the design of instruments that were about to be made during his lifetime
(C) suggest that early music advocates commonly perform music using scores that do not reflect revisions made to the music years after it was originally composed
(D) illustrate how composers like Beethoven sometimes composed music that called for notes that could not be played on instruments that were currently available
(E) provide an example of a piano composition that is especially amenable to being played on pianos available at the time the music was composed

16. The author suggests that the final movements of symphonies by Mozart and Beethoven might be played more slowly by today's orchestras if which one of the following were to occur?

(A) orchestras were to use instruments no more advanced in design than those used by orchestras at the time Mozart and Beethoven composed their symphonies

(B) audiences were to return to the custom of applauding at the end of each movement of a symphony

(C) audiences were to reserve their most enthusiastic applause for the most brilliantly played finales

(D) conductors were to return to the practice of playing the chords on an orchestral piano to keep the orchestra together

(E) conductors were to conduct the symphonies in the manner in which Beethoven and Mozart had conducted them

17. Which one of the following best describes the organization of the last paragraph?

(A) A generalization is made, evidence undermining it is presented, and a conclusion rejecting it is then drawn.

(B) A criticism is stated and then elaborated with two supporting examples.

(C) An assumption is identified and then evidence undermining its validity is presented.

(D) An assertion is made and evidence frequently provided in support of it is then critically evaluated.

(E) Two specific cases are presented and then a conclusion regarding their significance is drawn.

18. It can be inferred from the passage that the author's explanation in lines 50-54 would be most weakened if which one of the following were true?

(A) Musicians who perform in modern orchestras generally receive more extensive training than did their nineteenth-century counter-parts.

(B) Breaks between the movements of symphonies performed during the early nineteenth century often lasted longer than they do today because nineteenth-century musicians needed to retune their instruments between each movement.

(C) Early nineteenth-century orchestral musicians were generally as concerned with the audience's response to their music as are the musicians who perform today in modern orchestras.

(D) Early nineteenth-century audiences applauded only perfunctorily after the first three movements of symphonies and conventionally withheld their most enthusiastic applause until the final movement was completed.

(E) Early nineteenth-century audiences were generally more knowledgeable about music than are their modern counterparts.

19. It can be inferred from the passage that the author would be most likely to agree with which one of the following assertions regarding the early music recordings mentioned in the third paragraph?

(A) These recordings fail to recognize that the last movements of Haydn's and Mozart's symphonies were often played slower in the eighteenth century than they are played today.

(B) These recordings betray the influence of baroque musical styles on those early music advocates who have recently turned their attention to the music of Haydn and Mozart.

(C) By making audible the sound of an orchestral piano that was inaudible in eighteenth-century performances, these recordings attempt to achieve aesthetic integrity at the expense of historical authenticity.

(D) By making audible the sound of an orchestral piano that was inaudible in eighteenth-century performances, these recordings unwittingly create music that is unlike what eighteenth-century audiences heard.

(E) These recordings suggest that at least some advocates of early music recognize that concepts of musical intensity and excitement have changed since Haydn and Mozart composed their symphonies.

20. The author suggests that the modern audience's tendency to withhold applause until the end of a symphony's performance is primarily related to which one of the following?

(A) the replacement of the orchestral piano as a method of keeping the orchestra together

(B) a gradual increase since the time of Mozart and Beethoven in audiences' expectations regarding the ability of orchestral musicians

(C) a change since the early nineteenth century in audiences' concepts of musical excitement and intensity

(D) a more sophisticated appreciation of the structural integrity of the symphony as a piece of music

(E) the tendency of orchestral musicians to employ their most brilliant effects in the early movements of symphonies composed by Mozart and Beethoven

Critics have long been puzzled by the inner contradictions of major characters in John Webster's tragedies. In his *The Duchess of Malfi,* for instance, the Duchess is "good" in
(5) demonstrating the obvious tenderness and sincerity of her love for Antonio, but "bad" in ignoring the wishes and welfare of her family and in making religion a "cloak" hiding worldly self-indulgence. Bosola is "bad" in serving
(10) Ferdinand, "good" in turning the Duchess' thoughts toward heaven and in planning to avenge her murder. The ancient Greek philosopher Aristotle implied that such contradictions are virtually essential to the tragic personality, and yet critics
(15) keep coming back to this element of inconsistency as though it were an eccentric feature of Webster's own tragic vision.

The problem is that, as an Elizabethan playwright, Webster has become a prisoner of our
(20) critical presuppositions. We have, in recent years, been dazzled by the way the earlier Renaissance and medieval theater, particularly the morality play, illuminates Elizabethan drama. We now understand how the habit of mind that saw the world as a
(25) battleground between good and evil produced the morality play. Morality plays allegorized that conflict by presenting characters whose actions were defined as the embodiment of good or evil. This model of reality lived on, overlaid by different
(30) conventions, in the more sophisticated Elizabethan works of the following age. Yet Webster seems not to have been as heavily influenced by the morality play's model of reality as were his Elizabethan contemporaries; he was apparently more sensitive
(35) to the more morally complicated Italian drama than to these English sources. Consequently, his characters cannot be evaluated according to reductive formulas of good and evil, which is precisely what modern critics have tried to do. They
(40) choose what seem to be the most promising of the contradictory values that are dramatized in the play, and treat those values as if they were the only basis for analyzing the moral development of the play's major characters, attributing the
(45) inconsistencies in a character's behavior to artistic incompetence on Webster's part. The lack of consistency in Webster's characters can be better understood if we recognize that the ambiguity at the heart of his tragic vision lies not in the external
(50) world but in the duality of human nature. Webster establishes tension in his plays by setting up conflicting systems of value that appear immoral only when one value system is viewed exclusively from the perspective of the other. He presents us not
(55) only with characters that we condemn intellectually or ethically and at the same time impulsively approve of, but also with judgments we must accept as logically sound and yet find

emotionally repulsive. The dilemma is not only
(60) dramatic: it is tragic, because the conflict is irreconcilable, and because it is ours as much as that of the character.

8. The primary purpose of the passage is to

(A) clarify an ambiguous assertion
(B) provide evidence in support of a commonly held view
(C) analyze an unresolved question and propose an answer
(D) offer an alternative to a flawed interpretation
(E) describe and categorize opposing viewpoints

9. The author suggests which one of the following about the dramatic works that most influenced Webster's tragedies?

(A) They were not concerned with dramatizing the conflict between good and evil that was presented in morality plays.
(B) They were not as sophisticated as the Italian sources from which other Elizabethan tragedies were derived.
(C) They have never been adequately understood by critics.
(D) They have only recently been used to illuminate the conventions of Elizabethan drama.
(E) They have been considered by many critics to be the reason for Webster's apparent artistic incompetence.

10. The author's allusion to Aristotle's view of tragedy in lines 11-13 serves which one of the following functions in the passage?

(A) It introduces a commonly held view of Webster's tragedies that the author plans to defend.
(B) It supports the author's suggestion that Webster's conception of tragedy is not idiosyncratic.
(C) It provides an example of an approach to Webster's tragedies that the author criticizes.
(D) It establishes the similarity between classical and modern approaches to tragedy.
(E) It supports the author's assertion that Elizabethan tragedy cannot be fully understood without the help of recent scholarship.

11. It can be inferred from the passage that modern critics' interpretations of Webster's tragedies would be more valid if

(A)   the ambiguity inherent in Webster's tragic vision resulted from the duality of human nature
(B)   Webster's conception of the tragic personality were similar to that of Aristotle
(C)   Webster had been heavily influenced by the morality play
(D)   Elizabethan dramatists had been more sensitive to Italian sources of influence
(E)   the inner conflicts exhibited by Webster's characters were similar to those of modern audiences

12. With which one of the following statements regarding Elizabethan drama would the author be most likely to agree?

(A)   The skill of Elizabethan dramatists has in recent years been overestimated.
(B)   The conventions that shaped Elizabethan drama are best exemplified by Webster's drama.
(C)   Elizabethan drama, for the most part, can be viewed as being heavily influenced by the morality play.
(D)   Only by carefully examining the work of his Elizabethan contemporaries can Webster's achievement as a dramatist be accurately measured.
(E)   Elizabethan drama can best be described as influenced by a composite of Italian and classical sources.

13. It can be inferred from the passage that most modern critics assume which one of the following in their interpretation of Webster's tragedies?

(A)   Webster's plays tended to allegorize the conflict between good and evil more than did those of his contemporaries.
(B)   Webster's plays were derived more from Italian than from English sources.
(C)   The artistic flaws in Webster's tragedies were largely the result of his ignorance of the classical definition of tragedy.
(D)   Webster's tragedies provide no relevant basis for analyzing the moral development of their characters.
(E)   In writing his tragedies, Webster was influenced by the same sources as his contemporaries.

14. The author implies that Webster's conception of tragedy was

(A)   artistically flawed
(B)   highly conventional
(C)   largely derived from the morality play
(D)   somewhat different from the conventional Elizabethan conception of tragedy
(E)   uninfluenced by the classical conception of tragedy

Many argue that recent developments in electronic technology such as computers and videotape have enabled artists to vary their forms of expression. For example, video art can now achieve
(5) images whose effect is produced by "digitalization": breaking up the picture using computerized information processing. Such new technologies create new ways of seeing and hearing by adding different dimensions to older forms, rather than
(10) replacing those forms. Consider *Locale,* a film about a modern dance company. The camera operator wore a Steadicam™, an uncomplicated device that allows a camera to be mounted on a person so that the camera remains steady no matter
(15) how the operator moves. The Steadicam™ captures the dance in ways impossible with traditional mounts. Such new equipment also allows for the preservation of previously unrecordable aspects of performances, thus enriching archives.
(20) By contrast, others claim that technology subverts the artistic enterprise: that artistic efforts achieved with machines preempt human creativity, rather than being inspired by it. The originality of musical performance, for example, might suffer, as
(25) musicians would be deprived of the opportunity to spontaneously change pieces of music before live audiences. Some even worry that technology will eliminate live performance altogether; performances will be recorded for home viewing, abolishing the
(30) relationship between performer and audience. But these negative views assume both that technology poses an unprecedented challenge to the arts and that we are not committed enough to the artistic enterprise to preserve the live performance,
(35) assumptions that seem unnecessarily cynical. In fact, technology has traditionally assisted our capacity for creative expression and can refine our notions of any given art form.
For example, the portable camera and the
(40) snapshot were developed at the same time as the rise of Impressionist painting in the nineteenth century. These photographic technologies encouraged a new appreciation for the chance view and unpredictable angle, thus preparing an
(45) audience for a new style of painting. In addition, Impressionist artists like Degas studied the elements of light and movement captured by instantaneous photography and used their new understanding of the way our perceptions distort reality to try to
(50) more accurately capture reality in their work. Since photos can capture the "moments" of a movement, such as a hand partially raised in a gesture of greeting, Impressionist artists were inspired to paint such moments in order to more effectively convey
(55) the quality of spontaneous human action.

Photography freed artists from the preconception that a subject should be painted in a static, artificial entirety, and inspired them to capture the random and fragmentary qualities of our world. Finally,
(60) since photography preempted painting as the means of obtaining portraits, painters had more freedom to vary their subject matter, thus giving rise to the abstract creations characteristic of modern art.

1. Which one of the following statements best expresses the main idea of the passage?

    (A) The progress of art relies primarily on technology.
    (B) Technological innovation can be beneficial to art.
    (C) There are risks associated with using technology to create art.
    (D) Technology will transform the way the public responds to art.
    (E) The relationship between art and technology has a lengthy history.

2. It can be inferred from the passage that the author shares which one of the following opinions with the opponents of the use of new technology in art?

    (A) The live performance is an important aspect of the artistic enterprise.
    (B) The public's commitment to the artistic enterprise is questionable.
    (C) Recent technological innovations present an entirely new sort of challenge to art.
    (D) Technological innovations of the past have been very useful to artists.
    (E) The performing arts are especially vulnerable to technological innovation.

3. Which one of the following, if true, would most undermine the position held by opponents of the use of new technology in art concerning the effect of technology on live performance?

(A) Surveys show that when recordings of performances are made available for home viewing, the public becomes far more knowledgeable about different performing artists.

(B) Surveys show that some people feel comfortable responding spontaneously to artistic performances when they are viewing recordings of those performances at home.

(C) After a live performance, sales of recordings for home viewing of the particular performing artist generally increase.

(D) The distribution of recordings of artists' performances has begun to attract many new audience members to their live performances.

(E) Musicians are less apt to make creative changes in musical pieces during recorded performances than during live performances.

4. The author uses the example of the Steadicam™ primarily in order to suggest that

(A) the filming of performances should not be limited by inadequate equipment

(B) new technologies do not need to be very complex in order to benefit art

(C) the interaction of a traditional art form with a new technology will change attitudes toward technology in general

(D) the replacement of a traditional technology with a new technology will transform definitions of a traditional art form

(E) new technology does not so much preempt as enhance a traditional art form

5. According to the passage, proponents of the use of new electronic technology in the arts claim that which one of the following is true?

(A) Most people who reject the use of electronic technology in art forget that machines require a person to operate them.

(B) Electronic technology allows for the expansion of archives because longer performances can be recorded.

(C) Electronic technology assists artists in finding new ways to present their material.

(D) Electronic technology makes the practice of any art form more efficient by speeding up the creative process.

(E) Modern dance is the art form that will probably benefit most from the use of electronic technology.

6. It can be inferred from the passage that the author would agree with which one of the following statements regarding changes in painting since the nineteenth century?

(A) The artistic experiments of the nineteenth century led painters to use a variety of methods in creating portraits, which they then applied to other subject matter.

(B) The nineteenth-century knowledge of light and movement provided by photography inspired the abstract works characteristic of modern art.

(C) Once painters no longer felt that they had to paint conventional portraits, they turned exclusively to abstract portraiture.

(D) Once painters were less limited to the Impressionist style, they were able to experiment with a variety of styles of abstract art.

(E) Once painters painted fewer conventional portraits, they had greater opportunity to move beyond the literal depiction of objects.

Direct observation of contemporary societies at the threshold of widespread literacy has not assisted our understanding of how such literacy altered ancient Greek society, in particular its political
(5) culture. The discovery of what Goody has called the "enabling effects" of literacy in contemporary societies tends to seduce the observer into confusing often rudimentary knowledge of how to read with popular access to important books and documents;
(10) this confusion is then projected onto ancient societies. "In ancient Greece," Goody writes, "alphabetic reading and writing was important for the development of political democracy."

An examination of the ancient Greek city
(15) Athens exemplifies how this sort of confusion is detrimental to understanding ancient politics. In Athens, the early development of a written law code was retrospectively mythologized as the critical factor in breaking the power monopoly of the old
(20) aristocracy: hence the Greek tradition of the "law-giver," which has captured the imaginations of scholars like Goody. But the application and efficacy of all law codes depend on their interpretation by magistrates and courts, and unless
(25) the right of interpretation is "democratized," the mere existence of written laws changes little. In fact, never in antiquity did any but the elite consult documents and books. Even in Greek courts the juries heard only the relevant statutes read out
(30) during the proceedings, as they heard verbal testimony, and they then rendered their verdict on the spot, without the benefit of any discussion among themselves. True, in Athens the juries were representative of a broad spectrum of the
(35) population, and these juries, drawn from diverse social classes, both interpreted what they had heard and determined matters of fact. However, they were guided solely by the speeches prepared for the parties by professional pleaders and by the
(40) quotations of laws or decrees within the speeches, rather than by their own access to any kind of document or book.

Granted, people today also rely heavily on a truly knowledgeable minority for information and
(45) its interpretation, often transmitted orally. Yet this is still fundamentally different from an ancient society in which there was no "popular literature," i.e., no newspapers, magazines, or other media that dealt with sociopolitical issues. An ancient law code
(50) would have been analogous to the Latin Bible, a venerated document but a closed book. The resistance of the medieval Church to vernacular translations of the Bible, in the West at least, is therefore a pointer to the realities of ancient

(55) literacy. When fundamental documents are accessible for study only to an elite, the rest of the society is subject to the elite's interpretation of the rules of behavior, including right political behavior. Athens, insofar as it functioned as a democracy, did
(60) not because of widespread literacy, but because the elite had chosen to accept democratic institutions.

14. Which one of the following statements best expresses the main idea of the passage?

(A) Democratic political institutions grow organically from the traditions and conventions of a society.

(B) Democratic political institutions are not necessarily the outcome of literacy in a society.

(C) Religious authority, like political authority, can determine who in a given society will have access to important books and documents.

(D) Those who are best educated are most often those who control the institutions of authority in a society.

(E) Those in authority have a vested interest in ensuring that those under their control remain illiterate.

15. It can be inferred from the passage that the author assumes which one of the following about societies in which the people possess a rudimentary reading ability?

(A) They are more politically advanced than societies without rudimentary reading ability.

(B) They are unlikely to exhibit the positive effects of literacy.

(C) They are rapidly evolving toward widespread literacy.

(D) Many of their people might not have access to important documents and books.

(E) Most of their people would not participate in political decision-making.

16. The author refers to the truly knowledgeable minority in contemporary societies in the context of the fourth paragraph in order to imply which one of the following?

(A) Because they have a popular literature that closes the gap between the elite and the majority, contemporary societies rely far less on the knowledge of experts than did ancient societies.

(B) Contemporary societies rely on the knowledge of experts, as did ancient societies, because contemporary popular literature so frequently conveys specious information.

(C) Although contemporary societies rely heavily on the knowledge of experts, access to popular literature makes contemporary societies less dependent on experts for information about rules of behavior than were ancient societies.

(D) While only some members of the elite can become experts, popular literature gives the majority in contemporary society an opportunity to become members of such an elite.

(E) Access to popular literature distinguishes ancient from contemporary societies because it relies on a level of educational achievement attainable only by a contemporary elite.

17. According to the passage, each of the following statements concerning ancient Greek juries is true EXCEPT:

(A) They were somewhat democratic insofar as they were composed largely of people from the lowest social classes.

(B) They were exposed to the law only insofar as they heard relevant statutes read out during legal proceedings.

(C) They ascertained the facts of a case and interpreted the laws.

(D) They did not have direct access to important books and documents that were available to the elite.

(E) They rendered verdicts without benefit of private discussion among themselves.

18. The author characterizes the Greek tradition of the "law-giver" (line 21) as an effect of mythologizing most probably in order to

(A) illustrate the ancient Greek tendency to memorialize historical events by transforming them into myths

(B) convey the historical importance of the development of the early Athenian written law code

(C) convey the high regard in which the Athenians held their legal tradition

(D) suggest that the development of a written law code was not primarily responsible for diminishing the power of the Athenian aristocracy

(E) suggest that the Greek tradition of the "law-giver" should be understood in the larger context of Greek mythology

19. The author draws an analogy between the Latin Bible and an early law code (lines 49-51) in order to make which one of the following points?

(A) Documents were considered authoritative in premodern society in proportion to their inaccessibility to the majority.

(B) Documents that were perceived as highly influential in premodern societies were not necessarily accessible to the society's majority.

(C) What is most revered in a nondemocratic society is what is most frequently misunderstood.

(D) Political documents in premodern societies exerted a social influence similar to that exerted by religious documents.

(E) Political documents in premodern societies were inaccessible to the majority of the population because of the language in which they were written.

20. The primary purpose of the passage is to

(A) argue that a particular method of observing contemporary societies is inconsistent

(B) point out the weaknesses in a particular approach to understanding ancient societies

(C) present the disadvantages of a particular approach to understanding the relationship between ancient and contemporary societies

(D) examine the importance of developing an appropriate method for understanding ancient societies

(E) convey the difficulty of accurately understanding attitudes in ancient societies

The English who in the seventeenth and eighteenth centuries inhabited those colonies that would later become the United States shared a common political vocabulary with the English in
(5) England. Steeped as they were in the English political language, these colonials failed to observe that their experience in America had given the words a significance quite different from that accepted by the English with whom they debated;
(10) in fact, they claimed that they were more loyal to the English political tradition than were the English in England.

In many respects the political institutions of England were reproduced in these American
(15) colonies. By the middle of the eighteenth century, all of these colonies except four were headed by Royal Governors appointed by the King and perceived as bearing a relation to the people of the colony similar to that of the King to the English
(20) people. Moreover, each of these colonies enjoyed a representative assembly, which was consciously modeled, in powers and practices, after the English Parliament. In both England and these colonies, only property holders could vote.
(25) Nevertheless, though English and colonial institutions were structurally similar, attitudes toward those institutions differed. For example, English legal development from the early seventeenth century had been moving steadily
(30) toward the absolute power of Parliament. The most unmistakable sign of this tendency was the legal assertion that the King was subject to the law. Together with this resolute denial of the absolute right of kings went the assertion that Parliament
(35) was unlimited in its power: it could change even the Constitution by its ordinary acts of legislation. By the eighteenth century the English had accepted the idea that the parliamentary representatives of the people were omnipotent.
(40) The citizens of these colonies did not look upon the English Parliament with such fond eyes, nor did they concede that their own assemblies possessed such wide powers. There were good historical reasons for this. To the English the word
(45) "constitution" meant the whole body of law and legal custom formulated since the beginning of the kingdom, whereas to these colonials a constitution was a specific written document, enumerating specific powers. This distinction in meaning can be
(50) traced to the fact that the foundations of government in the various colonies were written charters granted by the Crown. These express authorizations to govern were tangible, definite things. Over the years these colonials had often
(55) repaired to the charters to justify themselves in the struggle against tyrannical governors or officials of the Crown. More than a century of government

under written constitutions convinced these colonists of the necessity for and efficacy of protecting their
(60) liberties against governmental encroachment by explicitly defining all governmental powers in a document.

21. Which one of the following best expresses the main idea of the passage?

(A) The colonials and the English mistakenly thought that they shared a common political vocabulary.

(B) The colonials and the English shared a variety of institutions.

(C) The colonials and the English had conflicting interpretations of the language and institutional structures that they shared.

(D) Colonial attitudes toward English institutions grew increasingly hostile in the eighteenth century.

(E) Seventeenth-century English legal development accounted for colonial attitudes toward constitutions.

22. The passage supports all of the following statements about the political conditions present by the middle of the eighteenth century in the American colonies discussed in the passage EXCEPT:

(A) Colonials who did not own property could not vote.

(B) All of these colonies had representative assemblies modeled after the British Parliament.

(C) Some of these colonies had Royal Governors.

(D) Royal Governors could be removed from office by colonial assemblies.

(E) In these colonies, Royal Governors were regarded as serving a function like that of a king.

23. The passage implies which one of the following about English kings prior to the early seventeenth century?

    (A) They were the source of all law.
    (B) They frequently flouted laws made by Parliament.
    (C) Their power relative to that of Parliament was considerably greater than it was in the eighteenth century.
    (D) They were more often the sources of legal reform than they were in the eighteenth century.
    (E) They had to combat those who believed that the power of Parliament was absolute.

24. The author mentions which one of the following as evidence for the eighteenth-century English attitude toward Parliament?

    (A) The English had become uncomfortable with institutions that could claim absolute authority.
    (B) The English realized that their interests were better guarded by Parliament than by the King.
    (C) The English allowed Parliament to make constitutional changes by legislative enactment.
    (D) The English felt that the King did not possess the knowledge that would enable him to rule responsibly.
    (E) The English had decided that it was time to reform their representative government.

25. The passage implies that the colonials discussed in the passage would have considered which one of the following to be a source of their debates with England?

    (A) their changed use of the English political vocabulary
    (B) English commitment to parliamentary representation
    (C) their uniquely English experience
    (D) their refusal to adopt any English political institutions
    (E) their greater loyalty to the English political traditions

26. According to the passage, the English attitude toward the English Constitution differed from the colonial attitude toward constitutions in that the English regarded their Constitution as

    (A) the legal foundation of the kingdom
    (B) a document containing a collection of customs
    (C) a cumulative corpus of legislation and legal traditions
    (D) a record alterable by royal authority
    (E) an unchangeable body of governmental powers

27. The primary purpose of the passage is to

    (A) expose the misunderstanding that has characterized descriptions of the relationship between seventeenth- and eighteenth-century England and certain of its American colonies
    (B) suggest a reason for England's treatment of certain of its American colonies in the seventeenth and eighteenth centuries
    (C) settle an ongoing debate about the relationship between England and certain of its American colonies in the seventeenth and eighteenth centuries
    (D) interpret the events leading up to the independence of certain of England's American colonies in the eighteenth century
    (E) explain an aspect of the relationship between England and certain of its American colonies in the seventeenth and eighteenth centuries

To critics accustomed to the style of fifteenth-century narrative paintings by Italian artists from Tuscany, the Venetian examples of narrative paintings with religious subjects that Patricia Fortini
(5) Brown analyzes in a recent book will come as a great surprise. While the Tuscan paintings present large-scale figures, clear narratives, and simple settings, the Venetians filled their pictures with dozens of small figures and elaborate buildings, in
(10) addition to a wealth of carefully observed anecdotal detail often irrelevant to the paintings' principal subjects—the religious stories they narrate. Although it occasionally obscured these stories, this accumulation of circumstantial detail from Venetian
(15) life—the inclusion of prominent Venetian citizens, for example—was considered appropriate to the narration of historical subjects and underlined the authenticity of the historical events depicted. Indeed, Brown argues that the distinctive style of
(20) the Venetian paintings—what she calls the "eyewitness style"—was influenced by Venetian affinity for a strongly parochial type of historical writing, consisting almost exclusively of vernacular chronicles of local events embroidered with all
(25) kinds of inconsequential detail.

And yet, while Venetian attitudes toward history that are reflected in their art account in part for the difference in style between Venetian and Tuscan narrative paintings, Brown has overlooked
(30) some practical influences, such as climate. Tuscan churches are filled with frescoes that, in contrast to Venetian narrative paintings, consist mainly of large figures and easily recognized religious stories, as one would expect of paintings that are normally
(35) viewed from a distance and are designed primarily to remind the faithful of their religious tenets. In Venice, where the damp climate is unsuited to fresco, narrative frescoes in churches were almost nonexistent, with the result that Venetian artists and
(40) their public had no practical experience of the large-scale representation of familiar religious stories. Their model for painted stories was the cycle of secular historical paintings in the Venetian magistrate's palace, which were indeed the
(45) counterpart of written history and were made all the more authoritative by a proliferation of circumstantial detail.

Moreover, because painting frescoes requires an unusually sure hand, particularly in the
(50) representation of the human form, the development of drawing skill was central to artistic training in Tuscany, and by 1500 the public there tended to distinguish artists on the basis of how well they could draw human figures. In Venice, a city

(55) virtually without frescoes, this kind of skill was acquired and appreciated much later. Gentile Bellini, for example, although regarded as one of the supreme painters of the day, was feeble at drawing. On the other hand, the emphasis on
(60) architecture so evident in the Venetian narrative paintings was something that local painters obviously prized, largely because painting architecture in perspective was seen as a particular test of the Venetian painter's skill.

9. Which one of the following best states the main idea of the passage?

(A) Tuscan painters' use of fresco explains the prominence of human figures in the narrative paintings that they produced during the fifteenth century.

(B) In addition to fifteenth-century Venetian attitudes toward history, other factors may help to explain the characteristic features of Venetian narrative paintings with religious subjects produced during that period.

(C) The inclusion of authentic detail from Venetian life distinguished fifteenth-century Venetian narrative paintings from those that were produced in Tuscany.

(D) Venetian painters were generally more skilled at painting buildings than Tuscan painters were at drawing human forms.

(E) The cycle of secular historical paintings in the Venetian magistrate's palace was the primary influence on fifteenth-century Venetian narrative paintings with religious subjects.

10. In the passage, the author is primarily concerned with

(A) pointing out the superiority of one painting style over another

(B) citing evidence that requires a reevaluation of a conventionally held view

(C) discussing factors that explain a difference in painting styles

(D) outlining the strengths and weaknesses of two opposing views regarding the evolution of a painting style

(E) arguing for the irrelevance of one theory and for its replacement by a more plausible alternative

11. As it is described in the passage, Brown's explanation of the use of the eyewitness style in Venetian narrative painting suggests that

(A) the painting of architecture in perspective requires greater drawing skill than does the representation of a human form in a fresco

(B) certain characteristics of a style of painting can reflect a style of historical writing that was common during the same period

(C) the eyewitness style in Venetian narrative paintings with religious subjects was largely the result of the influence of Tuscan artists who worked primarily in fresco

(D) the historical detail in Venetian narrative paintings with religious subjects can be traced primarily to the influence of the paintings in the Venetian magistrate's palace

(E) a style of painting can be dramatically transformed by a sudden influx of artists from another region

12. The author suggests that fifteenth-century Venetian narrative paintings with religious subjects were painted by artists who

(A) were able to draw human figures with more skill after they were apprenticed to painters in Tuscany

(B) assumed that their paintings would typically be viewed from a distance

(C) were a major influence on the artists who produced the cycle of historical paintings in the Venetian magistrate's palace

(D) were reluctant to paint frescoes primarily because they lacked the drawing skill that painting frescoes required

(E) were better at painting architecture in perspective than they were at drawing human figures

13. The author implies that Venetian narrative paintings with religious subjects included the representation of elaborate buildings in part because

(A) the ability to paint architecture in perspective was seen in Venice as proof of a painter's skill

(B) the subjects of such paintings were often religious stories

(C) large frescoes were especially conducive to representing architecture in perspective

(D) the architecture of Venice in the fifteenth century was more elaborate than was the architecture of Tuscany

(E) the paintings were imitations of a kind of historical writing that was popular in Tuscany

14. Which one of the following, if true, would most weaken the author's contention that fifteenth-century Venetian artists "had no practical experience of the large-scale representation of familiar religious stories" (lines 40-42)?

(A) The style of secular historical paintings in the palace of the Venetian magistrate was similar to that of Venetian narrative paintings with religious subjects.

(B) The style of the historical writing produced by fifteenth-century Venetian authors was similar in its inclusion of anecdotal details to secular paintings produced during that century in Tuscany.

(C) Many of the artists who produced Venetian narrative paintings with religious subjects served as apprentices in Tuscany, where they had become familiar with the technique of painting frescoes.

(D) Few of the frescoes painted in Tuscany during the fifteenth century had secular subjects, and those that did often betrayed the artist's inability to represent elaborate architecture in perspective.

(E) Few of the Venetian narrative paintings produced toward the end of the fifteenth century show evidence of the enhanced drawing skill that characterized the paintings produced in Venice a century later.

Years after the movement to obtain civil rights for black people in the United States made its most important gains, scholars are reaching for a theoretical perspective capable of clarifying its
(5) momentous developments. New theories of social movements are being discussed, not just among social psychologists, but also among political theorists.

Of the many competing formulations of the
(10) "classical" social psychological theory of social movement, three are prominent in the literature on the civil rights movement: "rising expectations," "relative deprivation," and "J-curve." Each conforms to a causal sequence characteristic of
(15) classical social movement theory, linking some unusual condition, or "system strain," to the generation of unrest. When these versions of the classical theory are applied to the civil rights movement, the source of strain is identified as a
(20) change in black socioeconomic status that occurred shortly before the widespread protest activity of the movement.

For example, the theory of rising expectations asserts that protest activity was a response to
(25) psychological tensions generated by gains experienced immediately prior to the civil rights movement. Advancement did not satisfy ambition, but created the desire for further advancement. Only slightly different is the theory of relative
(30) deprivation. Here the impetus to protest is identified as gains achieved during the premovement period, coupled with simultaneous failure to make any appreciable headway relative to the dominant group. The J-curve theory argues that the movement
(35) occurred because a prolonged period of rising expectations and gratification was followed by a sharp reversal.

Political theorists have been dismissive of these applications of classical theory to the civil rights
(40) movement. Their arguments rest on the conviction that, implicitly, the classical theory trivializes the political ends of movement participants, focusing rather on presumed psychological dysfunctions; reduction of complex social situations to simple
(45) paradigms of stimulus and response obviates the relevance of all but the shortest-term analysis. Furthermore, the theories lack predictive value: "strain" is always present to some degree, but social movement is not. How can we know which
(50) strain will provoke upheaval?

These very legitimate complaints having frequently been made, it remains to find a means of testing the strength of the theories. Problematically, while proponents of the various theories have
(55) contradictory interpretations of socioeconomic conditions leading to the civil rights movement, examination of various statistical records regarding the material status of black Americans yields ample evidence to support any of the three theories. The
(60) steady rise in median black family income supports the rising expectations hypothesis; the stability of the economic position of black vis-a-vis white Americans lends credence to the relative deprivation interpretation; unemployment data are consistent
(65) with the J-curve theory. A better test is the comparison of each of these economic indicators with the frequency of movement-initiated events reported in the press; unsurprisingly, none correlates significantly with the pace of reports
(70) about movement activity.

22. It can be inferred from the passage that the classical theory of social movement would not be appropriately applied to an annual general election because such an election

(A) may focus on personalities rather than on political issues
(B) is not provoked primarily by an unusual condition
(C) may be decided according to the psychological needs of voters
(D) may not entail momentous developments
(E) actually entails two or more distinct social movements

23. According to the passage, the "rising expectations" and "relative deprivation" models differ in which one of the following ways?

(A) They predict different responses to the same socioeconomic conditions.
(B) They disagree about the relevance of psychological explanations for protest movements.
(C) They are meant to explain different kinds of social change.
(D) They describe the motivation of protesters in slightly different ways.
(E) They disagree about the relevance of socioeconomic status to system strain.

24. The author implies that political theorists attribute which one of the following assumptions to social psychologists who apply the classical theory of social movements to the civil rights movement?

(A) Participants in any given social movement have conflicting motivations.
(B) Social movements are ultimately beneficial to society.
(C) Only strain of a socioeconomic nature can provoke a social movement.
(D) The political ends of movement participants are best analyzed in terms of participants' psychological motivations.
(E) Psychological motivations of movement participants better illuminate the causes of social movements than do participants' political motivations.

25. Which one of the following statements is supported by the results of the "better test" discussed in the last paragraph of the passage?

(A) The test confirms the three classical theories discussed in the passage.
(B) The test provides no basis for deciding among the three classical theories discussed in the passage.
(C) The test shows that it is impossible to apply any theory of social movements to the civil rights movement.
(D) The test indicates that press coverage of the civil rights movement was biased.
(E) The test verifies that the civil rights movement generated socioeconomic progress.

26. The validity of the "better test" (line 65) as proposed by the author might be undermined by the fact that

(A) the press is selective about the movement activities it chooses to cover
(B) not all economic indicators receive the same amount of press coverage
(C) economic indicators often contradict one another
(D) a movement-initiated event may not correlate significantly with any of the three economic indicators
(E) the pace of movement-initiated events is difficult to anticipate

27. The main purpose of the passage is to

(A) persuade historians of the indispensability of a theoretical framework for understanding recent history
(B) present a new model of social movement
(C) account for a shift in a theoretical debate
(D) show the unity underlying the diverse classical models of social movement
(E) discuss the reasoning behind and shortcomings of certain social psychological theories

Modern architecture has been criticized for emphasizing practical and technical issues at the expense of aesthetic concerns. The high-rise buildings constructed throughout the industrialized
(5) world in the 1960s and 1970s provide ample evidence that cost-efficiency and utility have become the overriding concerns of the modern architect. However, Otto Wagner's seminal text on modern architecture, first published in Germany
(10) in 1896, indicates that the failures of modern architecture cannot be blamed on the ideals of its founders.

Wagner's *Modern Architecture* called for a new style based on modern technologies and modes of
(15) construction. He insisted that there could be no return to traditional, preindustrial models; only by accepting wholeheartedly the political and technological revolutions of the nineteenth century could the architect establish the forms appropriate
(20) to a modern, urban society. "All modern creations," Wagner wrote, "must correspond to the new materials and demands of the present. . .must illustrate our own better, democratic, self-confident, ideal nature," and must incorporate the new
(25) "colossal technical and scientific achievements" of the age. This would indeed seem to be the basis of a purely materialist definition of architecture, a prototype for the simplistic form-follows-function dogma that opponents have identified as the
(30) intellectual basis of modern architecture.

But the picture was more complex, for Wagner was always careful to distinguish between art and engineering. Ultimately, he envisaged the architect developing the skills of the engineer without losing
(35) the powers of aesthetic judgment that Wagner felt were unique to the artist. "Since the engineer is seldom a born artist and the architect must learn as a rule to be an engineer, architects will in time succeed in extending their influence into the realm
(40) occupied by the engineers, so that legitimate aesthetic demands can be met in a satisfactory way." In this symbiotic relationship essential to Modernism, art was to exercise the controlling influence.
(45) No other prospect was imaginable for Wagner, who was firmly rooted as a designer and, indeed, as a teacher in the Classical tradition. The apparent inconsistency of a confessed Classicist advising against the mechanical imitation of historical
(50) models and arguing for new forms appropriate to the modern age created exactly the tension that made Wagner's writings and buildings so interesting. While he justified, for example, the choice of a circular ground plan for churches in

(55) terms of optimal sight-lines and the technology of the gasometer, the true inspiration was derived from the centralized churches of the Italian Renaissance. He acknowledged as a rationalist that there was no way back to the social and technological conditions
(60) that had produced the work of Michelangelo or Fischer von Erlach, but he recognized his emotional attachment to the great works of the Italian Renaissance and Austrian Baroque.

1. Which one of the following best expresses the main idea of the passage?

   (A) Modern architecture has been criticized for emphasizing practical and technical issues and for failing to focus on aesthetic concerns.

   (B) Critics have failed to take into account the technological innovations and aesthetic features that architects have incorporated into modern buildings.

   (C) Wagner's *Modern Architecture* provides architects with a chronicle of the origins of modern architecture.

   (D) Wagner's *Modern Architecture* indicates that the founders of modern architecture did not believe that practical issues should supersede the aesthetic concerns of the past.

   (E) Wagner's seminal text, *Modern Architecture,* provides the intellectual basis for the purely materialistic definition of modern architecture.

2. According to the passage, Wagner asserts which one of the following about the roles of architect and engineer?

   (A) The architect should make decisions about aesthetic issues and leave decisions about technical matters to the engineer.

   (B) The engineer has often developed the powers of aesthetic judgment previously thought to be unique to the architect.

   (C) The judgment of the engineer should be as important as the judgment of the architect when decisions are made about aesthetic issues.

   (D) The technical judgment of the engineer should prevail over the aesthetic judgment of the architect in the design of modern buildings.

   (E) The architect should acquire the knowledge of technical matters typically held by the engineer.

3. The passage suggests that Wagner would be LEAST likely to agree with which one of the following statements about classical architecture and the modern architect?

(A) The modern architect should avoid the mechanical imitation of the models of the Italian Renaissance and Austrian Baroque.

(B) The modern architect cannot design buildings appropriate to a modern, urban society and still retain emotional attachments to the forms of the Italian Renaissance and Austrian Baroque.

(C) The modern architect should possess knowledge of engineering as well as of the architecture of the past.

(D) The modern architect should not base designs on the technological conditions that underlay the designs of the models of The Italian Renaissance and Austrian Baroque.

(E) The designs of modern architects should reflect political ideals different from those reflected in the designs of classical architecture.

4. The passage suggests which one of the following about the quotations from *Modern Architecture* cited in the second paragraph?

(A) They represent the part of Wagner's work that has had the least influence on the architects who designed the high-rise buildings of the 1960s and 1970s.

(B) They describe the part of Wagner's work that is most often evoked by proponents of Wagner's ideas on art and technology.

(C) They do not adequately reflect the complexity of Wagner's ideas on the use of modern technology in architecture.

(D) They reflect Wagner's active participation in the political revolutions of the nineteenth century.

(E) They provide an overview of Wagner's ideas on the relationship between art and technology.

5. The author of the passage states which one of the following about the concerns of modern architecture?

(A) Cost-efficiency, utility, and aesthetic demands are the primary concerns of the modern architect.

(B) Practical issues supersede aesthetic concerns in the design of many modern buildings.

(C) Cost-efficiency is more important to the modern architect than are other practical concerns.

(D) The design of many new buildings suggests that modern architects are still inspired by architectural forms of the past.

(E) Many modern architects use current technology to design modern buildings that are aesthetically pleasing.

6. The author mentions Wagner's choice of a "circular ground plan for churches" (line 54) most likely in order to

(A) provide an example of the kinds of technological innovations Wagner introduced into modern architecture

(B) provide an example of Wagner's dismissal of historical forms from the Italian Renaissance

(C) provide an example of a modern building where technological issues were much less significant than aesthetic demands

(D) provide evidence of Wagner's tendency to imitate Italian Renaissance and Austrian Baroque models

(E) provide evidence of the tension between Wagner's commitment to modern technology and to the Classical tradition

7. The passage is primarily concerned with

(A) summarizing the history of a debate
(B) explaining a traditional argument
(C) describing and evaluating a recent approach
(D) justifying a recent criticism by presenting new evidence
(E) supporting an assertion by discussing an important work

In order to explain the socioeconomic achievement, in the face of disadvantages due to racial discrimination, of Chinese and Japanese immigrants to the United States and their
(5) descendants, sociologists have typically applied either culturally based or structurally based theories—but never both together. To use an economic metaphor, culturally based explanations assert the importance of the supply side of the labor
(10) market, emphasizing the qualities immigrant groups bring with them for competition in the United States labor market. Such explanations reflect a human-capital perspective in which status attainment is seen as a result of individuals' ability to generate
(15) resources. Structurally based explanations, on the other hand, examine the market condition of the immigrants' host society, particularly its discriminatory practices and their impact on the status attainment process of immigrant groups. In
(20) the economic metaphor, structural explanations assert the importance of the demand side of the labor market.

In order to understand the socioeconomic mobility of Chinese and Japanese immigrants and
(25) their descendants, only an analysis of supply-side and demand-side factors together, in the context of historical events, will suffice. On the cultural or supply side, differences in immigration pattern and family formation resulted in different rates of
(30) socioeconomic achievement for Chinese and Japanese immigrants. For various reasons, Chinese immigrants remained sojourners and did not (except for urban merchants) establish families. They were also hampered by ethnic conflict in the labor
(35) market. Japanese immigrants, on the other hand, were less constrained, made the transition from sojourner to settler within the first two decades of immigration, and left low-wage labor to establish small businesses based on a household mode of
(40) production. Chinese sojourners without families were more vulnerable to demoralization, whereas Japanese immigrants faced societal hostility with the emotional resources provided by a stable family life. Once Chinese immigrants began to establish
(45) nuclear families and produce a second generation, instituting household production similar to that established by Japanese immigrants, their socioeconomic attainment soon paralleled that of Japanese immigrants and their descendants.
(50) On the structural or demand side, changes in institutional constraints, immigration laws, labor markets, and societal hostility were rooted in the dynamics of capitalist economic development. Early capitalist development generated a demand for

(55) low-wage labor that could not be fulfilled. Early Chinese and Japanese immigration was a response to this demand. In an advanced capitalist economy, the demand for immigrant labor is more differentiated: skilled professional and technical
(60) labor fills empty positions in the primary labor market and, with the traditional unskilled low-wage labor, creates two immigrant streams. The high levels of education attained by the descendants of Chinese and Japanese immigrants and their
(65) concentration in strategic states such as California paved the way for the movement of the second generation into the expanding primary labor market in the advanced capitalist economy that existed after the Second World War.

8. Which one of the following best expresses the main idea of the passage?

(A) The socioeconomic achievement of Chinese and Japanese immigrants and their descendants is best explained by a historical examination of the economic structures prevalent in the United States when such immigrant groups arrived.

(B) The socioeconomic achievement of Chinese and Japanese immigrants and their descendants is best explained by an examination of their cultural backgrounds, in particular their level of educational attainment.

(C) The socioeconomic achievement of Chinese and Japanese immigrants and their descendants has taken place in the context of a culturally based emphasis on the economic welfare of the nuclear families.

(D) Only the market structure of the capitalist economy of the United States in which supply has historically been regulated by demand can account for the socioeconomic achievement of Chinese and Japanese immigrants and their descendants.

(E) Only an analysis that combines an examination of the culture of Chinese and Japanese immigrant groups and the socioeconomic structure of the host country can adequately explain the socioeconomic achievement of Chinese and Japanese immigrants and their descendants.

9. Which one of the following can best be described as a supply-side element in the labor market, as such elements are explained in the passage?

    (A) concentration of small businesses in a given geographical area
    (B) need for workers with varying degrees of skill
    (C) high value placed by immigrants on work
    (D) expansion of the primary labor market
    (E) development of an advanced capitalist economy

10. Which one of the following best states the function of the author's mention of "two immigrant streams" (line 62)?

    (A) It demonstrates the effects of changes in human capital.
    (B) It illustrates the operation of the primary labor market.
    (C) It explains the nature of early Chinese and Japanese immigration.
    (D) It characterizes the result of changing demand-side factors.
    (E) It underscores an influence on the labor market.

11. It can be inferred that the author's analysis of the socioeconomic achievement of Chinese and Japanese immigrants and their descendants differs from that of most sociologists primarily in that most sociologists

    (A) address the effects of the interaction of causal factors
    (B) exclude the factor of a developing capitalist economy
    (C) do not apply an economic metaphor
    (D) emphasize the disadvantageous effects of racial discrimination
    (E) focus on a single type of theoretical explanation

12. It can be inferred that which one of the following was an element of the experience of both Chinese and Japanese immigrants in the United States?

    (A) initial status as sojourners
    (B) slow accumulation of capital
    (C) quick transition from laborer to manager
    (D) rapid establishment of nuclear families
    (E) rapid acquisition of technical skills

13. The author is primarily concerned with

    (A) advancing a synthesis of approaches to an issue
    (B) challenging a tentative answer to a question
    (C) evaluating the soundness of theories
    (D) resolving the differences between schools of thought
    (E) outlining the achievements of a group

Late-nineteenth-century books about the French artist Watteau (1684-1721) betray a curious blind spot: more than any single artist before or since, Watteau provided his age with an influential image
(5) of itself, and nineteenth-century writers accepted this image as genuine. This was largely due to the enterprise of Watteau's friends who, soon after his death, organized the printing of engraved reproductions of the great bulk of his work—both
(10) his paintings and his drawings—so that Watteau's total artistic output became and continued to be more accessible than that of any other artist until the twentieth-century advent of art monographs illustrated with photographs. These engravings
(15) presented aristocratic (and would-be aristocratic) eighteenth-century French society with an image of itself that was highly acceptable and widely imitated by other artists, however little relationship that image bore to reality. By 1884, the bicentenary of
(20) Watteau's birth, it was standard practice for biographers to refer to him as "the personification of the witty and amiable eighteenth century."

In fact, Watteau saw little enough of that "witty and amiable" century for which so much nostalgia
(25) was generally felt between about 1870 and 1920, a period during which enthusiasm for the artist reached its peak. The eighteenth century's first decades, the period of his artistic activity, were fairly calamitous ones. During his short life, France
(30) was almost continually at war: his native region was overrun with foreign troops, and Paris was threatened by siege and by a rampaging army rabble. The dreadful winter of 1709, the year of Watteau's first Paris successes, was marked by
(35) military defeat and a disastrous famine.

Most of Watteau's nineteenth-century admirers simply ignored the grim background of the works they found so lyrical and charming. Those who took the inconvenient historical facts into consideration
(40) did so only in order to refute the widely held deterministic view that the content and style of an artist's work were absolutely dictated by heredity and environment. (For Watteau admirers, such determinism was unthinkable: the artist was born
(45) in a Flemish town only six years after it first became part of France, yet Watteau was quintessentially French. As one patriotic French biographer put it, "In Dresden, Potsdam, and Berlin I have never come across a Watteau without feeling refreshed by
(50) a breath of native air.") Even such writers, however, persisted in according Watteau's canvases a privileged status as representative "personifications" of the eighteenth century. The discrepancy between historical fact and artistic
(55) vision, useful in refuting the extreme deterministic position, merely forced these writers to seek a new formula that allowed them to preserve the desired

identity between image and reality, this time a rather suspiciously psychic one: Watteau did not
(60) record the society he knew, but rather "foresaw" a society that developed shortly after his death.

14. Which one of the following best describes the overall organization of the passage?

(A) A particular phenomenon is discussed, the reasons that it is atypical are put forward, and these reasons are evaluated and refined.

(B) An assumption is made, results deriving from it are compared with what is known to be true, and the assumption is finally rejected as counterfactual.

(C) A point of view is described, one hypothesis accounting for it is introduced and rejected, and a better hypothesis is offered for consideration.

(D) A general characterization is offered, examples supporting it are introduced, and its special applicability to a particular group is asserted.

(E) A particular viewpoint is explained, its shortcomings are discussed, and its persistence in the face of these is noted.

15. The passage suggests that late-nineteenth-century biographers of Watteau considered the eighteenth century to be "witty and amiable" in large part because of

(A) what they saw as Watteau's typical eighteenth century talent for transcending reality through art

(B) their opposition to the determinism that dominated late-nineteenth-century French thought

(C) a lack of access to historical source material concerning the early eighteenth century in France

(D) the nature of the image conveyed by the works of Watteau and his many imitators

(E) their political bias in favor of aristocratic regimes and societies

16. According to the passage, explanations of artistic production based on determinism were unthinkable to Watteau admirers for which one of the following reasons?

    (A)   If such explanations were widely accepted, too many people who would otherwise have admired Watteau would cease to appreciate Watteau's works.

    (B)   If such explanations were adopted, they would make it difficult for Watteau admirers to explain why Watteau's works were purchased and admired by foreigners.

    (C)   If such explanations were correct, many artists who, like Watteau, considered themselves French would have to be excluded from histories of French art.

    (D)   If such simple explanations were offered, other more complex arguments concerning what made Watteau's works especially charming would go unexplored.

    (E)   If such explanations were true, Watteau's works would reflect a "Flemish" sensibility rather than the especially "French" one these admirers saw in them.

17. The phrase "curious blind spot" (lines 2-3) can best be interpreted as referring to which one of the following?

    (A)   some biographers' persistent inability to appreciate what the author considers a particularly admirable quality

    (B)   certain writers' surprising lack of awareness of what the author considers an obvious discrepancy

    (C)   some writers' willful refusal to evaluate properly what the author considers a valuable source of information about the past

    (D)   an inexplicable tendency on the part of some writers to undervalue an artist whom the author considers extremely influential

    (E)   a marked bias in favor of a certain painter and a concomitant prejudice against contemporaries the author considers equally talented

18. It can be inferred from the passage that the author's view of Watteau's works differs most significantly from that of most late-nineteenth-century Watteau admirers in which one of the following ways?

    (A)   Unlike most late-nineteenth-century Watteau admirers, the author appreciates the importance of Watteau's artistic accomplishment.

    (B)   The author finds Watteau's works to be much less lyrical and charming than did most late-nineteenth-century admirers of the works.

    (C)   In contrast to most late-nineteenth-century Watteau admirers, the author finds it misleading to see Watteau's works as accurately reflecting social reality.

    (D)   The author is much more willing to entertain deterministic explanations of the origins of Watteau's works than were most late nineteenth-century Watteau admirers.

    (E)   Unlike most late-nineteenth-century admirers of Watteau, the author considers it impossible for any work of art to personify or represent a particular historical period.

19. The author asserts that during the period of Watteau's artistic activity French society was experiencing which one of the following?

    (A)   widespread social upheaval caused by war

    (B)   a pervasive sense of nostalgia for an idealized past

    (C)   increased domination of public affairs by a powerful aristocracy

    (D)   rapid adoption by the middle classes of aristocratic manners and life-styles

    (E)   a need to reconcile the French self-image with French social realities

20. The information given in the passage suggests that which one of the following principles accurately characterizes the relationship between an artist's work and the impact it is likely to have on a society?

    (A)   An artist's recognition by a society is most directly determined by the degree to which his or her works are perceived as lyrical and charming.

    (B)   An artist will have the greatest influence on a society that values art particularly highly.

    (C)   The works of an artist who captures the true and essential nature of a given society will probably have a great impact on that society.

    (D)   The degree of influence an artist's vision will have on a society is conditional on the visibility of the artist's work.

    (E)   An artist who is much imitated by contemporaries will usually fail to have an impact on a society unless the imitators are talented.

Innovations in language are never completely new. When the words used for familiar things change, or words for new things enter the language, they are usually borrowed or adapted from stock.
(5) Assuming new roles, they drag their old meanings along behind them like flickering shadows. This seems especially true of the language of the contemporary school of literary criticism that now prefers to describe its work simply and rather
(10) presumptuously as "theory" but is still popularly referred to as poststructuralism or deconstruction.

The first neologisms adopted by this movement were *signifier* and *signified,* employed to distinguish words from their referents, and to illustrate the
(15) arbitrariness of the terms we choose. The use of these particular terms (rather than, respectively, *word* and *thing)* underlined the seriousness of the naming process and its claim on our attention. Since in English "to signify" can also mean "to
(20) portend," these terms also suggest that words predict coming events.

With the use of the term *deconstruction* we move into another and more complex realm of meaning. The most common use of the terms *construction*
(25) and *deconstruction* is in the building trades, and their borrowing by literary theorists for a new type of criticism cannot help but have certain overtones to the outsider. First, the usage suggests that the creation and critical interpretation of literature are
(30) not organic but mechanical processes; that the author of any piece of writing is not an inspired, intuitive artist, but merely a laborer who cobbles existing materials (words) into more or less conventional structures. The term *deconstruction*
(35) implies that the text has been put together like a building or a piece of machinery, and that it is in need of being taken apart, not so much in order to repair it as to demonstrate underlying inadequacies, false assumptions, and inherent contradictions.
(40) This process can supposedly be repeated many times and by many literary hard hats; it is expected that each deconstruction will reveal additional flaws and expose the illusions or bad faith of the builder. The fact that deconstructionists prefer to
(45) describe their activities as *deconstruction* rather than *criticism* is also revealing. *Criticism* and *critic* derive from the Greek *kritikos,* "skillful in judging, decisive." *Deconstruction,* on the other hand, has no overtones of skill or wisdom; it merely suggests
(50) demolition of an existing building. In popular usage *criticism* suggests censure but not change. If we find fault with a building, we may condemn it, but we do not carry out the demolition ourselves. The deconstructionist, by implication, is both judge and
(55) executioner who leaves a text totally dismantled, if not reduced to a pile of rubble.

7. Which one of the following best expresses the main idea of the passage?

(A) Implicit in the terminology of the school of criticism known as *deconstruction* are meanings that reveal the true nature of the deconstructionist's endeavor.

(B) The appearance of the terms *signifier* and *signified* in the field of literary theory anticipated the appearance of an even more radical idea known as *deconstruction.*

(C) Innovations in language and the relations between old and new meanings of terms are a special concern of the new school of criticism known as *deconstruction.*

(D) Deconstructionists maintain that it is insufficient merely to judge a work; the critic must actively dismantle it.

(E) Progress in the field of literary theory is best achieved by looking for new terms like *signifier* and *deconstruction* that might suggest new critical approaches to a work.

8. Which one of the following is a claim that the author of the passage makes about deconstructionists?

(A) Deconstructionists would not have been able to formulate their views adequately without the terms *signifier* and *signified.*

(B) Deconstructionists had no particular purpose in mind in choosing to use neologisms.

(C) Deconstructionists do not recognize that their own theory contains inherent contradictions.

(D) Deconstructionists find little interest in the relationship between words and their referents.

(E) Deconstructionists use the terms *signifier* and *signified* to stress the importance of the process of naming.

9. Which one of the following generalizations about inventions is most analogous to the author's point about innovation in language?

   (A) A new invention usually consists of components that are specifically manufactured for the new invention.
   (B) A new invention is usually behind the times, never making as much use of all the available modern technology as it could.
   (C) A new invention usually consists of components that are already available but are made to function in new ways.
   (D) A new invention is most useful when it is created with attention to the historical tradition established by implements previously used to do the same job.
   (E) A new invention is rarely used to its full potential because it is surrounded by out-of-date technology that hinders its application.

10. The author of the passage uses the word "criticism" in lines 46-56 primarily in order to

    (A) give an example
    (B) introduce a contrast
    (C) undermine an argument
    (D) codify a system
    (E) dismiss an objection

11. Which one of the following best describes the function of the second paragraph within the passage as a whole?

    (A) It introduces a hypothesis that the author later expands upon.
    (B) It qualifies a claim made earlier by the author.
    (C) It develops an initial example of the author's general thesis.
    (D) It predicts a development.
    (E) It presents a contrasting view.

12. The passage suggests that the author most probably holds the view that an important characteristic of literary criticism is that it

    (A) demonstrate false assumptions and inherent contradictions
    (B) employ skill and insight
    (C) be carried out by one critic rather than many
    (D) reveal how a text is put together like a building
    (E) point out the superiority of conventional text structures

13. The passage suggests that which one of the following most accurately describes the author's view of deconstructionist thought?

    (A) The author is guardedly optimistic about the ability of deconstruction to reveal the intentions and biases of a writer.
    (B) The author endorses the utility of deconstruction for revealing the role of older meanings of words.
    (C) The author is enthusiastic about the significant neologisms that deconstruction has introduced into literary criticism.
    (D) The author regards deconstruction's tendency to focus only on the problems and faults of literary texts as too mechanical.
    (E) The author condemns deconstruction's attempts to define literary criticism as a creative act.

Until recently, few historians were interested in analyzing the similarities and differences between serfdom in Russia and slavery in the United States. Even Alexis de Tocqueville, who recognized the
(5) significant comparability of the two nations, never compared their systems of servitude, despite his interest in United States slavery. Moreover, the almost simultaneous abolition of Russian serfdom and United States slavery in the 1860s—a riveting
(10) coincidence that should have drawn more modern scholars to a comparative study of the two systems of servitude—has failed to arouse the interest of scholars. Though some historians may have been put off by the forbidding political differences
(15) between nineteenth-century Russia and the United States—one an imperial monarchy, the other a federal democracy—a recent study by Peter Kolchin identifies differences that are illuminating, especially with regard to the different kinds of
(20) rebellion exhibited by slaves and serfs.

Kolchin points out that nobles owning serfs in Russia constituted only a tiny proportion of the population, while in the southern United States, about a quarter of all White people were members
(25) of slave-owning families. And although in the southern United States only 2 percent of slaves worked on plantations where more than a hundred slaves worked, in Russia almost 80 percent of the serfs worked for nobles who owned more than a
(30) hundred serfs. In Russia most serfs rarely saw their owners, who tended to rely on intermediaries to manage their estates, while most southern planters lived on their land and interacted with slaves on a regular basis.
(35) These differences in demographics partly explain differences in the kinds of resistance that slaves and serfs practiced in their respective countries. Both serfs and slaves engaged in a wide variety of rebellious activity, from silent sabotage, much of
(40) which has escaped the historical record, to organized armed rebellions, which were more common in Russia. The practice of absentee ownership, combined with the large numbers in which serfs were owned, probably contributed
(45) significantly to the four great rebellions that swept across Russia at roughly fifty-year intervals in the seventeenth and eighteenth centuries. The last of these, occurring between 1773 and 1774, enlisted more than a million serfs in a futile attempt to
(50) overthrow the Russian nobility. Russian serfs also participated in smaller acts of collective defiance called the *volnenie,* which typically started with a group of serfs who complained of grievances by petition and went out on strike. Confrontations
(55) between slaves and plantation authorities were also common, but they tended to be much less collective in nature than those that occurred in Russia, probably in part because the number of workers on each estate was smaller in the United States than
(60) was the case in Russia.

21. Which one of the following best states the main idea of the passage?

(A) Differences in the demographics of United States slavery and Russian serfdom can help explain the different kinds of resistance practiced by slaves and serfs in their respective countries.
(B) Historians have yet to undertake an adequate comparison and contrast of Russian serfdom and United States slavery.
(C) Revolts by Russian serfs were commonly characterized by collective action.
(D) A recent study has questioned the value of comparing United States slavery to Russian serfdom, especially in light of the significant demographic and cultural differences between the two countries.
(E) De Tocqueville failed to recognize the fundamental differences between Russian serfdom and United States slavery which more recent historians have identified.

22. According to the author, de Tocqueville was similar to many modern historians in his

(A) interest in the demographic differences between Russia and the United States during the nineteenth century
(B) failure to undertake a comparison of Russian serfdom and United States slavery
(C) inability to explain why United States slavery and Russian serfdom were abolished during the same decade
(D) overestimation of the significance of the political differences between Russia and the United States
(E) recognition of the essential comparability of Russia and the United States

23. Which one of the following assertions, if true, would provide the most support for Kolchin's principal conclusion regarding the relationship of demographics to rebellion among Russian serfs and United States slaves?

(A) Collective defiance by serfs during the nineteenth century was confined almost exclusively to their participation in the *volnenie*.

(B) The rebellious activity of United States slaves was more likely to escape the historical record than was the rebellious activity of Russian serfs.

(C) Organized rebellions by slaves in the Western Hemisphere during the nineteenth century were most common in colonies with large estates that normally employed more than a hundred slaves.

(D) In the southern United States during the nineteenth century, those estates that were managed by intermediaries rather than by the owner generally relied upon the labor of at least a hundred slaves.

(E) The intermediaries who managed estates in Russia during the nineteenth century were in general much more competent as managers than the owners of the estates that they managed.

24. The fact that United States slavery and Russian serfdom were abolished during the same decade is cited by the author in the first paragraph primarily in order to

(A) emphasize that rebellions in both countries eventually led to the demise of the two institutions

(B) cite a coincidence that de Tocqueville should have been able to foresee

(C) suggest one reason why more historians should have been drawn to a comparative study of the two institutions

(D) cite a coincidence that Kolchin's study has failed to explain adequately

(E) emphasize the underlying similarities between the two institutions

25. The author cites which one of the following as a factor that might have discouraged historians from undertaking a comparative study of Russian serfdom and United States slavery?

(A) major differences in the political systems of the two countries

(B) major differences in the demographics of the two countries

(C) the failure of de Tocqueville to address the subject

(D) differences in the size of the estates on which slaves and serfs labored

(E) the comprehensiveness of Kolchin's own work

26. According to the passage, Kolchin's study asserts that which one of the following was true of Russian nobles during the nineteenth century?

(A) They agreed to the abolition of serfdom in the 1860s largely as a result of their having been influenced by the abolition of slavery in the United States.

(B) They became more directly involved in the management of their estates as a result of the rebellions that occurred in the previous century.

(C) They commonly agreed to at least some of the demands that arose out of the *volnenie*.

(D) They had relatively little direct contact with the serfs who worked on their estates.

(E) They hastened the abolition of serfdom by failing to devise an effective response to the collective nature of the serfs' rebellious activity.

27. The passage suggests that which one of the following was true of southern planters in the United States?

(A) They were as prepared for collective protest as were their Russian counterparts.

(B) Few of them owned plantations on which fewer than a hundred slaves worked.

(C) They managed their estates more efficiently than did their Russian counterparts.

(D) Few of them relied on intermediaries to manage their estates.

(E) The size of their estates was larger on average than the size of Russian estates.

J. G. A. Pocock's numerous investigations have all revolved around the fruitful assumption that a work of political thought can only be understood in light of the linguistic constraints to which its author
(5) was subject, for these prescribed both the choice of subject matter and the author's conceptualization of this subject matter. Only the occasional epic theorist, like Machiavelli or Hobbes, succeeded in breaking out of these bonds by redefining old terms
(10) and inventing new ones. The task of the modern commentator is to identify the "language" or "vocabulary" with and within which the author operated. While historians of literature have always been aware that writers work within particular
(15) traditions, the application of this notion to the history of political ideas forms a sharp contrast to the assumptions of the 1950s, when it was naively thought that the close reading of a text by an analytic philosopher was sufficient to establish its
(20) meaning, even if the philosopher had no knowledge of the period of the text's composition.

The language Pocock has most closely investigated is that of "civic humanism." For much of his career he has argued that eighteenth-century
(25) English political thought should be interpreted as a conflict between rival versions of the "virtue" central to civic humanism. On the one hand, he argues, this virtue is described by representatives of the Tory opposition using a vocabulary of public
(30) spirit and self-sufficiency. For these writers the societal ideal is the small, independent landowner in the countryside. On the other hand, Whig writers describe such virtue using a vocabulary of commerce and economic progress; for them the
(35) ideal is the merchant.

In making such linguistic discriminations Pocock has disassociated himself from historians like Namier, who deride all eighteenth-century English political language as "cant." But while Pocock's
(40) ideas have proved fertile when applied to England, they are more controversial when applied to the late-eighteenth-century United States. Pocock's assertion that Jefferson's attacks on the commercial policies of the Federalists simply echo the language
(45) of the Tory opposition in England is at odds with the fact that Jefferson rejected the elitist implications of that group's notion of virtue and asserted the right of all to participate in commercial society. Indeed, after promptings by Quentin
(50) Skinner, Pocock has admitted that a counterlanguage—one of rights and liberties—was probably as important in the political discourse of the late-eighteenth-century United States as the language of civic humanism. Fortunately, it is not
(55) necessary to rank the relative importance of all the different vocabularies in which eighteenth-century political argument was conducted. It is sufficient to recognize that any interesting text is probably a mixture of several of these vocabularies, and to
(60) applaud the historian who, though guilty of some exaggeration, has done the most to make us aware of their importance.

16. The main idea of the passage is that

(A) civic humanism, in any of its manifestations, cannot entirely explain eighteenth-century political discourse

(B) eighteenth-century political texts are less likely to reflect a single vocabulary than to combine several vocabularies

(C) Pocock's linguistic approach, though not applicable to all eighteenth-century political texts, provides a useful model for historians of political theory

(D) Pocock has more successfully accounted for the nature of political thought in eighteenth-century England than in the eighteenth-century United States

(E) Pocock's notion of the importance of language in political texts is a logical extension of the insights of historians of literature

17. According to the passage, Pocock most clearly associates the use of a vocabulary of economic progress with

(A) Jefferson
(B) Federalists
(C) English Whigs
(D) English Tories
(E) rural English landowners

18. The author's attitude toward Pocock is best revealed by which of the following pairs of words?

(A) "fruitful" (line 2) and "cant" (line 39)
(B) "sharp" (line 16) and "elitist" (line 46)
(C) "naively" (line 17) and "controversial" (line 41)
(D) "fertile" (line 40) and "applaud" (line 60)
(E) "simply" (line 44) and "importance" (line 55)

19. The passage suggests that one of the "assumptions of the 1950s" (line 17) regarding the meaning of a political text was that this meaning

    (A) could be established using an approach similar to that used by literary historians
    (B) could be definitively established without reference to the text's historical background
    (C) could be closely read in several different ways depending on one's philosophic approach
    (D) was constrained by certain linguistic preconceptions held by the text's author
    (E) could be expressed most clearly by an analytic philosopher who had studied its historical context

20. The author of the passage would most likely agree that which one of the following is a weakness found in Pocock's work?

    (A) the use of the term "language" to describe the expressive features of several diverse kinds of discourse
    (B) the overemphatic denigration of the role of the analytic philosopher in establishing the meaning of a political, or indeed any, text
    (C) the emphasis on the overriding importance of civic humanism in eighteenth-century English political thought
    (D) the insistence on a single linguistic dichotomy to account for political thought in eighteenth-century England and the United States
    (E) the assignment of certain vocabularies to particular parties in eighteenth-century England without taking note of how these vocabularies overlapped

21. Which one of the following best describes the organization of the passage?

    (A) A description of a thesis is offered, specific cases are considered, and an evaluation is given.
    (B) A thesis is brought forward, the thesis is qualified, and evidence that calls the qualification into question is stated.
    (C) A hypothesis is described, examples that suggest it is incorrect are summarized, and supporting examples are offered.
    (D) A series of evaluations are given, concrete reasons are put forward, and a future direction for research is suggested.
    (E) Comparisons and contrasts are made, some categories of evaluation are suggested, and a framework for applying these categories is implied.

Three kinds of study have been performed on Byron. There is the biographical study—the very valuable examination of Byron's psychology and the events in his life; Escarpit's 1958 work is an example
(5) of this kind of study, and biographers to this day continue to speculate about Byron's life. Equally valuable is the study of Byron as a figure important in the history of ideas; Russell and Praz have written studies of this kind. Finally, there are
(10) studies that primarily consider Byron's poetry. Such literary studies are valuable, however, only when they avoid concentrating solely on analyzing the verbal shadings of Byron's poetry to the exclusion of any discussion of biographical considerations. A
(15) study with such a concentration would be of questionable value because Byron's poetry, for the most part, is simply not a poetry of subtle verbal meanings. Rather, on the whole, Byron's poems record the emotional pressure of certain moments
(20) in his life. I believe we cannot often read a poem of Byron's, as we often can one of Shakespeare's, without wondering what events or circumstances in his life prompted him to write it.

No doubt the fact that most of Byron's poems
(25) cannot be convincingly read as subtle verbal creations indicates that Byron is not a "great" poet. It must be admitted too that Byron's literary craftsmanship is irregular and often his temperament disrupts even his lax literary method
(30) (although the result, an absence of method, has a significant purpose: it functions as a rebuke to a cosmos that Byron feels he cannot understand). If Byron is not a "great" poet, his poetry is nonetheless of extraordinary interest to us because
(35) of the pleasure it gives us. Our main pleasure in reading Byron's poetry is the contact with a singular personality. Reading his work gives us illumination—self-understanding—after we have seen our weaknesses and aspirations mirrored in
(40) the personality we usually find in the poems. Anyone who thinks that this kind of illumination is not a genuine reason for reading a poet should think carefully about why we read Donne's sonnets.

It is Byron and Byron's idea of himself that hold
(45) his work together (and that enthralled early-nineteenth-century Europe). Different characters speak in his poems, but finally it is usually he himself who is speaking: a far cry from the impersonal poet Keats. Byron's poetry alludes to
(50) Greek and Roman myth in the context of contemporary affairs, but his work remains generally of a piece because of his close presence in the poetry. In sum, the poetry is a shrewd personal performance, and to shut out Byron the
(55) man is to fabricate a work of pseudocriticism.

1. Which one of the following titles best expresses the main idea of the passage?

   (A) An Absence of Method: Why Byron Is Not a "Great" Poet
   (B) Byron: The Recurring Presence in Byron's Poetry
   (C) Personality and Poetry: The Biographical Dimension of Nineteenth-Century Poetry
   (D) Byron's Poetry: Its Influence on the Imagination of Early-Nineteenth-Century Europe
   (E) Verbal Shadings: The Fatal Flaw of Twentieth-Century Literary Criticism

2. The author's mention of Russell and Praz serves primarily to

   (A) differentiate them from one another
   (B) contrast their conclusions about Byron with those of Escarpit
   (C) point out the writers whose studies suggest a new direction for Byron scholarship
   (D) provide examples of writers who have written one kind of study of Byron
   (E) give credit to the writers who have composed the best studies of Byron

3. Which one of the following would the author most likely consider to be a valuable study of Byron?

    (A)   a study that compared Byron's poetic style with Keats' poetic style

    (B)   a study that argued that Byron's thought ought not to be analyzed in terms of its importance in the history of ideas

    (C)   a study that sought to identify the emotions felt by Byron at a particular time in his life

    (D)   a study in which a literary critic argues that the language of Byron's poetry was more subtle than that of Keats' poetry

    (E)   a study in which a literary critic drew on experiences from his or her own life

4. Which one of the following statements best describes the organization of the first paragraph of the passage?

    (A)   A generalization is made and then gradually refuted.

    (B)   A number of theories are discussed and then the author chooses the most convincing one.

    (C)   Several categories are mentioned and then one category is discussed in some detail.

    (D)   A historical trend is delineated and then a prediction about the future of the trend is offered.

    (E)   A classification is made and then a rival classification is substituted in its place.

5. The author mentions that "Byron's literary craftsmanship is irregular" (lines 27-28) most probably in order to

    (A)   contrast Byron's poetic skill with that of Shakespeare

    (B)   dismiss craftsmanship as a standard by which to judge poets

    (C)   offer another reason why Byron is not a "great" poet

    (D)   point out a negative consequence of Byron's belief that the cosmos is incomprehensible

    (E)   indicate the most-often-cited explanation of why Byron's poetry lacks subtle verbal nuances

6. According to the author, Shakespeare's poems differ from Byron's in that Shakespeare's poems

    (A)   have elicited a wider variety of responses from both literary critics and biographers

    (B)   are on the whole less susceptible to being read as subtle verbal creations

    (C)   do not grow out of, or are not motivated by, actual events or circumstances in the poet's life

    (D)   provide the attentive reader with a greater degree of illumination concerning his or her own weaknesses and aspirations

    (E)   can often be read without the reader's being curious about what biographical factors motivated the poet to write them

7. The author indicates which one of the following about biographers' speculation concerning Byron's life?

    (A)   Such speculation began in earnest with Escarpit's study.

    (B)   Such speculation continues today.

    (C)   Such speculation is less important than consideration of Byron's poetry.

    (D)   Such speculation has not given us a satisfactory sense of Byron's life.

    (E)   Such speculation has been carried out despite the objections of literary critics.

8. The passage supplies specific information that provides a definitive answer to which one of the following questions?

    (A)   What does the author consider to be the primary enjoyment derived from reading Byron?

    (B)   Who among literary critics has primarily studied Byron's poems?

    (C)   Which moments in Byron's life exerted the greatest pressure on his poetry?

    (D)   Has Byron ever been considered to be a "great" poet?

    (E)   Did Byron exert an influence on Europeans in the latter part of the nineteenth century?

Passage #16: December 1992 Questions 22-28

In the history of nineteenth-century landscape painting in the United States, the Luminists are distinguished by their focus on atmosphere and light. The accepted view of Luminist paintings is
(5) that they are basically spiritual and imply a tranquil mysticism that contrasts with earlier American artists' concept of nature as dynamic and energetic. According to this view, the Luminist atmosphere, characterized by "pure and constant light," guides
(10) the onlooker toward a lucid transcendentalism, an idealized vision of the world.

What this view fails to do is to identify the true significance of this transcendental atmosphere in Luminist paintings. The prosaic factors that are
(15) revealed by a closer examination of these works suggest that the glowing appearance of nature in Luminism is actually a sign of nature's domestication, its adaptation to human use. The idealized Luminist atmosphere thus seems to
(20) convey, not an intensification of human responses to nature, but rather a muting of those emotions, like awe and fear, which untamed nature elicits.

One critic, in describing the spiritual quality of harbor scenes by Fitz Hugh Lane, an important
(25) Luminist, carefully notes that "at the peak of Luminist development in the 1850s and 1860s, spiritualism in America was extremely widespread." It is also true, however, that the 1850s and 1860s were a time of trade expansion. From 1848 until his
(30) death in 1865, Lane lived in a house with a view of the harbor of Gloucester, Massachusetts, and he made short trips to Maine, New York, Baltimore, and probably Puerto Rico. In all of these places he painted the harbors with their ships—the
(35) instruments of expanding trade.

Lane usually depicts places like New York Harbor, with ships at anchor, but even when he depicts more remote, less commercially active harbors, nature appears pastoral and domesticated
(40) rather than primitive or unexplored. The ships, rather than the surrounding landscapes—including the sea—are generally the active element in his pictures. For Lane the sea is, in effect, a canal or a trade route for commercial activity, not a free,
(45) powerful element, as it is in the early pictures of his predecessor, Cole. For Lane nature is subdued, even when storms are approaching; thus, the sea is always a viable highway for the transport of goods. In sum, I consider Lane's sea simply an
(50) environment for human activity—nature no longer inviolate. The luminescence that Lane paints symbolizes nature's humbled state, for the light itself is as docile as the Luminist sea, and its tranquillity in a sense signifies no more than good

(55) conditions on the highway to progress. Progress, probably even more than transcendence, is the secret message of Luminism. In a sense, Luminist pictures are an ideological justification of the atmosphere necessary for business, if also an
(60) exaggerated, idealistic rendering of that atmosphere.

22. The passage is primarily concerned with discussing

(A) the importance of religion to the art of a particular period
(B) the way one artist's work illustrates a tradition of painting
(C) the significance of the sea in one artist's work
(D) differences in the treatment of nature as a more active or a less active force
(E) variations in the artistic treatment of light among nineteenth-century landscape painters

23. The author argues that nature is portrayed in Lane's pictures as

(A) wild and unexplored
(B) idealized and distant
(C) continually changing
(D) difficult to understand
(E) subordinate to human concerns

24. The passage contains information to suggest that the author would most probably agree with which one of the following statements?

(A) The prevailing religious principles of a given time can be reflected in the art of that time.
(B) In order to interest viewers, works of art must depict familiar subjects in detail.
(C) Because commerce is unusual as a subject in art, the painter of commercial activity must travel and observe it widely.
(D) Knowing about the environment in which an artist lived can aid in an understanding of a work by that artist.
(E) The most popular works of art at a given time are devoted to furthering economic or social progress.

HUMANITIES

25. According to the author, a supporter of the view of Luminism described in the first paragraph would most likely

    (A) be unimpressed by the paintings' glowing light
    (B) consider Luminist scenes to be undomesticated and wild
    (C) interpret the Luminist depiction of nature incorrectly
    (D) see Luminist paintings as practical rather than mystical
    (E) focus on the paintings' subject matter instead of on atmosphere and light

26. According to the author, the sea is significant in Lane's paintings because of its association with

    (A) exploration
    (B) commerce
    (C) canals
    (D) idealism
    (E) mysticism

27. The author's primary purpose is to

    (A) refute a new theory
    (B) replace an inadequate analysis
    (C) summarize current critics' attitudes
    (D) support another critic's evaluation
    (E) describe the history of a misinterpretation

28. The author quotes a critic writing about Lane (lines 25-27) most probably in order to

    (A) suggest that Luminism was the dominant mode of painting in the 1850s and 1860s
    (B) support the idea that Lane was interested in spiritualism
    (C) provide an example of the primary cultural factors that influenced the Luminists
    (D) explain why the development of Luminism coincided with that of spiritualism
    (E) illustrate a common misconception concerning an important characteristic of Lane's paintings

Wherever the crime novels of P. D. James are discussed by critics, there is a tendency on the one hand to exaggerate her merits and on the other to castigate her as a genre writer who is getting above
(5) herself. Perhaps underlying the debate is that familiar, false opposition set up between different kinds of fiction, according to which enjoyable novels are held to be somehow slightly lowbrow, and a novel is not considered true literature unless it
(10) is a tiny bit dull.

Those commentators who would elevate James's books to the status of high literature point to her painstakingly constructed characters, her elaborate settings, her sense of place, and her love of
(15) abstractions: notions about morality, duty, pain, and pleasure are never far from the lips of her police officers and murderers. Others find her pretentious and tiresome; an inverted snobbery accuses her of abandoning the time-honored conventions of the
(20) detective genre in favor of a highbrow literary style.

The critic Harriet Waugh wants P. D. James to get on with "the more taxing business of laying a tricky trail and then fooling the reader"; Philip Oakes in The Literary Review groans, "Could we
(25) please proceed with the business of clapping the handcuffs on the killer?"

James is certainly capable of strikingly good writing. She takes immense trouble to provide her characters with convincing histories and passions.
(30) Her descriptive digressions are part of the pleasure of her books and give them dignity and weight. But it is equally true that they frequently interfere with the story; the patinas and aromas of a country kitchen receive more loving attention than does the
(35) plot itself. Her devices to advance the story can be shameless and thin, and it is often impossible to see how her detective arrives at the truth; one is left to conclude that the detective solves crimes through intuition. At this stage in her career P. D. James
(40) seems to be less interested in the specifics of detection than in her characters' vulnerabilities and perplexities.

However, once the rules of a chosen genre cramp creative thought, there is no reason why an
(45) able and interesting writer should accept them. In her latest book, there are signs that James is beginning to feel constrained by the crime-novel genre. Here her determination to leave areas of ambiguity in the solution of the crime and to
(50) distribute guilt among the murderer, victim, and bystanders points to a conscious rebellion against the traditional neatness of detective fiction. It is fashionable, though reprehensible, for one writer to prescribe to another. But perhaps the time has come
(55) for P. D. James to slide out of her handcuffs and stride into the territory of the mainstream novel.

1. Which one of the following best states the author's main conclusion?

(A) Because P. D. James's potential as a writer is stifled by her chosen genre, she should turn her talents toward writing mainstream novels.

(B) Because the requirements of the popular novel are incompatible with true creative expression, P. D. James's promise as a serious author has been diminished.

(C) The dichotomy between popular and sophisticated literature is well illustrated in the crime novels of P. D. James.

(D) The critics who have condemned P. D. James's lack of attention to the specifics of detection fail to take into account her carefully constructed plots.

(E) Although her plots are not always neatly resolved, the beauty of her descriptive passages justifies P. D. James's decision to write in the crime-novel genre.

2. The author refers to the "patinas and aromas of a country kitchen" (line 33) most probably in order to

(A) illustrate James's gift for innovative phrasing
(B) highlight James's interest in rural society
(C) allow the reader to experience the pleasure of James's books
(D) explain how James typically constructs her plots
(E) exemplify James's preoccupation with descriptive writing

3. The second paragraph serves primarily to

(A) propose an alternative to two extreme opinions described earlier
(B) present previously mentioned positions in greater detail
(C) contradict an assertion cited previously
(D) introduce a controversial interpretation
(E) analyze a dilemma in greater depth

4. The passage supports which one of the following statements about detective fiction?

   (A) There are as many different detective-novel conventions as there are writers of crime novels.

   (B) Detective fiction has been characterized by extremely high literary quality.

   (C) Detective fiction has been largely ignored by literary critics.

   (D) There is very little agreement among critics about the basic elements of a typical detective novel.

   (E) Writers of detective fiction have customarily followed certain conventions in constructing their novels.

5. The passage suggests that both Waugh and Oakes consider James's novels to have

   (A) too much material that is extraneous to the solution of the crime

   (B) too little characterization to enable the reader to solve the crime

   (C) too few suspects to generate suspense

   (D) too simple a plot to hold the attention of the reader

   (E) too convoluted a plot for the reader to understand

6. It can be inferred from the passage that, in the author's view, traditional detective fiction is characterized by

   (A) concern for the weaknesses and doubts of the characters

   (B) transparent devices to advance the plot

   (C) the attribution of intuition to the detective

   (D) the straightforward assignment of culpability for the crime

   (E) attention to the concepts of morality and responsibility

7. The author characterizes the position of some critics as "inverted snobbery" (line 18) because they hold which one of the following views?

   (A) Critics of literature must acknowledge that they are less talented than creators of literature.

   (B) Critics should hesitate to disparage popular authors.

   (C) P. D. James's novels should focus less on characters from the English landed gentry.

   (D) Detective fiction should be content to remain an unambitious literary genre.

   (E) P. D. James should be less fastidious about portraying violence.

8. Which one of the following quotations about literature best exemplifies the "familiar" attitude mentioned in lines 5-10?

   (A) "The fantasy and whimsy characteristic of this writer's novels qualify them as truly great works of literature."

   (B) "The greatest work of early English literature happens to be a highly humorous collection of tales."

   (C) "A truly great work of literature should place demands upon its readers, rather than divert them."

   (D) "Although many critics are condescending about best-selling novels, I would not wish to challenge the opinion of millions of readers."

   (E) "A novel need only satisfy the requirements of its particular genre to be considered a true work of literature."

Passage #18: June 1996 Questions 21-27

Two impressive studies have reexamined Eric
Williams' conclusion that Britain's abolition of the
slave trade in 1807 and its emancipation of slaves in
its colonies in 1834 were driven primarily by
(5) economic rather than humanitarian motives.
Blighted by depleted soil, indebtedness, and the
inefficiency of coerced labor, these colonies,
according to Williams, had by 1807 become an
impediment to British economic progress.
(10) Seymour Drescher provides a more balanced
view. Rejecting interpretations based either on
economic interest or the moral vision of
abolitionists, Drescher has reconstructed the populist
characteristics of British abolitionism, which
(15) appears to have cut across lines of class, party,
and religion. Noting that between 1780 and 1830
antislavery petitions outnumbered those on any
other issue, including parliamentary reform,
Drescher concludes that such support cannot be
(20) explained by economic interest alone, especially
when much of it came from the unenfranchised
masses. Yet, aside from demonstrating that such
support must have resulted at least in part from
widespread literacy and a tradition of political
(25) activism, Drescher does not finally explain how
England, a nation deeply divided by class struggles,
could mobilize popular support for antislavery
measures proposed by otherwise conservative
politicians in the House of Lords and approved
(30) there with little dissent.
David Eltis' answer to that question actually
supports some of Williams' insights. Eschewing
Drescher's idealization of British traditions of
liberty, Eltis points to continuing use of low wages
(35) and Draconian vagrancy laws in the seventeenth and
eighteenth centuries to ensure the industriousness of
British workers. Indeed, certain notables even called
for the enslavement of unemployed laborers who
roamed the British countryside—an acceptance of
(40) coerced labor that Eltis attributes to a preindustrial
desire to keep labor costs low and exports
competitive. By the late eighteenth century,
however, a growing home market began to alert
capitalists to the importance of "want creation" and
(45) to incentives such as higher wages as a means of
increasing both worker productivity and the number
of consumers. Significantly, it was products grown
by slaves, such as sugar, coffee, and tobacco, that
stimulated new wants at all levels of British
(50) society and were the forerunners of products
intended in modern capitalist societies to satisfy
what Eltis describes as "nonsubsistence or
psychological needs." Eltis concludes that in an
economy that had begun to rely on voluntary labor
(55) to satisfy such needs, forced labor necessarily began

to appear both inappropriate and counterproductive
to employers. Eltis thus concludes that, while
Williams may well have underestimated the
economic viability of the British colonies employing
(60) forced labor in the early 1800s, his insight into the
economic motives for abolition was partly accurate.
British leaders became committed to colonial labor
reform only when they became convinced, for
reasons other than those cited by Williams, that free
(65) labor was more beneficial to the imperial economy.

21. Which one of the following best describes the main
idea of the passage?

(A) Although they disagree about the degree
to which economic motives influenced
Britain's abolition of slavery, Drescher and
Eltis both concede that moral persuasion by
abolitionists was a significant factor.
(B) Although both Drescher and Eltis have
questioned Williams' analysis of the
motivation behind Britain's abolition
of slavery, there is support for part of
Williams' conclusion.
(C) Because he has taken into account
the populist characteristics of British
abolitionism, Drescher's explanation of
what motivated Britain's abolition of
slavery is finally more persuasive than that
of Eltis.
(D) Neither Eltis nor Drescher has succeeded
in explaining why support for Britain's
abolition of slavery appears to have cut
across lines of party, class, and religion.
(E) Although flawed in certain respects,
Williams' conclusions regarding the
economic condition of British slave
colonies early in the nineteenth century
have been largely vindicated.

22. It can be inferred that Eltis cites the views of
"certain notables" (line 37) in order to

(A) support the claim that British traditions of
liberty were not as strong as Drescher
believed them to be
(B) support the contention that a strong labor
force was important to Britain's economy
(C) emphasize the importance of slavery as an
institution in preindustrial Britain
(D) indicate that the laboring classes provided
little support for the abolition of slavery
(E) establish that laborers in preindustrial
Britain had few civil rights

HUMANITIES

23. Which one of the following best states Williams' view of the primary reason for Britain's abolition of the slave trade and the emancipation of slaves in its colonies?

    (A)   British populism appealed to people of varied classes, parties, and religions.

    (B)   Both capitalists and workers in Britain accepted the moral precepts of abolitionists.

    (C)   Forced labor in the colonies could not produce enough goods to satisfy British consumers.

    (D)   The operation of colonies based on forced labor was no longer economically advantageous.

    (E)   British workers became convinced that forced labor in the colonies prevented paid workers from receiving higher wages.

24. According to Eltis, low wages and Draconian vagrancy laws in Britain in the seventeenth and eighteenth centuries were intended to

    (A)   protect laborers against unscrupulous employment practices

    (B)   counter the move to enslave unemployed laborers

    (C)   ensure a cheap and productive work force

    (D)   ensure that the work force experienced no unemployment

    (E)   ensure that products produced in British colonies employing forced labor could compete effectively with those produced in Britain

25. It can be inferred that the author of the passage views Drescher's presentation of British traditions concerning liberty as

    (A)   accurately stated
    (B)   somewhat unrealistic
    (C)   carefully researched
    (D)   unnecessarily tentative
    (E)   superficially convincing

26. The information in the passage suggests that Eltis and Drescher agree that

    (A)   people of all classes in Britain supported the abolition of slavery

    (B)   the motives behind Britain's abolition of slavery were primarily economic

    (C)   the moral vision of abolitionists played a vital part in Britain's abolition of slavery

    (D)   British traditions of liberty have been idealized by historians

    (E)   Britain's tradition of political activism was primarily responsible for Britain's abolition of slavery

27. According to the passage, Eltis argues against which one of the following contentions?

    (A)   Popular support for antislavery measures existed in Britain in the early nineteenth century.

    (B)   In the early nineteenth century, colonies that employed forced labor were still economically viable.

    (C)   British views concerning personal liberty motivated nineteenth-century British opposition to slavery.

    (D)   Widespread literacy in Britain contributed to public opposition to slavery in the early nineteenth century.

    (E)   Antislavery measures proposed by conservative politicians in the early nineteenth century met with little opposition.

Chapter 2: Diversity I

Passage #1: June 1991 Questions 1-8

1. C	(GR, MP)	All	
2. E	(GR, Parallel)	49-52	"Wheatley adopted......but replacements."
3. D	(CR, Must)	19-24	"African languages......spoke English."
4. D	(SR, Must, P)	31-40	"The standards......casual talk."
5. A	(CR, Must)	31-45	"The standards......reigning conventions."
6. E	(CR, Weaken)	26-31	"Wheatley's work......not exploit."
		54-56	"Wheatley's poetry......literary language."
7. D	(GR, Must, AP)	24-31	"Given her......not exploit."
8. B	(GR, Must, AP)	53-60	"Thus limited......American poet."
		26-31	"Wheatley's work......not exploit."

Passage #2: October 1991 Questions 1-6

1. C	(CR, Must)	39-40	"they contain…enumeration."
2. B	(SR, Must)	42-48	"There is…artfully crafted."
3. D	(GR, Must, AP)	26-32	"Jubilee…Europeanized."
4. B	(CR, Must, P)	19-32	"In 1862 white writers…Europeanized."
5. A	(GR, Must, AP)	29-32	"Clearly…Europeanized."
6. D	(GR, Must, AP)	33-37	"Even more…African American Literature."

Passage #3: February 1992 Questions 14-20

14. D	(GR, MP)	All	
15. C	(CR, Must, SP)	17-20	"Typical of......*of Women*."
16. B	(SR, Must)	20-26	"The emergence......for women."
17. D	(SR, Must, P)	1-13	"Women's participation......women's participation."
18. A	(CR, Must, SP)	43-47	"For Landes......resist suppression."
19. E	(SR, Must, P)	39-56	"What makes......political interests."
		63-66	"in the......borrowed voices."
20. B	(GR, Must, P)	All	

Passage #4: October 1992 Questions 7-12

7. E	(CR, Must)	15-16	"more typical…teams."
8. D	(CR, Must, P)	20-24	"What money…mission field.")
9. A	(GR, Must, O)	All	
10. A	(CR, Weaken)	20-30	"What money…women abroad."
11. D	(CR, Must)	33-38	"the advantages…female modesty."
12. D	(CR, Must)	33-38	"the advantages…female modesty."
		45-53	"The presence…in medicine."

Passage #5: June 1994 Questions 22-27

22. B	(GR, MP)	All	
23. B	(CR, Must)	5-19	"most historians…other healers."
24. E	(CR, Must, AP)	43-57	"The advantages…and 1530."
25. B	(CR, Must)	61-68	"Future studies…medieval society."
26. D	(CR, Must, P)	9-19	"although women…other healers."
27. D	(GR, Must, P)	All	

Passage #6: September 1995 Questions 22-27

22. C	(GR, MP)	All	
23. D	(CR, Must, P)	31-40	"Even scholars…middle-class women."
24. C	(SR, Must, AP)	25-35	"The contrast between…desirable past."
25. A	(SR, Must)	57-68	"…whereas…changes to women's lives."
26. A	(SR, Must)	41-48	"Recent publications…colonial women."
27. B	(SR, Must, SP)	48-57	"The new scholarship…colonial period."

Passage #7: December 1995 Questions 1-8

1. E	(GR, Must)	7-13	"There is no…literary canon."
2. B	(CR, Must)	14-18	"The details…upon its publication."
3. C	(GR, MP)	41-46	"Recent acclaim…Hurston's novel."
4. E	(CR, Must)	41-56	"Recent acclaim…within her work."
5. C	(CR, Must)	23-36	"the narration is exactly… "no message."
6. B	(CR, Must, SP)	29-33	"Black writers…the United States
7. C	(CR, Must, AP)	41-60	"Recent acclaim…in writing."
8. B	(GR, Must, P)	All	

Passage #8: October 1996 Questions 1-6

1. B	(GR, MP)	1-9	"The career......innovative sounds."
2. E	(CR, Must)	13-18	"think tank......jazz style."
3. A	(CR, Must)	14-17	"The work......to bebop"
4. E	(GR, Must, AP)	All	
5. D	(SR, Parallel)	40-44	"By 1969......movie director."
6. B	(CR, Weaken)	57-62	"But because…they cling."

Chapter 3: Diversity II

Passage #1: October 1991 Questions 7-13

7. E	(GR, Must-X)	9-12	(A): "the half…United States."
		1-5	(B): "Historians generally…Industrial Revolution."
		22-32	(C): "Thoreau and…unqualified improvement."
		51-53	(D): "(Had he…much stronger.)"
8. B	(SR, Must)	18-32	"What Stilgoe…unqualified improvement."
9. B	(CR, Must, SP)	33-51	"Stilgoe's assertion…and ambivalence."
10. E	(SR, Must, P)	33-42	"Stilgoe's assertion…the time."
11. C	(CR, Must, SP)	42-53	"The volume…much stronger.)"
12. D	(GR, Must, AP)	33-42	"Stilgoe's assertion…the time."
13 A	(GR, Must, P)	All	
		12-17	"In a…is unconvincing."

Passage #2: December 1991 Questions 21-28

21. E	(GR, Must, MP)	All	
22. A	(SR, Must, AP)	14-19	"The Anglo…enclosing pattern."
23. C	(CR, Must, AP)	40-52	"Second,…bordered styles."
24. D	(CR, Must-X)	1-12	"Amsden has…about 1890,"
25. D	(CR, Must)	50-61	"Third,…the border."
26. C	(CR, Must)	28-61	"Amsden's view…the border."
27. B	(SR, Must, P)	55-61	"In the…the border."
28. B	(GR, Must, P)	All	

Passage #3: February 1992 Questions 21-27

21. B	(GR, Must, MP)	All	
		15-22	"In a...finally, persuasive."
22. C	(CR, Must)	3-5	"Rewald's History...stylistic innovations."
23. C	(CR, Must)	23-25	"In attempting...of Impressionism."
		20-21	"his aim...sociocultural context."
24. A	(CR, Must)	11-13	"the Impressionists'...their pictures"
25. D	(GR, Must, O)	All	
26. D	(SR, Must, P)	56-62	"Not only...the other."
27. E	(CR, Must, AP)	59-62	"Their paintings...the other."

Passage #4: February 1993 Questions 1-7

1. E	(GR, Must)	All	
2. D	(GR, Must)	25-39	"In reconciling......full-time employment."
3. C	(CR, Must, AP)	16-24	"Although a......child-rearing responsibilities."
4. B	(CR, Must, AP)	12-15	"Conventional full-time......child-care responsibility."
5. D	(CR, Must X)	5-12	"Although day-care......their parents."
6. A	(GR, Must X)	16-68	"Although a......labor market."
7. A	(SR, Must, E)	All	

Passage #5: February 1993 Questions 21-27

21. C	(GR, MP)	All	
22. C	(CR, Strengthen)	48-51	"Additionally...political patronage."
23. D	(GR, Must, O)	All	
24. E	(CR, Must, AP)	27-36	"However...back to the tribe."
		48-56	"Additionally, politicians...government."
25. B	(CR, Must)	1-3	"In 1887...Native Americans."
		23-26	"Native Americans...of land."
26. B	(CR, Must)	1-15	"In 1887...the land."
27. D	(CR, Strengthen)	37-47	"When stated...and prestige."
		57-62	"One hypothesis...privatization system."

Passage #6: June 1993 Questions 14-20

14. D	(GR, MP)	All	
		1-9	"Any study......their subjects?"
		56-60	"Analysts should......their production."
15. E	(SR, Parallel)	23-27	"Even if......or germane."
16. B	(CR, Must, AP)	56-58	"Analysts should......authored texts."
17. D	(CR, Must)	28-37	"Readers of......American consciousness."
18. A	(SR, Must)	1-4	"Any study......and interpretation."
19. C	(CR, Must)	56-58	"Analysts should......authored texts."
20. B	(CR, Must, P)	15-23	"Blassingame has......faithfully produced."

Passage #7: October 1993 Questions 7-13

7. C	(CR, Must)	4-12	"Because...mainstream society."
8. A	(CR, Must)	55-59	"...they determined...for tribal members."
9. A	(SR, Must, O)	All	
10. C	(SR, Must, P)	4-12	"Because...mainstream society."
11. B	(CR, Must, SP)	5-12	"...life on reservations...society."
12. A	(CR, Must, SP)	51-53	"...Oneida deligates...upon the treaty."
13. B	(SR, Parallel)	33-35	"The efforts failed...similar offers before."

Passage #8: June 1995 Questions 22-27

22. E	(CR, Must)	1-11	"In 1964…work forces."
23. B	(CR, Must)	30-32	"in the mid-1940s…white schools"
24. C	(GR, Must, P)	All	
25. C	(CR, Must, SP)	12-16	"proponents of…and 1975."
26. A	(SR, Must, P)	57-70	"True,…economic progress."
27. D	(CR, Must)	12-17	"proponents of…historical forces."

Chapter 4: Diversity III

Passage #1: June 1992 Questions 22-27

22. C	(GR, MP)	All	
23. E	(SR, Must)	20-32	"For example……her people"
24. B	(SR, Must, P)	26-30	"Michelson's work……psychological motivation."
25. E	(CR, Must)	56-60	"Although Campbell……was written."
26. C	(CR, Must)	34-41	"The difference……patterns are."
27. C	(CR, Parallel)	4-18	"Life-passage……her culture."

Passage #2: December 1994 Questions 9-13

9. E	(GR, Must)	1-6	"For too…that institution."
10. B	(CR, Must)	43-48	"during the…status (1667)."
11. A	(CR, Must, P)	48-63	"Anthony Johnson,…in Virginia."
12. D	(CR, Must, AP)	All	
13. D	(GR, Must, P)	All	

Passage #3: June 1995 Questions 8-15

8. E	(GR, MP)	All	
9. E	(CR, Must, P)	22-27	"Perhaps more…folk performers."
10. C	(SR, Must)	49-59	"These recent…particular culture."
11. B	(CR, Must)	7-9	"since the…of creativity."
12. A	(CR, Must, SP)	1-10	"It has…in writing."
13. A	(CR, Parallel)	1-6	"It has…oral culture."
14. D	(SR, Must, P)	34-52	"Recent works…use it."
15. B	(CR, Must, AP)	43-48	"Another notable…repertoire analysis."

Passage #4: December 1992 Questions 16-21

16. B	(GR, MP)	All	
17. B	(CR, Must, AP)	53-60	"Because his……the Cherokee."
18. D	(CR, Must)	45-49	"most members……White settlers."
19. E	(CR, Must, SP)	35-44	"Traditionalist Cherokee……White allies."
20. C	(CR, Must)	19-30	"Missionaries did……and practices."
21. D	(CR, Weaken)	15-30	"William G. McLoughlin…practices."

Passage #5: October 1996 Questions 22-26

22. D	(GR, Must, O)	All	
23. E	(GR, Must, MP)	25-27	"Lowe sets...archeological evidence."
		50-54	"it is...available data."
24. E	(CR, Parallel, SP)	9-11	"Lowe assumes...been abandoned."
		57-62	"Lowe's assumption...had ceased."
25. B	(CR, Must, AP)	5	"Like previous...relies on."
		25-28	"Lowe sets...archeological evidence."
		47-52	"If there...historic activity."
26. E	(GR, Must, AP)	47-54	"If there...available data."

Chapter 5: Law

Passage #1: June 1991 Questions 17-21

17. A	(CR, Must)	46-50	"Fact-finding......adversarial system)"
18. E	(CR, Must, AP)	43-45	"the inquisitorial......and protective."
19. B	(CR, Must)	1-13	"There are......of society"
20. D	(CR, Must, X)	26-45	(A): "By contrast...protection."
		38-40	(B): "The system mandates...possession."
		43-44	(C): "...the inquisitional...trial."
		55-59	(E): "...if given the choice...system."
21. B	(CR, Must, AP)	26-59	"By contrast...adversarial system."

Passage #2: October 1991 Questions 22-28

22. B	(GR, Must, P)	All	
23. E	(CR, Must, AP)	1-25	"The Constitution......such decisions."
24. B	(GR, Must X)	37-54	"the Vietnam......been deployed."
25. B	(SR, Must)	9-10	"The constitution......declare war,"
		49-54	"The resolution......been deployed."
26. C	(GR, Must, AP)	21-25	"the spirit......such decisions."
27. A	(CR, Must, AP)	21-23	"the spirit......deploy troops,"
		29-34	"One scholar......Vietnam conflict"
28. D	(CR, Must)	49-54	"The resolution......been deployed."

Passage #3: June 1992 Questions 1-8

1. A	(GR, Must, P)	All	
2. D	(SR, Must, AP)	11-29	"In order......two counts."
3. D	(CR, Must)	1-11	"Governments of......for itself."
4. E	(CR, Must)	36-39	"the contracting......civil contracts."
5. E	(SR, Must)	51-57	"In both......specific provision."
6. C	(SR, Must, P)	48-57	"Second,......specific provision."
7. D	(GR, Must, MP)	All	
8. A	(SR, Weaken)	57-62	"Indeed,......state power."

Passage #4: February 1994 Questions 15-21

15. E	(CR, Must)	34-36	"The realists...distinction loosely."
16. E	(CR, Must)	28-30	"...the holding...reasons for it."
17. B	(CR, Must, SP)	46-51	"When judging...contradictory one."
18. A	(GR, Must, SP)	3-6	"These scholars believe...unclear."
19. D	(CR, Must, SP)	31-36	"...and the dicta...distinction loosely."
20. D	(GR, O)	All	
21. D	(GR, Must, E)	All	

Passage #5: October 1994 Questions 14-20

14. C	(GR, Must)	All	
15. E	(CR, Must, SP)	18-41	"Consider, ...not observed."
16. E	(SR, Must)	18-47	"Consider,......or enforcement."
17. D	(GR, Must X)	1-3	(A): "Although the legal...differ profoundly..."
		All	(B): "Although the legal...ignored altogether."
		18-19	(C): "For example...legally ineffective."
		35-37	(E): "Consider, for example...parks."
18. A	(SR, Must, P)	48-57	"Legal scholars......ignored altogether."
19. C	(GR, Must)	41-47	"Once the......or enforcement."
20. A	(GR, Must)	12-15	"Substantive reasons......to speak."

Passage #6: December 1994 Questions 21-27

21. A	(GR, Must, MP)	All	
		9-13	"In certain......the truth."
		37-40	"Recent empirical......predictable circumstances."
22. D	(GR, Must, AP)	49-60	"The notion......by lawyers."
23. D	(SR, Must, P)	14-36	"Although juries......evidence entirely."
24. C	(GR, Must, AP)	54-60	"most judges......by lawyers."
25. B	(CR, Weaken)	37-60	"Recent empirical......by lawyers."
26. A	(GR, Must, AP)	54-60	"most judges......by lawyers."
27. E	(CR, Must, AP)	27	"a jury"
		30-32	"may underestimate......persuasive manner."

Passage #7: September 1995 Questions 9-15

9. E	(SR, Must)	4-5	"Many…products of political compromise."
10. A	(SR, Must)	18-21	"Some critics…reviewing a case."
11. C	(SR, Must, P)	10-24	"Despite…judicial power."
12. B	(CR, Must, AP)	All	
13. D	(CR, Must, AP)	48-60	"A second achievement…possessed historically."
14. E	(GR, Must, P)	All	
15. B	(CR, Must, AP)	11-16	"…it is worth noting…important issues."

Passage #8: December 1995 Questions 9-15

9. C	(GR, MP)	All	
10. C	(CR, Must)	38-41	"For Dworkin…legal rules."
11. D	(CR, Must, AP)	49-56	"…we should expect…clearer meaning."
12. D	(SR, Must, P)	18-22	" 'Vehicle' has a core…prohibited."
13. B	(CR, Must, AP)	8-11	"H.L.A. Hart's…on which it rests."
14. B	(SR, Must)	4-7	"The ongoing debate…existing law."
15. E	(GR, Must, P)	All	

Passage #9: December 1992 Questions 1-7

1. A	(GR, Must, P)	All	
2. E	(GR, Parallel)	13-59	"Indeed,......academic circles."
3. A	(GR, Must, SP)	37-41	"Posner argues......single meaning."
4. C	(GR, Must)	25-27	"Legal questions......in literature."
5. B	(SR, Must, P)	10-13	"there can......law schools."
6. A	(GR, Must, SP)	20-30	"Critiquing the......might suppose."
7. A	(GR, Must, SP)	36-41	"the notion......single meaning."

Passage #10: June 1996 Questions 9-14

9. C	(GR, Must, P)	All	
10. E	(CR, Must)	18-22	"in cases......this regard.' "
11. D	(CR, Must)	23-26	"in most......common law."
12. B	(CR, Must)	39-42	"the practice......a stranger,"
13. A	(SR, Must, P)	36-39	"the common......the deceased."
14. D	(GR, MP)	26-29	"In cases......and museums."

Passage #11: October 1996 Questions 7-14

7. C	(GR, MP)	All	
		7-14	"One might......erring members."
8. A	(GR, Must)	43-45	"there was......ecclesiastical bar."
9. B	(SR, Must, P)	14-18	"Some even......guild members."
10. C	(CR, Must, P)	46-57	"church authorities......very common."
11. A	(CR Must)	18-21	"In the few......fellow lawyers."
12. B	(SR, Parallel)	58-68	"Such criticisms......own ranks."
13. B	(CR, Must)	7-10	"One might......often did,"
14. C	(CR, Must, AP)	All	

Chapter 6: Law-Regulation

Passage #1: February 1992 Questions 1-6

1. B	(CR, Must)	25-27	"since there......between nations."
2. C	(CR, Must)	8-12	"A nation......all activities."
3. A	(CR, Must)	14-15	"most nations......territorial waters."
		17-18	"large ocean......or restrictions."
		25-26	"there were......'open seas'"
		28-35	"The lack......by navigation."
4. C	(CR, Must)	48-52	"the establishment......larger ecosystems."
5. C	(CR, Must)	13-15	"because this......territorial waters."
6. D	(GR, Must)	All	

Passage #2: October 1992 Questions 1-6

1. E	(SR, Parallel)	9-17	"Much of......no effect."
2. C	(GR, Must)	17-24	"Carroll argues......right-to-work states."
3. A	(CR, Must, AP)	49-53	"craft unionism......labor market"
4. E	(CR, Must)	53-58	"strong positive......3 percent."
5. B	(CR, Must)	58-66	"If state......up wages."
6. D	(GR, Must, P)	All	

Passage #3: June 1993 Questions 7-13

7. A	(GR, MP)	All	
		26-27	"Trademark owners......marketing practices"
		59-63	"Since only......marketing cases."
8. D	(GR, Must, P)	All	
9. B	(SR, Must)	32-35	"authorized distributors......unauthorized channels."
10. A	(CR, Must— Point at Issue)	48-58	"The exhaustion......their trademarks."
11. B	(CR, Must, P)	26-32	"Trademark owners......postsale service."
12. C	(CR, Must, AP)	59-63	"Since only......marketing cases."
13. C	(CR, Must)	5-15	"Gray marketing......market channels."

Passage #4: February 1995 Questions 14-20

14. C	(GR, MP)	All	
15. B	(SR, Must)	1-23	"The legislature......cultural property."
16. C	(CR, Must, SP)	13-23	"Testifying in......cultural property."
17. C	(CR, Must, SP)	13-25	"Testifying in......for museums."
18. A	(SR, Must)	13-28	"Testifying in......Burke's concern."
19. D	(CR, Must, AP)	26-58	"However,......stolen works."
20. E	(CR, Must, AP)	28-38	"the proposed......searched for."
		54-58	"what is......stolen works."

Passage #5: December 1995 Questions 16-21

16. B	(CR, Must)	13-16	"Such a tax…use of energy."
17. A	(SR, Must, P)	19-27	"At first glance…Toronto conference."
18. A	(SR, Weaken)	10-16	"Because oil emits…use of energy."
19. B	(GR, Must, P)	All	
20. C	(SR, Must, AP)	51-54	"As a consequence."
21. E	(SR, Parallel)	35-43	"There are very…elusive."

Chapter 7: Social Science

Passage #1: June 1991 Questions 9-16

9. B	(GR, MP)	All	
10. E	(CR, Must)	19-21	"They also……cell division."
11. A	(SR, Must)	25-29	"Also,……or foamlike."
12. B	(CR, Must, SP)	35-37	"cytologists considered……living cell."
13. A	(SR, Must, P)	55-64	"This interaction……the past."
14. A	(GR, Must)	15	"in the……nineteenth century"
		31-32	"the newly……of life."
		44-46	"But in……molecular biology"
15. B	(CR, Must SP)	29-31	"Their interest……of protoplasm"
		33-35	"In general……basic processes"
16. C	(GR, Must, O)	All	

Passage #2: December 1991 Questions 8-15

8. C	(GR, MP)	All	
		25-64	"Boyle turned……their employers."
9. E	(SR, Must)	1-27	"Historians attempting……paid technicians"
10. C	(CR, Must)	48-54	"To seventeenth-century……their employers."
11. D	(CR, Must)	7-19	"Leaders of……Christian piety."
12. A	(GR, Must)	32-39	"Why were……and skill."
13. D	(SR, Must, O)	32-64	"Why were……their employers."
14. A	(SR, Must, P)	32-33	"Why were……their employers?"
		46-64	"all of……their employers."
15. D	(SR, Must)	40-41	"the clamor……scientific rhetoric"
		1-11	"Historians attempting……scientists themselves."

Passage #3: December 1991 Questions 16-20

16. E	(CR, Must, AP)	34-65	"Antitrust laws……to consumers."
17. E	(CR, Must)	7-13	"In order……related markets."
		48-60	"The antitrust……computer systems."
18. D	(SR, Must, P)	28-49	"Supracompetitive prices……monopoly power"
19. B	(CR, Must)	All	
20. A	(SR, Must)	All	

Passage #4: June 1992 Questions 9-15

9. C	(GR, Must, MP)	All	
		1-8	"Nico Frijda…raise counterexamples."
10. C	(CR, Must)	1-6	"Nico Frijda…as real."
11. C	(CR, Must)	49-56	"Frijda does…is pretending."
12. B	(CR, Must-X)	31-45	"Most psychologists,…illusory stimuli."
13. E	(SR, Must, O)	1-30	"Nico Frijda…is real."
14. B	(CR, Cannot-X)	13-22	"suppose I…with reality."
15. D	(CR, Must, SP)	40-45	"These debates…illusory stimuli."

Passage #5: October 1992 Questions 21-27

21. C	(GR, MP)	All	
		17-23	"Both minimills......becomes available."
		49-56	"Integrated producers......furnace operation."
22. A	(CR, Must X)	59-60	(B): "...they sell their finished products locally."
		51-55	(C): "...the minimills have dispensed...the mining."
		21-22	(D): "Both take advantage of new technology..."
		8-11	(E): "The minimills......for concrete."
		17-26	"Both minimills......geographic area"
23. C	(SR, Must, P)	39-45	"One might......economic trouble."
24. E	(SR, Must, O)	29-48	"Among the......nineteenth century."
25. E	(CR, Must)	49-56	"Integrated producers......furnace operation."
26. A	(GR, Parallel X)	29-56	"Among the......furnace operation."
27. E	(CR, Strengthen)	45-56	"The fact......furnace operation."

Passage #6: June 1993 Questions 1-6

1. D	(GR, Must, P)	All	
2. A	(CR, Must)	1-10	"After thirty......genetic code."
3. D	(GR, Must X)	32-33	(A): "...waste disposal may benefit..."
		18-21	(B): "Proponents of......organism's development."
		35-38	(C): "Agriculture might also take..soil."
		32-33	(E): "Energy...may benefit."
4. A	(GR, Weaken)	39-41	"A major......the laboratory."
5. E	(SR, Must, P)	60-65	"The implications......specific roles."
6. B	(GR, Strengthen)	47-52	"The effect......existing ecosystem."

Passage #7: June 1993 Questions 21-27

21. C	(GR, Must, MP)	All	
22. D	(CR, Must)	15-42	"Rubinstein's claim......worth investigating."
23. A	(CR, Must)	29-32	"What the......market values."
24. E	(CR, Must)	43-55	"The orthodox......middle-class income."
25. B	(CR, Must, P)	34-42	"A further......worth investigating."
26. D	(CR, Strengthen)	7-42	"A new......worth investigating."
27. E	(CR, Weaken)	50-53	"Rubinstein dismisses......manufacturing companies."

Passage #8: June 1994 Questions 1-7

1. D	(GR, MP)	All	
2. E	(GR, Must, AP)	1-10	"Nearly every...morally unjust."
3. B	(SR, Must, P)	1-23	"Nearly every...his own."
4. E	(CR, Must)	10-23	"this emphasis...his own."
5. D	(CR, Must)	26-29	"Thoreau...of society."
6. C	(CR, Must)	10-23	"this emphasis...his own."
7. C	(SR/CR, Must)	41-60	"Most transcendentalists...nineteenth century."

Passage #9: June 1994 Questions 8-14

8. A	(SR, Must, P)	19-23	"polyarchy reinforces......centrifugal characteristic,"
9. E	(SR, Must, P)	1-3	"In *Democracy*......or polyarchies"
		35-36	"During the......was vigorous."
10. B	(CR, Must)	25-32	"Polyarchy achieves......particular groups."
11. A	(CR, Must, SP)	7-16	"Of course,......defends polyarchy."
		22-25	"It is......democratic ideal."
12. B	(CR, Parallel)	7-16	"Of course,......defends polyarchy."
13. E	(CR, Strengthen)	22-46	"It is......decision-making."
14. D	(GR, Must)	All	

Passage #10: September 1995 Questions 16-21

16. C	(GR, Must, X)	27-29	(A): "many large…to a critical state."
		24-26	(B): "many large…traditional analysis."
		10-11	(D): "In a large…to a catastrophe."
		31-32	(E): "such systems…catastrophes."
17. E	(CR, Must)	42-45	"The system…edge of the disc."
18. A	(SR, Must)	20-22	"…they…proportionate to that disturbance."
19. E	(GR, Must, O)	All	
20. E	(SR, Parallel)	46-53	"Now when…remain unpredictable."
21. D	(GR, Must, AP)	23-31	"During the past few…the system."
		57-58	"Criticality is a global…sandpile."

Passage #11: December 1992 Questions 8-15

8. C	(CR, Must, AP)	32-39	"science's accumulation......and observation."
9. A	(GR, Must, SP)	41-44	"new scientific......to Kepler's)."
10. C	(SR, Must, P)	22-54	"While this......achieve prominence."
11. E	(SR, Must, P)	22-31	"While this......be falsified."
12. B	(SR, Must, AP)	1-21	"A recent......the historians."
13. D	(CR, Must, AP)	22-57	"While this......scientists believe."
14. A	(SR, Must, P)	57-62	"What the......scientific acceptance."
15. D	(SR, Must, AP)	55-57	"But one......scientists believe."
		17-24	"While these......deeply implausible."

Chapter 8: Hard Science

Passage #1: October 1991 Questions 14-21

14. D	(GR, Must, P)	All	
15. D	(CR, Must)	32-44	"The summer......to meet."
16. A	(CR, Must)	60-68	"Those eggs......macropterous offspring."
17. A	(CR, Must)	57-65	"Eggs laid......normal wings."
18. B	(CR, Must)	6-10	"Regulatory responses......for example."
19. E	(CR, Must)	21-36	"Most water-bug......for flight."
20. C	(SR, Must, P)	47-68	"The individual's......macropterous offspring."
21. A	(GR, Must, O)	All	

Passage #2: December 1991 Questions 1-7

1. E	(GR, Must, MP)	All	
2. D	(CR, Must)	21-30	"The most......strongly indicated."
3. A	(CR, Must, SP)	48-60	"Yet even......occulting body."
4. C	(GR, Must)	37-39	"With the......commonly reported."
5. C	(GR, Must)	48-51	"Yet even......secondary event."
6. D	(CR, Must)	37-46	"With the......secondary event"
7. C	(GR, Must, P)	All	

Passage #3: February 1992 Questions 7-13

7. E	(GR, Must)	All	
8. E	(SR, Parallel)	10-18	"The history......all-time high."
9. D	(CR, Must)	27-30	"But the......species perished."
10. B	(CR, Must, P)	39-43	"Hundreds of......is extensive."
11. B	(GR, Must X)	36-38	(A): "Half of the bird...through hunting..."
		36-38	(C): "Half of the...desruction of native forests."
		3-6	(D): "Today, as human populations expand...era."
		38-42	(E): "Hundreds...careless introduction of one fish..."
12. A	(CR, Must)	49-52	"unlike material......for granted."
13. C	(CR, Must, AP)	6-9	"The ultimate......be harmful."

Passage #4: June 1992 Questions 16-21

16. B	(CR, Must)	44-56	"Researchers reasoned......be uniform."
17. E	(CR, Must)	1-5	"Although bacteria......harmful substances."
		15-31	"One clue......change direction."
18. E	(SR, Must)	15-20	"One clue......is stronger."
		44-50	"Researchers reasoned......few tumbles."
19. C	(CR, Must)	15-31	"One clue......change direction."
20. B	(SR, Must, O)	32-58	"Biologists have......different times."
21. A	(GR, Must)	All	

Passage #5: February 1993 Questions 15-20

15. B	(GR, Must, MP)	All	
16. E	(CR, Must)	1-8	"Cultivation of......of time."
17. D	(SR, Must, P)	26-29	"These improvements......specific purposes."
18. C	(CR, Must)	1-19	"Cultivation of......suppresses phytopathogens."
19. A	(CR, Must, SP)	41-45	"Proponents,......was derived."
20. D	(CR, Weaken)	34-45	"Some experiments......was derived."

Passage #6: February 1994 Questions 1-8

1. A	(GR, MP)	All	
2. D	(CR, Must)	12-16	"These pumps......the wellhead."
3. B	(SR, Must, O)	1-47	"Oil companies......it operates."
4. E	(SR, Must)	26	" 'head,'......a pump,"
5. C	(CR, Must, AP)	5-12	"because processing......handle crude."
6. B	(CR, Must)	16-29	"Currently,......the shore."
7. E	(SR, Must)	30-41	"Of the......the other."
8. D	(GR, Must)	1-4	"Oil companies......substances ashore."

Passage #7: June 1994 Questions 15-21

15. C	(SR, Must)	14-20	"Sanders argued...this view."
16. C	(SR, Must, AP)	54-61	"Although no...rain forest today."
17. D	(CR, Must)	37-38	"in the Amazon...drier than uplands."
18. A	(GR, Must, O)	All	
19. E	(CR, Must, P)	48-53	"...the periodic...changing climates."
20. E	(CR, Must)	29-33	"This pattern...a stable climate?"
21. E	(SR, Strengthen)	48-53	"...the periodic...changing climates."

Passage #8: October 1994 Questions 21-27

21. D	(GR, Must, MP)	All		
22. A	(SR, Must)	15-30	"Serotonin is......into serotonin."
23. B	(CR, Must)	50-54	"drugs that......weight gain."
24. A	(CR, Must)	33-54	"Rats that......weight gain."
25. E	(SR, Must, P)	15-30	"Serotonin is......into serotonin."
26. C	(CR, Must)	44-50	"In human......crave carbohydrates."
27. E	(GR, Must, P)	All	

Passage #9: December 1994 Questions 1-8

1. A	(GR, Must, MP)	All	
2. D	(CR, Must)	21-40	"After each......replace them."
3. B	(CR, Must X, AP)	48-58	"Although the......adult brain."
4. C	(SR, Weaken)	40-47	"A possible......a lifetime."
5. D	(SR, Must, P)	12-24	"Young canaries......juvenile bird."
6. A	(CR, Must)	40-42	"A possible......life span"
7. C	(SR, Must, O)	28-47	"Recent neurological......a lifetime."
8. C	(CR, Must, AP)	40-41	"A possible......nerve cells"
		52-54	"Whether such......not known"

Passage #10: February 1995 Questions 1-6

1. C	(CR, Must)	16-21	"It is......inner core."
2. E	(CR, Must)	38-49	"A more......magnetic field."
		59-63	"But theories......the mantle."
3. A	(SR, Must, P)	31-38	"One proposal......heat-circulation pattern."
4. B	(CR, Must)	6-9	"Geological evidence......increasing rate."
5. D	(CR, Must)	30-31	"Several explanations......been proposed."
6. D	(CR, Must X)	30-49	"Several explanations......magnetic field."

Passage #11: June 1995 Questions 1-7

1. C	(CR, Must)	10-18	"This view......the dinosaurs."
2. A	(CR, Must)	40-41	"the lower......as meteorites"
3. D	(CR, Must)	38-47	"Although iridium......meteorite impact."
4. A	(GR, Must, P)	All	
5. B	(CR, Must)	47-60	"the volcanic-eruption......Earth's surface."
6. D	(SR, Must)	44-47	"a gas......meteorite impact."
7. B	(SR, Weaken)	19-34	"Currently available......Earth's crust."

Passage #12: December 1995 Questions 22-27

22. B	(GR, MP)	All	
23. B	(CR, Must, AP)	50-52	"The notion...not well supported."
24. D	(CR, Must)	29-34	"supporters of the cooling...vortex."
25. A	(CR, Must)	9-13	"between 1945 and...Celsius."
26. D	(GR, Must,O)	All	
27. E	(CR, Must, SP)	27-40	"...supporters...bring sub-Saharan rain."

Passage #13: June 1996 Questions #15-20

15. C	(GR, MP)	All	
		46-48	"A fourth and most plausible...extinction."
16. E	(CR, Must)	18-24	"the species-energy...number of species."
17. A	(CR, Must)	9-14	"...the 'time theory'...succession of ice ages."
18. E	(CR, Weaken)	62-66	"Since sub-groups...become new species."
19. D	(CR, Must)	1-4	"When the same...from pole to equator."
20. B	(GR, Must, AP)	37-52	"However, the ecology...extinction."

Passage #14: October 1996 Questions 15-21

15. B	(CR, Must)	11-17	"birds possessing......such attribute."
16. A	(SR, Must, P)	30-36	"There are......undyed juveniles."
17. B	(SR, Weaken)	47-50	"demonstrated social......held constant."
18. A	(GR, Must, O)	All	
19. E	(CR, Must)	26-27	"Rohwer's data......his assertions:"
20. D	(CR, Must)	5-7	"each bird......higher status."
21. B	(CR, Must)	33-34	"adults,......light-throated;"

Chapter 9: Humanities

Passage #1: June 1991 Questions 22-28

22. E	(GR, Must, AP)	21-23	"A profession......devotion."
		56-63	"Being a......of life"
23. D	(GR, Must, MP)	44-66	"Physicians are......continuing devotion"
24. C	(SR, Must, P)	All	
25. D	(GR, Must X)	40-43	"the prestige......they receive."
		53-56	"just as......and wholesomeness."
		60-65	"Professing oneself......a livelihood"
26. E	(GR, Must, AP)	56-66	"Being a......continuing devotion"
27. B	(SR, Must, E)	All	
28. C	(SR, Must, P)	19-44	" 'To profess"......their profession."

Passage #2: October 1992 Questions 13-20

13. D	(SR, Must)	20-33	"In the…to play."
14. A	(GR,MP)	All	
		11-13	"the early…troubling questions."
15. D	(SR, Must, P)	14-33	"Early music…to play."
16. B	(CR, Must)	47-56	"although in…are now."
17. B	(SR, Must, O)	34-60	"In addition…simply, changed."
18. D	(SR, Weaken)	47-56	"although in…are now."
19. D	(SR, Must, AP)	37-46	"The discovery…was found."
20. C	(CR, Must)	47-60	"although in…simply, changed."

Passage #3: February 1993 Questions 8-14

8. D	(GR, Must, P)	All	
9. A	(CR, Must)	23-36	"We now…English sources."
10. B	(SR, Must, P)	1-17	"Critics have…tragic vision."
11. C	(GR, Strengthen)	18-39	"The problem…to do."
12. C	(CR, Must, AP)	20-31	"We have…following age."
13. E	(GR, Must, SP)	18-39	"The problem…to do."
14. D	(CR, Must)	18-62	"The problem…the character."

Passage #4: October 1993 Questions 1-6

1. B	(GR, Must, MP)	All	
2. A	(GR, Must, AP/SP)	27-35	"Some even......unnecessarily cynical."
3. D	(CR, Weaken)	27-30	"Some even......and audience."
4. E	(CR, Must, P)	7-17	"Such new......traditional mounts."
5. C	(GR, Must)	1-4	"Many argue......of expression."
6. E	(CR, Must, AP)	59-63	"Finally,......modern art."

Passage #5: October 1993 Questions 14-20

14. B	(GR, Must, MP)	All		
		11-16	" 'In ancient…ancient politics."	
		59-61	"Athens,…democratic institutions."	
15. D	(CR, Must)	5-11	"The discovery…ancient societies."	
16. C	(SR, Must, P)	43-58	"Granted,…of behavior."	
17. A	(GR, Must-X)	27-42	"In fact,…or book."	
18. D	(SR, Must, P)	16-21	"In Athens,…'Law-giver.' "	
19. B	(SR, Must, P)	49-58	"An ancient…of behavior."	
20. B	(GR, Must, P)	All		

Passage #6: October 1993 Questions 21-27

21. C	(GR, Must, MP)	All	
		25-27	"though English……institutions differed."
22. D	(CR, Must X)	13-24	"In many……could vote."
23. C	(CR, Must)	28-39	"English legal……were omnipotent."
24. C	(CR, Must)	33-36	"Together with……of legislation."
25. E	(CR, Must)	5-12	"Steeped as……in England."
26. C	(CR, Must)	44-49	"To the……specific powers."
27. E	(GR, Must, P)	All	

Passage #7: February 1994 Questions 9-14

9. B	(GR, MP)	All	
		19-30	"Brown argues…as climate."
10. C	(GR, Must, P)	All	
11. B	(CR, Must)	19-25	"Brown argues…inconsequential detail."
12. E	(CR, Must)	50-64	"the development…painter's skill."
13. A	(CR, Must)	59-64	"the emphasis…painter's skill."
14. C	(SR, Weaken)	30-42	"Tuscan churches…religious stories."

Passage #8: February 1994 Questions 22-27

22. B	(CR, Must)	9-17	"Of the……of unrest."
23. D	(CR, Must)	23-33	"the theory……dominant group."
24. E	(CR, Must, SP)	38-43	"Political theorists……psychological dysfunctions;"
25. B	(SR, Must)	65-70	"A better……movement activity."
26. A	(SR, Weaken)	65-68	"A better……the press;"
27. E	(GR, MP)	All	

Passage #9: October 1994 Questions 1-7

1. D	(GR, MP)	All	
		1-12	"Modern architecture…its founders."
2. E	(GR, Must, SP)	31-42	"Wagner was…satisfactory way."
3. B	(GR, Must, SP)	47-63	"The apparent…Austrian Baroque."
4. C	(SR, Must)	20-31	"All modern…more complex."
5. B	(GR, Must)	1-8	"Modern architecture…modern architect."
6. E	(SR, Must, P)	47-57	"The apparent…Italian Renaissance."
7. E	(GR, Must, P)	All	
		8-12	"Otto Wagner's…its founders."

Passage #10: October 1994 Questions 8-13

8. E		(GR, Must, MP)	All	
			1-7	"In order......both together."
			23-27	"In order......will suffice."
9. C		(CR, Must)	7-12	"To use......labor market."
10. D		(SR, Must, P)	50-62	"On the......immigrant streams."
11. E		(CR, Must, AP)	1-7	"In order......both together."
			23-27	"In order......will suffice."
12. A		(GR, Must)	31-33	"For various......establish families."
			35-38	"Japanese immigrants......of immigration"
13. A		(GR, Must, AP)	All	
			23-27	"In order......will suffice."

Passage #11: December 1994 Questions 14-20

14. E	(GR, Must, O)	All	
15. D	(CR, Must, SP)	1-22	"Late-nineteenth-century......eighteenth century.' "
16. E	(CR, Must, SP)	36-50	"Most of......native air.' "
17. B	(SR, Must, P)	All	
		1-19	"Late-nineteenth-century......to reality."
		36-38	"Most of......and charming."
18. C	(CR, Must, AP)	All	
19. A	(CR, Must)	23-33	"In fact,......army rabble."
20. D	(CR, Must, Pr)	3-14	"more than......with photographs."

Passage #12: February 1995 Questions 7-13

7. A	(GR, MP)	All	
8. E	(GR, Must)	12-18	"The first......our attention."
9. C	(CR, Parallel)	1-4	"Innovations in......from stock."
10. B	(SR, Must, P)	44-56	"The fact......of rubble."
11. C	(SR, Must, O)	1-21	"Innovations in......coming events."
12. B	(CR, Must, AP)	44-50	"The fact......existing building."
13. D	(CR, Must, AP)	22-56	"With the......of rubble."

Passage #13: February 1995 Questions 21-27

21. A	(GR, Must, MP)	All	
		35-37	"These differences.....respective countries."
22. B	(CR, Must)	1-7	"Until recently,......States slavery."
23. C	(CR, Strengthen)	21-60	"Kolchin points......in Russia."
24. C	(SR. Must, P)	7-13	"the almost......of scholars."
25. A	(CR, Must)	13-17	"some historians......federal democracy—"
26. D	(CR, Must)	28-32	"in Russia......their estates,"
27. D	(CR, Must)	30-34	"In Russia......regular basis."

Passage #14: June 1995 Questions 16-21

16. C	(GR, MP)	All	
17. C	(CR, Must)	22-35	"The language…the merchant."
18. D	(CR, Must, AP)	39-40	"Pocock's ideas…proved fertile."
		57-62	"It is…their importance."
19. B	(SR, Must)	13-21	"While historians…text's composition."
20. D	(GR, Must, AP)	22-54	"The language…civic humanism."
21. A	(GR, Must, O)	All	

Passage #15: September 1995 Questions 1-8

1. B	(GR, MP)	All	
2. D	(CR, Must, P)	6-9	"Equally valuable…studies of this kind."
3. C	(GR, Must, AP)	16-20	"Byron's poetry…his life."
4. C	(SR, Must, O)	1-23	"Three kinds…to write it."
5. C	(SR, Must, P)	24-29	"No doubt…his lax literary method."
6. E	(CR, Must)	20-23	"I believe we…write it."
7. B	(CR, Must)	5-6	"biographers to this day…Byron's life."
8. A	(GR, Must)	35-37	"Our main pleasure…singular personality."

Passage #16: December 1992 Question 22-28

22. B	(GR, Must, P)	All	
23. E	(CR, Must)	36-60	"Lane usually…that atmosphere."
24. D	(GR, Must, AP)	28-35	"It is…expanding trade."
25. C	(SR, Must, SP)	4-14	"The accepted…Luminist paintings."
26. B	(CR, Must, AP)	43-51	"For Lane…longer inviolate."
27. B	(GR, Must, P)	All	
28. E	(SR, Must, P)	4-35	"The accepted…expanding trade."

Passage #17: June 1996 Questions 1-8

1. A	(GR, Must, MP)	All	
		46-48	"In her……crime-novel genre."
		54-56	"But perhaps……mainstream novel."
2. E	(SR, Must, P)	30-35	"Her descriptive……plot itself
3. B	(SR, Must, P)	5-10	"underlying the……bit dull."
		11-20	"Those commentators……literary style."
4. E	(GR, Must)	19-20	"the time……detective genre."
		51-52	"a conscious……detective fiction."
5. A	(CR, Must, SP)	21-26	"The critic……the killer?"
6. D	(GR, Must, AP)	39-42	"James seems……and perplexities."
		24-26	"Could we……the killer?"
		48-52	"her determination……detective fiction."
7. D	(SR, Must)	18-20	"an inverted……literary style."
8. C	(SR, Must)	All	

Passage #18: June 1996 Questions 21-27

21. B	(GR, Must, MP)	All	
		31-32	"Eltis' answer……Williams' insights."
22. A	(SR, Must, P)	32-37	"Eschewing Drescher's……British workers."
23. D	(CR, Must, SP)	2-9	"Britain's abolition……economic progress."
24. C	(CR, Must, SP)	34-37	"use of……British workers."
		39-42	"an acceptance……exports competitive."
25. B	(CR, Must, AP)	All	
		25-28	"Drescher does……little dissent."
		33-34	"Drescher's idealization……of liberty,"
26. A	(CR, Must, SP)	13-16	"Drescher has……and religion."
		31-65	"David Eltis'……imperial economy."
27. C	(CR, Must)	32-34	"Eschewing Drescher's……of liberty,"
		62-66	"British leaders……imperial economy."

APPENDIX

Test-by-Test Passage Location Identifier ████████████████████

This section contains a reverse lookup that references every passage in this book according to the source LSAT. The tests are listed in order of PrepTest number, from PrepTest 1 (June 1991) to PrepTest 20 (October 1996). All other LSAC publication identifiers are also listed. Thereafter, the chapter, and page number where each passage can be found in this book is listed.

If you choose, you can use this lookup to find the four passages from an individual test and then do those four passages in order, re-creating that test section.

Passage   Book Location

June 1991 (LSAT PrepTest 1)

Passage #1: Chapter 2, page 20
Passage #2: Chapter 7, page 104
Passage #3: Chapter 5, page 68
Passage #4: Chapter 9, page 158

October 1991 (LSAT PrepTest 2; LSAT TriplePrep, Volume 1)

Passage #1: Chapter 2, page 22
Passage #2: Chapter 3, page 38
Passage #3: Chapter 8, page 128
Passage #4: Chapter 5, page 70

December 1991 (LSAT PrepTest 3; LSAT TriplePrep, Volume 2)

Passage #1: Chapter 8, page 130
Passage #2: Chapter 7, page 106
Passage #3: Chapter 7, page 108
Passage #4: Chapter 3, page 40

February 1992 (LSAT PrepTest 4; LSAT TriplePrep, Volume 1)

Passage #1: Chapter 6, page 92
Passage #2: Chapter 8, page 132
Passage #3: Chapter 2, page 24
Passage #4: Chapter 3, page 42

June 1992 (LSAT PrepTest 5; LSAT TriplePrep, Volume 1)

Passage #1: Chapter 5, page 72
Passage #2: Chapter 7, page 110
Passage #3: Chapter 8, page 134
Passage #4: Chapter 4, page 56

October 1992 (LSAT PrepTest 6; LSAT TriplePrep, Volume 2)

Passage #1: Chapter 6, page 94
Passage #2: Chapter 2, page 26
Passage #3: Chapter 9, page 160
Passage #4: Chapter 7, page 112

December 1992 (LSAT PrepTest 18; 10 Actual, Official LSAT PrepTests)

Passage #1: Chapter 5, page 84
Passage #2: Chapter 7, page 124
Passage #3: Chapter 4, page 62
Passage #4: Chapter 9, page 188

February 1993 (LSAT PrepTest 7; LSAT TriplePrep, Volume 2; 10 Actual, Official LSAT PrepTests)

Passage #1: Chapter 3, page 44
Passage #2: Chapter 9, page 162
Passage #3: Chapter 8, page 136
Passage #4: Chapter 3, page 46

June 1993 (LSAT PrepTest 8; LSAT TriplePrep, Volume 3)

Passage #1: Chapter 7, page 114
Passage #2: Chapter 6, page 96
Passage #3: Chapter 3, page 48
Passage #4: Chapter 7, page 116

October 1993 (LSAT PrepTest 9; LSAT TriplePrep, Volume 3; 10 Actual, Official LSAT PrepTests)

Passage #1: Chapter 9, page 164
Passage #2: Chapter 3, page 50
Passage #3: Chapter 9, page 166
Passage #4: Chapter 9, page 168

February 1994 (LSAT PrepTest 10; LSAT TriplePrep, Volume 3; 10 Actual, Official LSAT PrepTests)

Passage #1: Chapter 8, page 138
Passage #2: Chapter 9, page 170
Passage #3: Chapter 5, page 74
Passage #4: Chapter 9, page 172

June 1994 (LSAT PrepTest 11; LSAT TriplePrep Plus with Explanations; 10 Actual, Official LSAT PrepTests)

Passage #1: Chapter 7, page 118
Passage #2: Chapter 7, page 120
Passage #3: Chapter 8, page 140
Passage #4: Chapter 2, page 28

October 1994 (LSAT PrepTest 12; LSAT TriplePrep Plus with Explanations; 10 Actual, Official LSAT PrepTests)

Passage #1: Chapter 9, page 174
Passage #2: Chapter 9, page 176
Passage #3: Chapter 5, page 76
Passage #4: Chapter 8, page 142

December 1994 (LSAT PrepTest 13; LSAT TriplePrep Plus with Explanations; 10 Actual, Official LSAT PrepTests)

Passage #1: Chapter 8, page 144
Passage #2: Chapter 4, page 58
Passage #3: Chapter 9, page 178
Passage #4: Chapter 5, page 78

February 1995 (LSAT PrepTest 14; 10 Actual, Official LSAT PrepTests)

Passage #1: Chapter 8, page 146
Passage #2: Chapter 9, page 180
Passage #3: Chapter 6, page 98
Passage #4: Chapter 9, page 182

June 1995 (LSAT PrepTest 15; 10 Actual, Official LSAT PrepTests)

Passage #1: Chapter 8, page 148
Passage #2: Chapter 4, page 60
Passage #3: Chapter 9, page 184
Passage #4: Chapter 3, page 52

September 1995 (LSAT PrepTest 16; 10 Actual, Official LSAT PrepTests)

Passage #1: Chapter 9, page 186
Passage #2: Chapter 5, page 80
Passage #3: Chapter 7, page 122
Passage #4: Chapter 2, page 30

December 1995 (LSAT PrepTest 17)

Passage #1: Chapter 2, page 32
Passage #2: Chapter 5, page 82
Passage #3: Chapter 6, page 100
Passage #4: Chapter 8, page 150

June 1996 (LSAT PrepTest 19; 10 More Actual, Official LSAT PrepTests)

Passage #1: Chapter 9, page 190
Passage #2: Chapter 5, page 86
Passage #3: Chapter 8, page 152
Passage #4: Chapter 9, page 192

October 1996 (PrepTest 20; 10 More Actual, Official LSAT PrepTests; The Official LSAT Sample PrepTest—free online

Passage #1: Chapter 2, page 34
Passage #2: Chapter 5, page 88
Passage #3: Chapter 8, page 154
Passage #4: Chapter 4, page 64

LSAT Classification Notes:

1. The December 1993 LSAT was nondisclosed. It was later administered as the September 1995 LSAT and then released as PrepTest 16.

2. Starting in 1996, the February LSATs have been nondisclosed. In April 2000, the February 1997 LSAT was released as the Official LSAT PrepTest with Explanations, Volume One. In May 2004, the February 1996, February 1999, and February 2000 LSATs were released in The Official LSAT SuperPrep.